MW00444521

Angie Smith has written an excellent study for women on the often misunderstood Epistle of James. Her 6-week study probes, with bulldog-like tenacity, the depths of this grand epistle. Students will find within the pages of her work biblical exegesis at its best.

Understanding the Bible isn't limited to the gifted few. Understanding the Bible is for everyone. Angie's study on James opens the door of understanding to anyone willing to roll up her sleeves and get dirty by digging deep into Scripture. Her helpful insights into Scripture can clear up many misconceptions and help one grasp the meaning of James and its application to your twenty-first century life.

~Mike Piburn, Director, Non-Traditional Studies, Calvary Bible College & Theological Seminary

This study is the most powerful in depth study I have ever done. It moved me from "knowing" to "applying" in many areas I thought I had already addressed. I can't even begin to describe its impact on my life!

~Brandy P.

I found this study to be just what our women's Bible study needed: challenging but also easy to understand. The women in the group repeatedly said that this has been our best study yet in the two years of studying together. It has been thrilling as a leader to watch God's hand use Angie Smith's study of James to deepen their relationship with the Lord.

~Johanna P.

The study was life changing at a time when I needed life change and focus. It directed me to the Scripture, led me to a depth of understanding that I had not experienced, and helped me to deepen my relationship with the Father.

~Kourtney G.

This is a great tool if you want to take apart the book of James and learn more. A quality 'in-depth' tool for studying.

~Christa F.

It is a fabulous study and I was in the heat of the fire as I went through it. It provided great insight that helped me keep my eyes on Christ.

~Jennifer H.

I am so grateful for this study. It was just what I needed during a season of trials and temptations in my life.

~Kristen B.

James

Living a Life of Faith

Angie K. Smith

LIFE SENTENCE
Publishing, LLC

www.lifesentencepublishing.com

Like us on Facebook

Visit www.asiamministries.org

James - Living a Life of Faith – Angie K. Smith and Dave Vitt

Copyright © 2014

All rights reserved. No part of this book may be reproduced, stored in a retrieval system, or transmitted in any form or by any means – electronic, mechanical, photocopying, recording, or otherwise, without written permission from the publisher.

Scripture taken from the *NEW AMERICAN STANDARD BIBLE*®, © Copyright 1960, 1962, 1963, 1968, 1971, 1972, 1973, 1975, 1977, 1995 by The Lockman Foundation Used by permission. www.Lockman.org

Scripture quotations marked (NIV) are taken from the Holy Bible, New International Version®, NIV®. Copyright © 1973, 1978, 1984, 2011 by Biblica, Inc.™ Used by permission of Zondervan. All rights reserved worldwide. www.zondervan.com.

The "NIV" and "New International Version" are trademarks registered in the United States Patent and Trademark Office by Biblica, Inc.™

Scripture quotations marked (NLT) are taken from the Holy Bible, New Living Translation, copyright © 1996, 2004, 2007 by Tyndale House Foundation. Used by permission of Tyndale House Publishers, Inc., Carol Stream, Illinois 60188. All rights reserved.

Scripture quotations marked (ESV) are from The Holy Bible, English Standard Version® (ESV®), copyright © 2001 by Crossway, a publishing ministry of Good News Publishers. Used by permission. All rights reserved.

Printed in the United States of America

First edition published 2011

LIFE SENTENCE Publishing books are available at discounted prices for ministries and other outreach.

Find out more by contacting
info@lifesentencepublishing.com

LIFE SENTENCE Publishing and its logo are trademarks of

LIFE SENTENCE Publishing, LLC
P.O. Box 652
Abbotsford, WI 54405

Paperback ISBN: 978-1-62245-155-5

Ebook ISBN: 978-1-62245-156-2

10 9 8 7 6 5 4 3 2 1

This book is available from www.amazon.com, Barnes & Noble, and your local Christian bookstore.

Cover Design: Amber Burger

Contributing, Content Editor - Dave Vitt

Additional Editing by Mary Vesperman

Cover Image: © Adam Gryko / Fotolia

CONTENTS

FOREWORD

The book you are holding is not a Bible study for those who are looking for fluff. In a day when so many Bible study materials are superficial, the church desperately needs materials that take Christians deeper into the Word.

James, being a book of applied Christianity, is such an important study for modern Christians. It challenges the disciple of Christ to walk in holiness in areas such as speech, business, personal relationships and suffering. James emphasizes the need to apply Scripture to one's personal life, demonstrating the reality of one's faith – for true holiness is demonstrated in the details of life. In an age when the Church shows so little difference from the culture that surrounds it, the message of James is vital.

In this study, author Angie Smith and contributing editor, Dave Vitt, consistently demonstrate excellent Bible study methods, making them accessible to all students – especially those who haven't done in-depth studies before. Word studies, historical context, and explanation of grammatical detail will lead the student into the heart of the text. Yet, this is not a dry, academic exercise. Personal illustrations and humor are also employed to demonstrate the relevance of the Word in a 21st century context, assisting in personal application. Study questions provide an opportunity for individual interaction with the Scriptures, but the homework is not overwhelming for working adults with multiple commitments.

It is also a privilege to recommend this study because of my personal knowledge of the authors. Both Angie and Dave are deeply committed to walking out the principles they teach, both in their homes and in the community. Together they founded "as I AM ministries," an organization that produces Bible studies, serves others by growing and distributing food for the poor, and sponsors local mission trips that extend love to underprivileged children. With strong marriages, and families deeply committed to Christ, Dave and Angie have actively enjoyed ministry within their local churches for over a decade.

I trust you will benefit from the study, just as I have, as you make your way through its pages.

In Christ,

Rev. Keith Gibson
Pastor – Word of Life Community Church
Director - Apologetics Resource Center, Kansas City, MO

ABOUT THE AUTHOR

Angela K. Smith, known to those who love her as simply "Angie," was raised in a loving Christian home, the youngest of three children, all of whom have devoted the entirety of their adult lives to serving their Lord. While a junior at Blue Ridge Christian High School, Angie genuinely fell in love with God's Word, and it was then that she first felt God's calling. After devoting the early years of her adult life to being a wife, mother, and then home-schooling mom, Angie took a step of faith by sending her children to school and beginning classes herself at Calvary Bible College in Kansas City. Soon after, Angie knew it was time to begin the ministry God had called her to 18 years earlier. The study you hold in your hands is the culmination of nearly 20 years of waiting, learning, studying, and finally writing.

Currently, Angie lives outside of the metropolitan Kansas City area with her husband of 19 years, and their two beautiful daughters. Over the years, Angie's anchor for all outside ministry has been her activity within the local church as a teacher, speaker, worship leader, and musician. In addition, her energetic work with children and youth groups has earned her the endearing title of "Momma A." Recently, she and cofounder Dave Vitt, launched *as I AM ministries* – a non-profit organization that produces Bible study curriculum, daily devotions, and provides service opportunities for those in their community who want to be the hands and feet of Christ. Such opportunities include working in their community garden, which produces thousands of pounds of food for the hungry each summer, and staffing weeks of summer camp that ministers to underprivileged children. A more devoted student of God's Word and lover of God's people would be hard to find. What Angie writes, she lives. I trust you will find traces of both as you enjoy your time in *James – Living a Life of Faith.*

~~~~~~

Dave Vitt wrote the Leader Guide, the "About the Author" description above, and contributed to this study as collaborator and content editor. He resides in Raymore, Missouri, where he has served in his local churches in the music and men's ministries, as well as being a respected adult Sunday School teacher for many years. He is the loving husband of his wife, Davina, and devoted father to his two daughters, Amanda and Amy. As a graduate of the University of Kansas, Dave received his Bachelors of Science in Pharmacy and later went on to earn his Masters of Arts in Christian Counseling and Psychology. After working in the pharmaceutical industry as a medical writer and editor for 25 years, having owned his own business (Advanced Response Management) for 10 of those years, Dave felt the Lord leading him to retire from a successful secular career in order to commit his life more fully to ministry. His passion for God's Word, his gift for writing and editing, and a teaching style similar to that of Angie's, led to the makings of their special writing team and made his work in this study invaluable. He has recently adapted James – Living a Life of Faith, for male audiences in order to reach men and their families with the life-changing messages found in the book of James.

~~~~~~

Angie and/or Dave are available to speak at your upcoming event.
For more information, or to schedule, please visit: www.asIAMministries.org

ACKNOWLEDGMENTS

A warm thank you to my husband, Brett, and daughters, Cassidy and Charity, who have shown tremendous amounts of patience and support as my passion for God's Word consumes a great deal of my time and often covers our house with Bibles, commentaries, and scriptural research materials. Your acknowledgment of God's calling in my life and your understanding that His call sometimes demands sacrifices for our family is a gift and treasure.

Thank you, as well, to my dear friends, the Vitt ladies – Davina, Amanda, and Amy – for your patience and support while Dave scrutinized my theology, rearranged my sometimes dizzying thoughts, and helped me to articulate on paper what was sometimes stuck in my heart and mind!

To my unsuspecting class of ladies who were willing to go out on a limb and walk through this study with me without a clue of what you were getting into – thank you from the bottom of my heart. Your support, encouragement, and devotion to digging into God's Word together blessed my socks off! God used you in my life in ways you can't imagine. Thank you for being willing to take the time to be His tools of encouragement.

Finally, a thank you that brings tears to my eyes. To Jesse Wesselink, my high school Bible teacher – there are not sufficient words to fully thank you for teaching me to study my Bible inductively and to fall in love with God's Word so many years ago. Never doubt the impact of your passion for God's Word; the effects of your teaching will continue to ripple into eternity. Bless you!

PERSONAL NOTE FROM THE AUTHOR...

Dear Sister,

Welcome to *James – Living a Life of Faith*! I am so thrilled that in the unfathomable depths of His will, God somehow arranged for our paths to cross for a season of study. Over the course of the next 6 weeks, we will dig into the amazing book of James, a book that literally changed my life as I studied and applied its truths. I pray that as you work your way through the study, His Spirit will lead you to new understanding, resulting in a more genuine and practical relationship with our Lord.

After reading the introduction (don't skip this as it has valuable background information for your study), your study time will consist of 5 daily "homework" assignments for the duration of 6 weeks* in preparation for weekly group discussion. Take your time; soak in God's Word as you go. I know that we all have busy schedules, and if you're like so many of us, you'll be tempted to save all five days for the last day or two and "cram" it in before it's time for your weekly meeting with the other ladies who are taking this journey with you. May I implore you – please don't! This study has been written with the intention of delving deeply into God's Word and deeply into the heart of the reader. That simply cannot be done in a rush. God's Word was meant to change your life – will you give it the time and opportunity to do just that?

I promise you that, despite my inadequacies as a writer and teacher, you will get out of this study exactly what you are willing to put into it. I can say this with confidence because these pages will have you immersed in God's Word, and we know that His Word never returns void, but always accomplishes the purpose He has for it. Will you commit to giving it your all for the next 6 weeks*? If you will, you will have developed a habit that can change your life.

As a side note, while you are entirely welcome to use your favorite translation of Scripture, I have selected the New American Standard Bible (NASB), as it is a word-for-word, literal translation of the original Hebrew and Greek texts. In some instances, subtle variations in the English words used, make significant differences. Therefore, it is important that we have a common frame of reference as we discuss particular words and topics. Again, you may use your preferred Bible, but be aware that any "fill in the blank" exercises will be based upon the NASB. I have provided all five chapters of James in this version for your convenience. You will notice that they are spaced as widely on the page as possible – this is to give you the opportunity to take notes in the margins and between the lines concerning insights you learn along the way. I do this in my own Bible regularly so I can recall my studies and findings easily. Some of you may prefer not to write in your Bibles. Please feel free to do so on these pages instead. For those of you who might like to store your findings in your Bible, but are tentative – use these pages for your "rough draft" and then copy them over into your Bible when our six weeks is complete.

No matter your method, however you study, make it personal. Your God treasures you and desperately wants you to treasure Him! I trust that the Lord has an incredible purpose for our time together. I can hardly wait for you to find it – so let's get started!

In Christ alone,

Angie

*Note: Some individuals or groups may wish to extend the study over 12 weeks rather than 6. If so, we have provided a 12-week study schedule as Appendix A, on page 163.

INTRODUCTION

To get the most from any Bible passage or book, it is important to understand the historical background of both the writer and the readers. Most Bible scholars agree that the book of James was written by James, the half-brother of Jesus. Our look into the historical background of this book will begin with him.

Imagine if your brother started telling everyone he was the Messiah / God. James was **used** to Jesus; He was just another guy to him. Perhaps they had made mud pies together, they'd played games together, and goodness – James would have even known Jesus' bathroom habits! ☺ When you are closely-related to someone, you can easily take their uniqueness for granted as you see their common qualities every day. Sometimes I wonder how much Mary and Joseph shared with the rest of the family concerning Jesus' birth. We are left entirely in the dark on that topic. We know that upon Mary's pregnancy, she and Joseph KNEW that Jesus was God's Son, but somewhere along the line, as described in the passages below, there was apparently a disconnect of some sort.

> *For not even His brothers were believing in Him. (John 7:5)*

> *When His own people heard of this, they went out to take custody of Him; for they were saying, "He has lost His senses." (Mark 3:21)*

As the above passages show us, not only did His brothers not believe in Him, His family (His own people) thought He was crazy. James was part of a group of brothers who thought Jesus had lost His senses. Can you imagine the confusion, frustration, and likely division within their family?

But, just as it should in our own lives, the death and resurrection of Jesus changed everything. The Brother, whom James thought was "just a man," conquered death and rose again. James' world was about to turn upside down.

> *After that, He appeared to more than five hundred brethren at one time, most of whom remain until now, but some have fallen asleep; **then He appeared to James**, then to all the apostles. (1 Cor. 15:6-7)*

…then He appeared to James. Notice that after Jesus' resurrection, He appeared to more than 500 people, and the apostles, but James was singled out by name. Imagine the moment. We often hear about the moment "doubting Thomas" saw Jesus and was humbled by his disbelief. Imagine this moment when the brother who hadn't believed all along, who'd called Him a lunatic, who'd thought He was an embarrassment to the family, stood face to face with Him, his Brother – risen from the dead!

Many of us have experienced the pain of losing a loved one. There is a longing there to just be able to go back and talk to them one more time. I wonder if James wished he could apologize for the way he'd scorned Jesus. He hadn't had faith in Him yet, but I can't imagine he'd wanted Him dead. He was, after all, still His brother. I can't even fathom the moment when he saw Jesus resurrected. What a flood of emotion it must have been. Besides seeing a dead man alive again, besides having the chance to say the "if onlys" to his family member, this was the moment when <u>all reality must have flooded in.</u> He really had been who He'd said, the Son of God! What remorse must have rushed into James' heart. *What have I done? I thought I knew so much, but I've been such a fool.*

You know what happens after something that has been hidden is finally realized. Little by little, past details fall into place. I'm sure James had a rush of those revelations; a lifetime of things that suddenly made sense, but had seemed so ridiculous before. Things Jesus may have said and done, even as a child, may have suddenly made sense. Sermons He'd preached that had seemed ludicrous at the time, all seemed clearer. We have no Scriptural evidence for what the encounter between James and the risen Jesus entailed exactly, but James was human, and it's only human for the past to flood in when the present reality proves that we'd entirely misunderstood what we thought was so clear.

What remorse James must have felt as the realization of who Jesus was flooded in upon him.

Regardless of what his immediate reaction was, once James saw Jesus for who He really was, we begin seeing James in an entirely new light. He sat with the disciples in the upper room after Jesus' ascension into heaven (Acts 1:14), he received the Holy Spirit at Pentecost (Acts 2), and he became a prominent leader in the early church. While he may have doubted and denied before, what he'd now witnessed with his own eyes transformed his life, making him into a man who would faithfully follow his Brother even though the path would be dangerous. This is proven by his faithfulness to Christ even after Stephen was martyred (Acts 6 and 7). James had learned that the One who'd come to die for him was worth dying for.

It is not hard to imagine that James' passion and faithfulness to Christ was driven by indebtedness.

As mentioned, James became a prominent leader in the church. I imagine that his passion was driven by indebtedness. His sorrow over his disobedience in the past must have inspired his obedience now. The example he'd seen in Jesus to present the truth without expecting accolades may have been what drove him to seek no glory for himself in the writing of this book. Jesus' only desire was to share the gospel; this was now James' message. Understanding his own previous blindness to the truth must have driven him to have compassion for those who did not yet believe. He could so easily relate with their doubt and skepticism. Knowing he'd lived with Jesus 24/7 and not believed may have given him a great compassion for those who had only heard and not believed. What a responsibility he must have felt to clearly present the truth. He'd been given the chance to see Jesus alive in order to change his mind – **others must now be able to see Jesus alive in him in order to do the same**. He suddenly realized that he had a message of life and death in his hands. As a result, his life became consumed with the urgency of conveying it to all who were dying because of the same stubbornness he'd once had.

Understanding the recipients is also important.

As previously noted, it is just as important to understand the recipients of this letter as it is to get to know the author. At the time James wrote this letter, the churches, filled with Jews who had converted to Christianity, were under a great deal of persecution and had been forced out of Jerusalem and surrounding areas. This group, known as the Diaspora (the Jews dispersed abroad), is precisely who James was writing to. We will look more closely at some of their trials in the weeks to come, but a broad overview shows us that being a Christian Jew invited trouble on all sides. Bearing that title could certainly cost them their life.

And he found a Jew named Aquila, a native of Pontus, having recently come from Italy with his wife Priscilla, because Claudius had commanded all the Jews to leave Rome. (Acts 18:2)

At nearly the same time that James wrote his letter, all the Jews were driven out of Rome under the Roman emperor, Claudius. So the first wave of trouble came to them for simply being Jews. Their homes were taken, their property was looted, their businesses were boycotted, they'd lost all normal means of income, they were ripped away from family and friends, and their children were unwelcome in the schools. Dealing with these pressures alone, on a day-to-day basis, would have caused them to be weary and heavily burdened. But, their problems didn't end there.

> *Saul was in hearty agreement with putting him to death. And on that day a great persecution began against the church in Jerusalem, and they were all scattered throughout the regions of Judea and Samaria, except the apostles. Some devout men buried Stephen, and made loud lamentation over him. But Saul began ravaging the church, entering house after house, and dragging off men and women, he would put them in prison. Therefore, those who had been scattered preached the word wherever they went. (Acts 8:1-4)*

James wrote to Jewish Christians who had been dispersed from Jerusalem and Rome.

On top of being ostracized by the government, the Christian Jews were also hated by the Jews who did not share their newfound faith. The passage in Acts follows on the heels of the murder of Stephen. Saul, who would become a believer himself by the time James wrote his book, is shown looking on while Stephen is murdered, giving his hearty approval. This began a horrible season of persecution for Christian Jews by other Jews. People of their own former faith, who refused to accept the Messiah, were killing them, dragging men and women out of their houses in order to throw them in jail as public examples. To the Jew, the Jewish Christian was committing blasphemy, and it was simply unforgiveable. Not only were these displaced Christians despondent due to the upheaval of their lives, they were now afraid for their lives, living in fear that at the least, they would be thrown into jail.

> *Now about that time Herod the king laid hands on some who belonged to the church in order to mistreat them. And he had James the brother of John put to death with a sword. When he saw that it pleased the Jews, he proceeded to arrest Peter also. Now it was during the days of Unleavened Bread. When he had seized him, he put him in prison, delivering him to four squads of soldiers to guard him, intending after the Passover to bring him out before the people. (Acts 12:1-4)*

If these two sources of persecution weren't enough, there was still more available. Herod Agrippa I was appointed ruler of Judea under Claudius the emperor, and he was ambitious about pleasing his non-Christian Jewish subjects. This ambition led him to be a murderous persecutor of the Christian Jews. As we can see in Acts 12, he had James (the son of Zebedee, brother of John) put to death and sought to do the same to Peter at this time.

Life for these Christians who had stepped out in faith and accepted the Messiah was gruesome and lonely. Yet, James writes to them expecting them to hold fast to their faith and to grow in the Lord. If he could expect that from them in the midst of those circumstances, I believe he can expect the same from us today as well.

Our precious James became such a man of God that he was affectionately known as "Camel Knees" due to the calluses he developed from the many years spent on his knees in prayer. Eventually, he would give his life for his faith. Differing accounts of his death are given, ranging from being stoned, to being thrown from the temple and beaten with a club. Either way, he was martyred for his faith in 62AD and was joyfully reunited with his Brother once again. Until the day of our reunion with Christ in heaven, may we follow James' message of "*Living a Life of Faith.*"

May God bless you as you study His Word.

JAMES 1 (NASB)

¹ James, a bond-servant of God and of the Lord Jesus Christ, to the twelve tribes who are dispersed abroad, greetings. ² Consider it all joy, my brethren, when you encounter various trials, ³ knowing that the testing of your faith produces endurance. ⁴ And let endurance have its perfect result, so that you may be perfect and complete, lacking in nothing. ⁵ But if any of you lacks wisdom, let him ask of God, who gives to all generously and without reproach, and it will be given to him. ⁶ But he must ask in faith without any doubting, for the one who doubts is like the surf of the sea, driven and tossed by the wind. ⁷ For that man ought not to expect that he will receive anything from the Lord, ⁸ being a double-minded man, unstable in all his ways. ⁹ But the brother of humble circumstances is to glory in his high position; ¹⁰ and the rich man is to glory in his humiliation, because like flowering grass he will pass away. ¹¹ For the sun rises with a scorching wind and withers the grass; and its flower falls off and the beauty of its appearance is destroyed; so too the rich man in the midst of his pursuits will fade away. ¹² Blessed is a man who perseveres under trial; for once he has been approved, he will receive the crown of life which the Lord has promised to those who love Him. ¹³ Let no one say when he is tempted, "I am being tempted by God"; for God cannot be tempted by evil, and He Himself does not tempt anyone. ¹⁴ But each one is tempted when he is carried away and enticed by his own lust. ¹⁵ Then when lust has conceived, it gives birth to sin; and when sin is accomplished, it brings forth death. ¹⁶ Do not be deceived, my beloved brethren. ¹⁷ Every good thing given and every perfect gift is from above, coming down from the Father of lights, with whom there is no variation or shifting shadow. ¹⁸ In the exercise of His will He brought us forth by the word of truth, so that we would be a kind of first fruits among His creatures. ¹⁹ This you know, my beloved brethren. But everyone must be quick to hear, slow to speak and slow to anger; ²⁰ for the anger of man does not achieve the righteousness of God. ²¹ Therefore, putting aside all filthiness and all that remains of wickedness, in humility receive the word implanted, which is able to save your souls. ²² But prove yourselves doers of the word, and not merely hearers who delude themselves. ²³ For if anyone is a hearer of the word and not a doer, he is like a man who looks at his natural face in a mirror; ²⁴ for once he has looked at himself and gone away, he has immediately forgotten what kind of person he was. ²⁵ But one who looks intently at the perfect law, the law of liberty, and abides by it, not having become a forgetful hearer but an effectual doer, this man will be blessed in what he does. ²⁶ If anyone thinks himself to be religious, and yet does not bridle his tongue but deceives his own heart, this man's religion is worthless. ²⁷ Pure and undefiled religion in the sight of our God and Father is this: to visit orphans and widows in their distress, and to keep oneself unstained by the world.

JAMES 2 (NASB)

¹ My brethren, do not hold your faith in our glorious Lord Jesus Christ with *an attitude of* personal favoritism. ² For if a man comes into your assembly with a gold ring and dressed in fine clothes, and there also comes in a poor man in dirty clothes, ³ you pay special attention to the one who is wearing the fine clothes, and say, "You sit here in a good place," and you say to the poor man, "You stand over there, or sit down by my footstool," ⁴ have you not made distinctions among yourselves, and become judges with evil motives? ⁵ Listen, my beloved brethren: did not God choose the poor of this world *to be* rich in faith and heirs of the kingdom which He promised to those who love Him? ⁶ But you have dishonored the poor man. Is it not the rich who oppress you and personally drag you into court? ⁷ Do they not blaspheme the fair name by which you have been called? ⁸ If, however, you are fulfilling the royal law according to the Scripture, "YOU SHALL LOVE YOUR NEIGHBOR AS YOURSELF," you are doing well. ⁹ But if you show partiality, you are committing sin *and* are convicted by the law as transgressors. ¹⁰ For whoever keeps the whole law and yet stumbles in one *point,* he has become guilty of all. ¹¹ For He who said, "DO NOT COMMIT ADULTERY," also said, "DO NOT COMMIT MURDER." Now if you do not commit adultery, but do commit murder, you have become a transgressor of the law. ¹² So speak and so act as those who are to be judged by *the* law of liberty. ¹³ For judgment *will be* merciless to one who has shown no mercy; mercy triumphs over judgment. ¹⁴ What use is it, my brethren, if someone says he has faith but he has no works? Can that faith save him? ¹⁵ If a brother or sister is without clothing and in need of daily food, ¹⁶ and one of you says to them, "Go in peace, be warmed and be filled," and yet you do not give them what is necessary for *their* body, what use is that? ¹⁷ Even so faith, if it has no works, is dead, *being* by itself. ¹⁸ But someone may *well* say, "You have faith and I have works; show me your faith without the works, and I will show you my faith by my works." ¹⁹ You believe that God is one. You do well; the demons also believe, and shudder. ²⁰ But are you willing to recognize, you foolish fellow, that faith without works is useless? ²¹ Was not Abraham our father justified by works when he offered up Isaac his son on the altar? ²² You see that faith was working with his works, and as a result of the works, faith was perfected; ²³ and the Scripture was fulfilled which says, "AND ABRAHAM BELIEVED GOD, AND IT WAS RECKONED TO HIM AS RIGHTEOUSNESS," and he was called the friend of God. ²⁴ You see that a man is justified by works and not by faith alone. ²⁵ In the same way, was not Rahab the harlot also justified by works when she received the messengers and sent them out by another way? ²⁶ For just as the body without *the* spirit is dead, so also faith without works is dead.

JAMES 3 (NASB)

[1] Let not many *of you* become teachers, my brethren, knowing that as such we will incur a stricter judgment. [2] For we all stumble in many *ways*. If anyone does not stumble in what he says, he is a perfect man, able to bridle the whole body as well. [3] Now if we put the bits into the horses' mouths so that they will obey us, we direct their entire body as well. [4] Look at the ships also, though they are so great and are driven by strong winds, are still directed by a very small rudder wherever the inclination of the pilot desires. [5] So also the tongue is a small part of the body, and *yet* it boasts of great things. See how great a forest is set aflame by such a small fire! [6] And the tongue is a fire, the *very* world of iniquity; the tongue is set among our members as that which defiles the entire body, and sets on fire the course of *our* life, and is set on fire by hell. [7] For every species of beasts and birds, of reptiles and creatures of the sea, is tamed and has been tamed by the human race. [8] But no one can tame the tongue; *it is* a restless evil *and* full of deadly poison. [9] With it we bless *our* Lord and Father, and with it we curse men, who have been made in the likeness of God; [10] from the same mouth come *both* blessing and cursing. My brethren, these things ought not to be this way. [11] Does a fountain send out from the same opening *both* fresh and bitter *water*? [12] Can a fig tree, my brethren, produce olives, or a vine produce figs? Nor *can* salt water produce fresh. [13] Who among you is wise and understanding? Let him show by his good behavior his deeds in the gentleness of wisdom. [14] But if you have bitter jealousy and selfish ambition in your heart, do not be arrogant and *so* lie against the truth. [15] This wisdom is not that which comes down from above, but is earthly, natural, demonic. [16] For where jealousy and selfish ambition exist, there is disorder and every evil thing. [17] But the wisdom from above is first pure, then peaceable, gentle, reasonable, full of mercy and good fruits, unwavering, without hypocrisy. [18] And the seed whose fruit is righteousness is sown in peace by those who make peace.

JAMES 4 (NASB)

¹What is the source of quarrels and conflicts among you? Is not the source your pleasures that wage war in your members? ²You lust and do not have; *so* you commit murder. You are envious and cannot obtain; *so* you fight and quarrel. You do not have because you do not ask. ³You ask and do not receive, because you ask with wrong motives, so that you may spend *it* on your pleasures. ⁴You adulteresses, do you not know that friendship with the world is hostility toward God? Therefore whoever wishes to be a friend of the world makes himself an enemy of God. ⁵Or do you think that the Scripture speaks to no purpose: "He jealously desires the Spirit which He has made to dwell in us"? ⁶But He gives a greater grace. Therefore *it* says, "GOD IS OPPOSED TO THE PROUD, BUT GIVES GRACE TO THE HUMBLE." ⁷Submit therefore to God. Resist the devil and he will flee from you. ⁸Draw near to God and He will draw near to you. Cleanse your hands, you sinners; and purify your hearts, you double-minded. ⁹Be miserable and mourn and weep; let your laughter be turned into mourning and your joy to gloom. ¹⁰Humble yourselves in the presence of the Lord, and He will exalt you. ¹¹Do not speak against one another, brethren. He who speaks against a brother or judges his brother, speaks against the law and judges the law; but if you judge the law, you are not a doer of the law but a judge *of it*. ¹²There is *only* one Lawgiver and Judge, the One who is able to save and to destroy; but who are you who judge your neighbor? ¹³Come now, you who say, "Today or tomorrow we will go to such and such a city, and spend a year there and engage in business and make a profit." ¹⁴Yet you do not know what your life will be like tomorrow. You are *just* a vapor that appears for a little while and then vanishes away. ¹⁵Instead, *you ought* to say, "If the Lord wills, we will live and also do this or that." ¹⁶But as it is, you boast in your arrogance; all such boasting is evil. ¹⁷Therefore, to one who knows *the* right thing to do and does not do it, to him it is sin.

JAMES 5 (NASB)

¹ Come now, you rich, weep and howl for your miseries which are coming upon you. ² Your riches have rotted and your garments have become moth-eaten. ³ Your gold and your silver have rusted; and their rust will be a witness against you and will consume your flesh like fire. It is in the last days that you have stored up your treasure! ⁴ Behold, the pay of the laborers who mowed your fields, *and* which has been withheld by you, cries out *against you;* and the outcry of those who did the harvesting has reached the ears of the Lord of Sabaoth. ⁵ You have lived luxuriously on the earth and led a life of wanton pleasure; you have fattened your hearts in a day of slaughter. ⁶ You have condemned and put to death the righteous *man;* he does not resist you. ⁷ Therefore be patient, brethren, until the coming of the Lord. The farmer waits for the precious produce of the soil, being patient about it, until it gets the early and late rains. ⁸ You too be patient; strengthen your hearts, for the coming of the Lord is near. ⁹ Do not complain, brethren, against one another, so that you yourselves may not be judged; behold, the Judge is standing right at the door. ¹⁰ As an example, brethren, of suffering and patience, take the prophets who spoke in the name of the Lord. ¹¹ We count those blessed who endured. You have heard of the endurance of Job and have seen the outcome of the Lord's dealings, that the Lord is full of compassion and *is* merciful. ¹² But above all, my brethren, do not swear, either by heaven or by earth or with any other oath; but your yes is to be yes, and your no, no, so that you may not fall under judgment. ¹³ Is anyone among you suffering? *Then* he must pray. Is anyone cheerful? He is to sing praises. ¹⁴ Is anyone among you sick? *Then* he must call for the elders of the church and they are to pray over him, anointing him with oil in the name of the Lord; ¹⁵ and the prayer offered in faith will restore the one who is sick, and the Lord will raise him up, and if he has committed sins, they will be forgiven him. ¹⁶ Therefore, confess your sins to one another, and pray for one another so that you may be healed. The effective prayer of a righteous man can accomplish much. ¹⁷ Elijah was a man with a nature like ours, and he prayed earnestly that it would not rain, and it did not rain on the earth for three years and six months. ¹⁸ Then he prayed again, and the sky poured rain and the earth produced its fruit. ¹⁹ My brethren, if any among you strays from the truth and one turns him back, ²⁰ let him know that he who turns a sinner from the error of his way will save his soul from death and will cover a multitude of sins.

WEEK ONE: A TRIED FAITH

Day One - The Other Side of the Trees

Over the centuries, the book of James has been fiercely debated due to its strong stance on works. The great reformer, Martin Luther, denounced it, claiming that it should be stricken from Scripture as he felt it contradicted the clear teachings of Paul concerning salvation through faith alone. What Luther failed to see, at that time, was that the book of James does not clash with the rest of Scripture, but rather creates a beautiful harmony line to an already established melody.

Paul and James, the half-brother of Jesus, had a common goal, but they targeted different audiences. Because of this, their tone and emphasis varied from one another. Just as I find it necessary to address and discipline my two daughters differently depending on their personalities, level of maturity, and individual situations, these two authors found themselves addressing audiences with different struggles, temptations, and needs. In the books of Romans and Galatians, Paul pressed the issue of salvation by faith alone, because the recipients were struggling with understanding that works had nothing to do with eternal security. His emphasis was on the Christian finding liberty in his or her faith. On the other hand, the original readers of the book of James needed to hear that although their salvation was secure through faith, that very faith needed to be *demonstrated* by an outpouring of works in obedience to the God in whom their faith was placed. Paul emphasized the *origin* of their salvation; James emphasized its *evidence*.

Recognizing who the recipients of the book of James are is imperative for understanding this difference.

Read James 1:1-2.

In these verses, James refers to the recipients in two ways. What are they?

_____

First, he refers to them as the twelve tribes who are dispersed abroad. You most likely recognize the twelve tribes as the twelve tribes of Israel, the Jews, God's chosen people. This in itself is significant, but the second description completes our understanding. As James repeatedly refers to his recipients as "brethren," he is letting us know that these Jews are also Christians. Therefore, his message to them through this letter is equally applicable to us in our daily lives as Christians. It is important that we never take promises or instructions intended for a specific group of people within Scripture and claim them as our own, unless they are restated for us in Scripture elsewhere. For example – the promise of a land flowing with milk and honey (Ex. 3:8) is intended exclusively for the children of Israel. Through our study of James, though, we will discover that although distinct technicalities are addressed

Welcome to Day One! I'm so glad you've chosen to study this great book of the Bible with me. I pray you'll grow in your walk with Christ as a result of our time together!

Paul emphasized the origin of their salvation; James emphasized its evidence.

for the recipient's particular situations, every principle is valuable to us and meant for our instruction as fellow Christians.

Now that we have identified the original readers as Jewish Christians, we have more insight into the tone in which James is writing his letter. The Christians that James addressed apparently already knew that their salvation was secured through faith, and we can conclude that this was not a point he needed to reinforce in the manner that Paul was compelled to on other occasions. Instead, James was able to write his letter with the intention of building upon the Christian's foundational understanding of saving faith, expounding on the works that demonstrate the faith of a true believer.

At times, topics such as faith and works found in books such as James and Galatians can cause doubt in the mind of readers, as the two books appear to say two different things. Remember, Scripture never contradicts itself. When it seems to, historical context and other Scripture will always reveal truth that may not be clear upon first glance.

As the overarching theme of James is the manifestation of true faith in a believer's life, he begins the book with an ultimate test of faith: trials.

When you hear the word "trial," what thoughts first come to mind?

_____

_____

Throughout my life, as with many of you, my own concept of the word "trial" has evolved. Somehow through life's hard knocks, we go from stressing over having a toy taken away from us in Kindergarten to coping with cancer as an adult. What was once earth-shattering becomes trivial as we stretch and grow in our faith.

Read James 1:1-4, specifically noting the word "trial."

The word trial, as it is used in this passage, is the Greek word *peirasmós*, which holds two meanings. The first meaning refers to a testing that challenges the strength and integrity of one's faith. The second refers to temptations that challenge one's moral strength and integrity.[1] We will see both meanings used within the first chapter of James, but our immediate attention will be directed to the first. How we interpret life in full, its challenges as well as its joys, depends entirely on our perspective. **How we see things outwardly, fully affects how we receive them inwardly**. During our study of trials, it will be my personal challenge to all of us, that we learn to see trials and suffering in this life through new lenses, with a new perspective that allows us to recognize trials as tools in the hands of a loving God, rather than merely negative setbacks and tragedies.

In order to change our perspectives, it is important for us to identify our current perspective so we recognize our starting place while working toward our end goal. When you think of the trials in your life, past and present, what is your knee-jerk reaction to them?

_____

_____

Margin notes

Scripture never contradicts itself

The overarching theme of James is the manifestation of true faith

peirasmós – 1) testing of one's faith; and 2) temptations to one's moral strength and integrity

---

1   Charles R. Swindoll, *Swindoll's New Testament Insights, Insights on James, 1 & 2 Peter*, p. 25

Looking back to the introduction, what are some of the trials that the Christian Jews who had been "dispersed abroad" had to endure?

_____

_____

Because James, himself, was a Christian Jew, he was well-versed and experienced in the trials and sufferings his readers had endured. He understood the cruelties of life, even to the extent of watching his own Brother, Jesus, die a merciless death on a cross. Make no mistake, when James used the word trial, he wasn't speaking of getting stuck in traffic, being late to a ball game, not meeting a work deadline, or the fact that someone's husband refuses to put the toilet seat down or squeeze from the right end of the tube of toothpaste! No, James knew that the trials his readers were undergoing involved life and death, fear and great suffering. Even so, he did not coddle his brothers and sisters in Christ with excuses to give up.

James knew the trials his readers were undergoing!

Certainly these Christians had their faith tested by their trials. What questions and struggles might have gone through your mind had you been among them in these years of early church persecution?

_____

_____

Do you think they could have endured such trials and suffering had they taken their faith lightly or considered it optional? Why or why not?

_____

_____

Reread James 1:1-4. How should we *consider* trials that come our way? _____

Joy seems like a pretty strange way to consider trials, doesn't it? Immediately, though, we see that James has called for a change in the perspective of his readers as we have already discussed. He made a pretty bold request of them that he realizes is going to seem like a hard pill to swallow. Instead of lambasting them with an outright statement such as, "Trials should bring you joy," he calls on them to change their thinking, their consideration, in order for them to absorb the profound truth that he is about to share; truth that can only be truly understood through a godly mindset. Are we ready to change our thinking? Are we ready to see our lives through the lenses of God's sovereignty rather than with our limited vision?

We're called upon to change our thinking about the trials we face

Nearly two years ago, I was driving on a cold winter afternoon after an ice storm had hit our city the night before. I need to preface this with the reality that I do not delight in winter, nor do I relish cold; when it's 80 degrees outside, I'm in hog heaven! This being the case, when ice not only lines every blade of grass, but the streets as well, I'm in no hurry to drive anywhere. I much prefer to hunker down in my home and keep the fire burning until spring! Nevertheless, necessity required that I run an errand, and I found myself with both fists clinching the steering wheel while driving on our ice-covered country roads. As much as I could handle eliminating the entire winter season, there is one thing about a Missouri ice storm I've always found breathtaking – the trees. As I drove along on this frigid day, I noticed the sun absolutely twinkling off the ice-laden trees as if they were diamond-crested visions of splendor; it was magnificent. I didn't mind driving slowly; I simply could not get enough of their beauty.

Eventually, I reached my destination, accomplished my task, and began my journey home. I was anxious to get to the particular country road that had so grasped my attention, and yet when I got there, the view had changed. The trees that were dancing with light only an hour before were now dark, cold, and dreary. Their limbs that had broken under the heavy weight of ice were now readily apparent and to be completely honest, the new vision was quite depressing. My heart sank as I had so recently been praising the Lord for the beauty of His creation and had looked forward to basking in it once again. Like a child disappointed on Christmas morning, I wondered what had changed so quickly. I must have just caught the sun at the perfect time; my chance to see its beauty must have been over. A bit saddened by the whole account, upon coming to the end of the road, I turned around to look once more at the trees that had brought me such joy - as well as such disappointment. To my amazement, they were ablaze with light, dancing with beauty that now seemed to surpass any beauty they had provided before. The sun had not changed. The trees had not changed, nor their beauty. The only factor that had changed was the direction in which I was driving; my perspective had completely been altered. On my way, I had seen the same trees, burdened with the weight of ice, brittle and breaking under their heavy load, but beautiful in the midst of their trial as the sun shone so brilliantly upon their weakened branches and filled them with light. On my way home, as my perspective had changed, so did my focus. I saw only their burden, their brokenness, the devastation, and the darkness. In no way, though, had their beauty disappeared… it was simply my choice as to which side of the trees I would set my gaze.

There are always two sides to every trial; will you set your mind to finding God's perspective?

We've only just begun our look at trials, but we've begun in a place where we can decide which side of our trials we will choose to set our gaze. There are always two sides of every ice-laden tree. Will you set your mind to finding God's perspective – to looking for the beauty that will come from the ashes of even the darkest trial? Are you able, even now, to look back on a storm of life and see beauty amidst the brokenness?

Take time now to reflect, asking God to show you what He's brought you through that has made you a more usable vessel for Him, a more beautiful creation, a greater reflection of His light.

Thank Him below for bringing you through past trials, for holding you through current suffering. Use this space to cry out to Him, if you need, to help you to see the light in a trial that has so far seemed to provide only darkness. Ask Him to open your eyes to a new and fresh perspective, not only as you turn to look at the trees in your past, but as you drive into the seasons ahead.

_____

_____

_____

_____

_____

Day Two - Endurance Training

As I sit here daunted by the task ahead of me, I realize that it is for no lesser reason than the fact that I am asking you to delve into the deepest recesses of your minds and souls, places that I find quite intimidating in my own life. If given the choice, I prefer to stay on "safe" ground where I can go about my daily business, not subjecting my heart to vulnerability. May I ask, though, that for today, we remove our veils that we so often hide behind in order to call on our past experiences and trials? For it is in our most vulnerable moments that we often hear our Lord's voice the clearest. *Lord, open our eyes, and as You do, please speak to our hearts.*

Read James 1:1-4 again.

If you're tempted to skip reading these verses again because of repetition, please don't. It is through the process of repeatedly reading passages of Scripture and focusing on a different facet each time that our eyes open to what the Holy Spirit desires to convey. It is through this process that the Word comes alive, providing everything we need for our weary hearts.

Yesterday we discussed the fact that the book of James challenges us to see our trials with a new perspective, to consider them joy. I don't know about you, but I'm not easily swayed by requests that seem unreasonable. Thankfully, we serve an entirely reasonable God, and He always supports His requests with sovereign wisdom. Knowing that the request in verse 2 goes against the grain of natural human thinking, James uses verse 3 to support it with logical rationale.

What are we to *know* about trials that test our faith? _____

When James says, "*knowing that the testing of your faith produces endurance*" immediately after his request to consider trials as joy, he is not commanding that they now learn that the testing of faith does so. Rather, he is presuming that the persecuted Jewish Christians already understand, through experience, that the testing of their faith brings about endurance; therefore, they can consider it joy when they encounter the trials that they do. Reversing the order of verses 2 and 3 may give us a better idea of what James had in mind - "…knowing that the testing of your faith produces endurance, consider it all joy when you encounter them." The assumption here is that the Christian actually desires to build endurance.

Can you look back on your life and recognize ways in which you have learned to endure greater burdens as a result of previous suffering? In what ways have you seen your endurance grow?

_____

_____

Although I would be willing to bet that you would not desire to relive those trials, are you

In our most vulnerable moments, we may hear God's voice the clearest.

Reading passages of Scripture repeatedly opens our eyes to what the Spirit wants to convey.

grateful for the growth they have brought you and the endurance they have built? That is what James is seeking to convey here. He is giving a logical foundation for what seems to be an illogical request, laying out a reasonable process for us in regard to our trials. First, we see that we are to *consider* our suffering in a new way – as joy. It is therefore supposed to seem reasonable to do such because we *know* that the testing of our faith brings a positive result – endurance.

Read verse 4. What are we to *let* happen as we endure trials? _____

_____

Seeing our trials as tools in the hands of a loving God is not enough; we must let God accomplish what He desires.

This next part of the process is a daily challenge for me. I can learn to consider my trials as tools in the hands of a loving Father; I can know that it will eventually bring a positive result, but I often struggle to *let* God accomplish that task in me, by fighting Him during my suffering.

My daughters both love swimming and participated in our town's swim team for a few years. During one particular year, they did endurance training all year long, early in the mornings before their school days began. It was hard getting up out of a warm bed that early in the morning only to jump into a cold pool. It was difficult swimming 2000 meters after just crawling out of bed, and it really wasn't much fun dragging themselves out of the pool only to get cleaned up and start a full day of school. One of my daughters is very compliant and constantly had her eye on the prize. She knew she was becoming one of the girls to beat, and although the hardship of training was just as difficult for her, she rarely ever voiced a word of complaint. My other daughter, who really needs her proverbial cup of coffee every morning, did not find it as easy to bite her tongue. Every day she expressed her disapproval of the hardships of endurance training. She, too, wanted the benefit of the training in the end, but she didn't want to let the endurance do its work in her while it was stretching and strengthening her muscles.

We may miss out on the joy He has in mind for us if our attitudes during trials aren't correct.

My friends, we cannot have one without the other. We cannot grow spiritually without spiritual strength training and we cannot realize the effect of that training if we do not *let* it have its perfect result. As applicable as a swimming illustration is, the two stories diverge upon the end result. Both of my daughters built their muscles and skills regardless of what their attitudes were, and they both happily claimed their medals at the end of the year. One daughter let endurance do its work; the other was made to endure under duress and both of their medals appeared the same. We do not have that option. We will suffer trials in this life, but depending on how we endure, our "medals" will look quite different. God may reward obedience one way or the other; however, we will miss out on the joy He has in mind for us if our attitudes during trials aren't correct. If we set our minds to growing during our suffering, letting God use our hurt to mold us and reach others, our endurance will have its perfect result. If we fight our heavenly Trainer and refuse to *let* Him work in us and through our trial, our reward will be bitterness rather than joy.

Considering the swimming illustration above, give other examples of what positive and negative spiritual endurance might look like.

_____

_____

Why do we want to strive for positive spiritual endurance? Does it really matter?

_____

_____

The true answer to that question lies in another question. Do you want to live a life of peace and hope - or a life of turmoil? The answer to that question seems obvious, but we so often fight against the way God desires to bring us peace that we choose our own turmoil.

Read 1 Peter 1:3-9.

In what is our hope that causes us to rejoice? _____

Will this hope fade even in the darkest trial? _____

According to verse 6, how long will our trials last? _____

When distressed, what does our endurance prove according to verse 7? _____

What does that proof result in? _____

How we endure trials in our lives proves the genuineness of our faith.

Ultimately, how we endure the trials in our lives proves our faith; it is an evidence of our ultimate trust in Jesus Christ to adequately cover not only our salvation, but our daily needs as well. If our faith is the cornerstone of who we are, as it should be, then that in itself should spur us on to begin enduring our trials in a Christ-like manner. But, beyond proving our faith, God gives us additional practical, everyday reasons for positive, rather than negative, endurance.

Read Romans 5:1-5. Verse 2 tells us that we can exult in hope of the glory of God from whom we have obtained grace by faith. What does verse 3 also tell us to exult in?

_____

This passage in Romans 5 is similar to what we have been looking at in James. Just like James, Paul tells us that we can look on our trials positively because we *know* their result. Chart the progression of their positive result below.

_____ brings _____ brings _____ brings _____

In our brokenness, we grow in grace and wisdom.

As much as we'd sometimes like for there to be a shortcut from our suffering to our hope, there is none.. If we never have anything to endure, we will never learn endurance; if we are never forced to persevere, we will never grow in maturity. It is in the trenches of hardship that we learn the most; it is in our brokenness that we grow in grace and wisdom. If I were capable of living a perfect life, I would expect perfection of those around me. If, though, I am forced to live a life of hardship, exposing my own inadequacies and need for a merciful God, those very hardships give me the opportunity to absorb grace from Him, which in turn makes me want to lavish it on others. Through this process, we are all given the opportunity to become more Christ-like as we give grace where it is not deserved.

Read James 1:4 again and finish the sentence: Let endurance have its perfect result, that you may be _____ and _____, _____.

I often call myself "a recovered perfectionist." I grew up holding myself to such a high standard that it was eventually suffocating. I've since learned to bask in God's grace and not have such unreasonable expectations of myself (and consequently of others). If you're anything like me, reading a verse that mentions a goal of perfection makes you cringe. I know I can't reach perfection and it causes me stress to think that I need to attain a perfect goal.

What do you think this verse might be saying when it suggests that endurance will make us perfect and complete, lacking in nothing?

téleios – perfection toward a given end

_____

_____

Thankfully, we can understand more about this goal of perfection by digging into the meaning of the Greek word for perfect, *téleios*. *Téleios* implies perfection toward a given end. It is not as much about reaching an unattainable standard as it is reaching a maturity in order to fulfill a task. In other words, our endurance in trials will mature us into the servant of God we were born to become; it is up to us to allow that work to be done.

Remember, from our time together yesterday, that this kind of testing challenges the strength and integrity of our faith. It isn't an easy road, but if we stand back and look at the big picture, what are our options? On one hand, we have the option of shaking our fists at God, expressing our disapproval at the trials He allows to come our way. We can tell Him that we don't want Him to use this trial for our growth and we really don't care to allow Him to use it for the encouragement or growth of others; we just want out. But, trials are inevitable and shaking our fist at God, or even sulking in the midst of them, only causes us to fight against the trial as well as God, Himself. As I have learned, this road is unfortunately paved with more hurt than healing. On the other hand, we have the option of endurance and surrender. It does not guarantee that the trial will disappear, quite the contrary, some of the most beloved of God have taken their trials to their last breath. What it does guarantee is that we can put our fighting gloves down and find incomprehensible peace in the midst of the darkest storm (Phil. 4:7). By surrendering to endure suffering in order to be used in

It is better to hurt peacefully within the hands of our Father, than to hopelessly fight outside of them.

a greater way that will bless us and others around us, we are allowing God to mature us in ways that we cannot imagine. The ripple effects in our lives and the lives of others will know no end. Trials will continue to hurt; they wouldn't be trials if they didn't. In my own life, I have come to the point where I have decided that I much prefer to hurt peacefully in the hands of my Father than to hopelessly fight outside of them. Through this, we press on toward becoming *téleios*.

The book of James is not intended for those who desire to remain baby Christians; it is a book of instruction concerning how to grow up in Christ, how to let our lives become molded to spiritual maturity, even when we don't feel like subjecting ourselves to the growing pains. It is at this point that we realize the choice is ours. We are confronted with two alternatives. Do we let endurance have its perfect effect, or do we tell God, "I don't deserve this! I want out of this situation and refuse to allow it to do a work in me!" It is our human nature to want to escape suffering; we aren't masochists. Suffering is inevitable, though, and it will inevitably plant seeds in our hearts. Will those seeds grow into something beautiful that can refresh others or into bitterness that will crush the spirits of those we come in contact with?

I cannot conclude this time without looking to the example of our Savior, after whom we are called to model our lives. As we are tempted to look on our trials and ask our God the question, "Why?" we need look no further than the cross to understand that suffering plays no favorites and knows no bounds. As my Savior walked this earth, He didn't deserve the ridicule or the scorn; He didn't deserve to be misunderstood by His own family or mocked by His own peers. He didn't deserve to be born in a manger; He didn't deserve to die on a cross. When He asked His heavenly Father if this cup might pass from Him, the answer didn't reflect what He deserved. The answer made it clear that there was a greater purpose and for that purpose, He needed to endure – to *let* endurance have its perfect result. There was matchless beauty that would come from His life and death of suffering, and His responsibility was to allow it to happen. The fact that He willingly did that for me is what I don't deserve. If in return, He asks me to find joy in my trials and let endurance through suffering do a work in my life, I find I can justify no other answer than to say, "I will." Believe me, this is not easy; we will have to say it today, and we'll likely have to say it tomorrow as well.

Will you conclude your time today by laying your trials out before the Lord and being very honest with Him about the way in which you've chosen to endure them thus far? Will you consider handing them over to Him, letting go of any bitterness their seeds have grown, asking Him for peace in the storm and for Him to use them in whatever manner He would choose in order to make you perfect and complete, lacking in nothing?

_____

_____

_____

_____

_____

_____

In every trial, we have two alternatives: to let endurance have its perfect effect; or to tell God, "I don't deserve this!"

The example of Christ shows us that suffering plays no favorites and knows no bounds.

Day Three - Wisdom for the Weary

Y ou may be wondering how in the world we are going to get through the entire book of James at the pace we are currently moving! I am happy to tell you that today, we will double the number of verses we have looked at thus far and we will eventually work at a more rapid pace. However, I believe it was necessary to take our time as we gingerly stepped into the turbulent waters of trials and suffering, because James immediately presents us with a request that is so contrary to our human nature. A call to change our entire perspective concerning something that affects us so deeply needs to be communicated and absorbed slowly. Thank you for wading through it with me.

A call to change our perspective concerning trials needs to be communicated and absorbed slowly.

Trials continue to be the emphasis of James 1, but today we are able to shift our emphasis a bit. Before we do that, let's briefly revisit what we've covered so far.

With what perspective are we to *consider* trials and suffering?

_____

What are we to *let* happen through those trials?

_____

Read James 1:1-8. Pay close attention to the use of the word faith as you read.

Verses 1-4 have painted a best-case scenario for us. They have shown us the ideal way to see and meet our trials. Verse 5 begins with a word that lets us know that God understands our humanity and that it will be an ongoing struggle to accomplish the goals of the previous verses. Although some translations have excluded this word, the NASB, which has been provided for you, is a literal translation of the original Greek, and this word is included.

What is the first word of James 1:5? _____

In other words, "There is a perfect way to handle trials, BUT you're going to need to ask a perfect God to not only help you see it that way, but to help you to live it out."

Be assured as you go through your trials that God understands your humanity.

When struggling through our trials, what are we to ask of God? _____

When you personally ask for wisdom, what do you feel you are requesting of God?

_____

_____

I believe that we often see wisdom as an end – the answer or solution. We pray for wisdom as if it is the insight needed to solve our problems and end our suffering. Yet, wisdom is the vehicle needed for endurance and insight in the midst of the trial, not necessarily the way out of it. Wisdom is a goal that has no end but is characterized by an ever-growing, life-long process. Ironically, it is often when we hit rock bottom and realize that we have no answers on our own, that we become our wisest and humbly choose to look up for guidance rather than focusing on ourselves and our circumstances.

Daniel 2:21 says, *"He gives wisdom to the wise..."* This seems peculiar, as it would make more sense for God to give wisdom to the unwise in order that they might become wise.

Read Proverbs 9:10. What is the beginning of wisdom? _____

The fear of the Lord is a multifaceted thing, but for our purpose today, we will only focus on one aspect. A proper fear of the Lord acknowledges His position of sovereignty as well as our position of submission. The fruit of wisdom is born of its first seed – the desire for wisdom and the recognition of its need. The birth of wisdom occurs the moment one realizes his need for wisdom and his inadequacy to attain it on his own.

Just as you will never find a truly humble person proclaiming his humility, you will never find the wise broadcasting their gift of wisdom or discernment. The wiser we become, the more we realize how weak we are on our own and how little we truly understand. A fool rushes in believing he has all the answers (Pro. 14:3), but the wise man recognizes his own need for further wisdom in every circumstance. In our context of trials, this is entirely applicable. I can't begin to count how many times I've heard a fellow hurting Christian say, "I don't think God realizes that I'm not strong enough for this…" We've all thought this at times; you may be in a circumstance where you're thinking it now. It is at this time, when we are on the cusp of a breaking point, where healing begins and wisdom blooms. This breaking point is exactly where He desires to bring us in order for us to recognize our inadequacy in contrast to His adequacy. It is from this point that we grow in maturity; and in future trials, we will call on wisdom earlier and it will multiply itself within us.

We now know that God will give wisdom to the wise and that it takes true wisdom to realize our need for additional wisdom. What does James 1:5 tell us we must do in order to receive wisdom?

_____

Barnes' notes on the Bible states it this way:

> *"...no man can feel that he has a right to hope for the favor of God, who does not value it enough to pray for it; no one ought to obtain it, who does not prize it enough to ask for it..."*[2]

Simply stated, God is waiting to give us all the wisdom we can possess, but we have to ask for it. What a blessing it is to know beyond the shadow of a doubt that every single time we ask for wisdom in the midst of our trials, He will give it. This verse doesn't say wisdom **might** be given, it says it **will**. On the days when we have no idea how to pray because we have nothing but groaning in our hearts and we can't begin to know how to pray God's will in a matter, we can rest assured that we are always within His will when we ask for wisdom. We can rest assured that He is always ready and willing to give it to us.

How does verse 5 say that God gives wisdom to those who seek it in the midst of their trials?

_____

Wisdom is the vehicle for endurance and insight during a trial, not necessarily a way out of it.

The wise man realizes his need for further wisdom in every circumstance.

Rest assured – you are always within God's will when you ask Him for wisdom.

---

2   http://bible.cc/james/1-5.htm

Do you ever feel foolish asking for help? There is irony in that, isn't there? We've now been told that there is wisdom in humbly admitting that we don't have all the answers, and yet our human nature makes us feel childish for admitting such. It seems pretty clear to me that this is a ploy on the part of the enemy who has a goal of keeping us as foolish as possible. Foolishness isn't the only fear we often face when asking for help. Intimidation and shame come to mind as well. James is very clear in this verse concerning the confidence in which you can approach the Father when asking for wisdom in times of suffering. In the midst of a bold statement, he softens it with comfort and assurance. In your trial, no matter what it is, no matter its origin, no matter your level of responsibility in it, you can humbly come to your Father without shame in this request. He will not only respond with generosity, He will look on you with love without scolding. There will be no record of past wrongs held over our head; there will be no mention of ways that He knows you will disappoint Him in the future. A humble request for His wisdom in trials will always be met with a loving "yes."

A humble request for wisdom during trials will always be met with a loving "yes."

Read Matthew 7:7-11. What do these verses explain about the desire of your heavenly Father to give you good things?

_____

_____

There are times when we all worry about whether or not what we are asking of God is truly in His will. Read Proverbs 4:1-9. How does God esteem wisdom?

You need never feel foolish or ashamed when requesting wisdom.

_____

_____

There is such enthusiasm in the description of wisdom in these verses that it reminds me of someone just returning from vacation wanting to describe the beauty of something they just can't seem to find adequate words to describe! There are two things in Scripture that are promised to us upon our humble request: salvation and wisdom. Sweet sister, you can come to God with this request, never feeling ashamed or foolish, but with confidence that you are merely asking Him for the gift He is aching for you to receive.

At the beginning of verse 6, we find another instance of the word "but." It does not nullify anything previously said; it does not need to deflate the sails of confidence in what we've just learned. It does, though, give us the stipulation upon which it all rests. There must be faith in the request for wisdom.

The request for wisdom must be accompanied by faith.

Read James 1:6-8 again. The doubting one who lacks faith is likened to something in v. 6 and directly called something else in v. 8. List the two descriptions below.

_____

_____

Verses 1 through 5 have painted the picture of one who handles trials with unwavering consistency. This person has built maturity upon maturity that is only realized through a stable faith in God. This steadfast trust is now contrasted with the one who is lacking faith.

The reference to being like the surf of the sea, driven and tossed by the wind, uses the same language we find in one of the gospel scenes.

Read Luke 8:22-24. What was the source of the disciples' fear? _____.

Did you say the storm? Let me ask you…was it the wind, or the waves threatening to drown them that caused their fear? There is no doubt the wind caused the waves, but the wind and the storm would not solely cause their demise. Their fear was worsened because of the waves that were tossing them to and fro in the midst of the storm. The word in James 1:6 used for "surf" is *kludón.* This is the same word used for the waves in Luke. Simultaneously, the word for doubt in our focal passage is *diakrinó,* which gives a picture of disputing with oneself and wavering about. The image in James is not merely of a man burdened with a trial, but of a man wavering so much in his beliefs that he has a conflict of loyalties that prevent him from standing on his own two feet, as if tossed about by the sea. When the storms of life come his way, he has no foundation of faith or wisdom to stand on, consequently he creates his own waves, causing additional instability and detriment.

kludón – surf or waves

James 1:7-8 further develops this description by calling the doubting man *dipsuchos,* which transliterates as "double-minded." With the same basic theme of a wavering person, this description gives the image of one who simultaneously wants God's will but refuses to give up his own. He is entirely divided and unstable in all his ways. This person is told to expect that he will receive nothing from the Lord.

Now read Luke 8:25. What did Jesus ask them? _____

diakrinó – doubt represented by a man disputing with himself or wavering about

He promised them so much and only asked for faith in return. Had they not already seen Him raise the dead and heal countless others? Were they truly fearful of the waves of the sea when they were with the Man they had witnessed doing miracle after miracle? Had they not seen enough?

What was the disciples' response to the calming of the storm?

_____

_____

For one, they were fearful and amazed. What did we say was the beginning of all wisdom? The fear of the Lord. He'd done nothing to technically scare them; this was good, old-fashioned awe striking, respectful and reverent fear. Sometimes we need to be reminded that although our faith is in a loving God, it is also in the Creator of the universe, and we need to bow our knee accordingly.

dipsuchos – doubleminded

Secondly, they didn't take for granted the magnitude of what they had witnessed. They looked at one another in amazement and said, "Who is this?" Why this drove them to ask this question after they had already witnessed Him raise two people from the dead will never cease to amaze me. But, may I ask you; aren't we so often tempted to do the same thing? We serve the God of creation, the God of infinite wonder, and the God of our daily provision, yet when we see Him step in and provide in the midst of our storm, we are so often surprised. It is often easier to trust the God of the universe to provide for the needs of others during their crises; but will He truly come through for us in ours? Where is our faith? It was upon this experience that the disciples were given the opportunity to add to their wisdom. By hiding this experience in their hearts, their maturity would develop, their wisdom would increase, and perhaps the next time, their faith would trump their fear in the storm. We know they wouldn't be perfect, but they were growing in wisdom. Are we? When trials come our way, are we willing to call on the Lord for wisdom and hand the details over to Him while we calmly rest in His hands? Or are we so convinced that we have to hold on to every detail, that we are like the double-minded man, unstable in all our ways? Are we creating our own waves in the midst of the storm by allowing our hearts and minds to be torn between loyalty to ourselves and to our God? Do we, today, need to be reminded of the One who can calm the storm? If we stand back and allow ourselves to be awestruck with the majesty of our God, saying, "Who are You really?" are we willing to hear His answer and accept Him for who He is?

Faith gives birth to the effective prayer for wisdom in the midst of the darkest storm. As we conclude today, will you place your trials into the hands that are strong enough to handle them, setting your feet on the firm foundation of wisdom rather than subjecting yourself to the raging sea? Below, list at least one trial that you will take out of your own hands and place into the hands of your Father. Then pray that you will leave it there.

We serve the God of creation, the God of infinite power, yet are we surprised when He provides for us in the midst of our storms?

Place your trials into the hands that are strong enough to handle them – and leave them there!

_____

_____

_____

_____

_____

Day Four - "Perspection"

Thus far, we've discussed joy, endurance, wisdom, and faith in trials. Today we will find glory in them; what an oxymoron! It is that sort of comment that makes the world call us foolish. It is only by the indwelling of the Holy Spirit that we realize the difference between the faulty wisdom of the world and the infinite wisdom of our God.

Read Mark 3:20-22. What did Jesus' own family say about Him? _____

It is interesting to consider this verse at this time, for it is quite likely that James, the half-brother of Christ, was among the family members reprimanding our Lord for His apparent insanity. He was not yet able to see wisdom through the grace-tinted lens of the Holy Spirit.

Read 1 Corinthians 1:18-25. According to these verses:

What is the message of the cross to the unsaved? _____

What is it to those who have accepted Jesus Christ? _____

Was the world able to recognize who Jesus was in their own wisdom? _____

What "foolishness" was preached that pleased God, yet proved to be a stumbling block to the Jews and foolishness to the Gentiles? _____

Finish the sentence: The foolishness of God is _____.

The very means by which we can be saved seems foolish to the world; it should be no less surprising to us that the way in which we are called to find peace and joy in the midst of life's storms seems equally foolish. But, I know Whom I have believed and am persuaded that He is able to secure my salvation (2 Tim. 1:12); I will choose to equally trust Him concerning how to handle my trials.

I'd like to revisit a concept we touched on in Day One. As we looked at considering our trials as joy, we discussed the need for a change in perspective. Fill in the blanks using the comment in **bold** on page 2 from Day One.

How we see things_____, fully affects how we receive them _____.

Every situation in life has a positive and negative side. If you listen carefully to conversations all around you, you will soon notice that the human nature invariably gravitates toward focusing on the negative. When walking into a pristine room with everything in its place, a stain on the carpet would stand out and be remembered. Dozens of other items in the room could be in perfect order and completely unnoticed, yet the appearance of the stain will naturally catch the eye and be internally processed as negative. Consider this: You're outside on a bitterly cold day in the midst of a winter storm. Your nose is frozen from the biting wind, your teeth are chattering, your cheeks are flushed, and your fingers are numb. Your dream would be to walk into a toasty house, with a roaring fire and thaw out while

By the indwelling Spirit, we distinguish between the faulty wisdom of the world and the infinite wisdom of God.

Every situation has a positive and negative side; human nature invariably gravitates toward the negative.

— 15 —

sipping a cup of hot cocoa. Upon entering your house, to your delight, the fire is lit and there is a mug full of cocoa waiting for you on the hearth. But, as you sit by the fire, sipping your cocoa, the raging storm outside catches your attention through the nearby window and the joy of your moment is shot down. All you can think about now is the fact that you are going to have to return to the bitter cold at some point; instead of enjoying the positive moment you've been given, your mind cannot escape the negative scene your eyes have landed on. Your perspective (your outward view) is changing your perception (your internal view) of the moment.

When taking an art class, one of the basic skills taught is perspective. You learn how to draw things in a realistic manner that is convincing to the eye. What you physically set your eyes upon is your **perspective**. On the other hand, how you internally receive and process that information is your **perception**. One truly never happens without the other, for we always translate and internalize what we set our eyes upon in either a positive or a negative manner. As I've realized this throughout the years, I've come to understand that this entire process begins and ends with my heart. It is my heart that chooses what I set my gaze upon, and it is equally my heart that chooses whether to let the object of my set gaze affect me in a positive or negative manner. Will I choose to be thankful for the blessing of the cocoa or will I refuse to peel my eyes away from the storm raging outside my window? Because perspective and perception are so inseparably intertwined, I call the entire process my "**perspection**." As we look at these next verses, as well as the ones that have preceded them, using wisdom, we will need to alter our perspection in order to absorb them with the eternal mindset that God desires.

Read James 1:9-11. In what is the brother of humble circumstances to glory?

___

Because verse 10 speaks of the rich man, our minds immediately assume that the "brother of humble circumstances" in verse 9 concerns the poor. Indeed, this is correct, but not exclusive. The Greek word describing this brother is *tapeinos*, also translated as "lowly." This sense of the word *tapeinos* is often used in a descriptive manner in the Old Testament.[3] Read the following verses and list the different ways this "lowly" man is described.

Psalm 10:18 ___

Psalm 34:18 ___

Psalm 102:17 ___

I don't know about you, but when I read words like oppressed, broken-hearted, crushed, and destitute, I don't automatically perceive them as something to glory in, nor do I think of them in terms of a high position! This, though, is where God is requesting of us a change in perspective. We need to see these words in the light of His purpose, and therefore respond to them in the light of His glory.

In this context, to "glory" means to boast. This lowly person is to boast in his high position.

Your outward view (your perspective) changes your internal view (your perception).

Because perspective and perception are intertwined, the process can be called "perspection."

tapeinos – means lowly.

---
3   Douglas J. Moo, *Tyndale New Testament Commentaries, James*, p. 69

What is it about his position that he could possibly boast about?

_____

_____

When Scripture calls us to boast, it is never from a place of pride in our positions or our-selves. We are to boast in what God finds valuable. The English Standard Version translates James 1:9 this way: "*Let the lowly brother boast in his exaltation.*" Exaltation here is *hypsos*, a word used to describe the heavenly realm.

Read Philippians 3:20. Where is our citizenship? _____

Read Ephesians 1:18-21.

According to verse 18, what are our true riches? _____

According to verse 20, where is Christ now seated? _____

Now Read Ephesians 2:4-7. Finish this sentence using a portion of verse 6:

Our God, rich in mercy, gave us the riches of His grace by raising us up with Him, seating us

_____ .

This is eternal security! This is richness beyond comparison! When we were saved, we were **seated** with Christ. These types of concepts are mind-boggling to me, because God's ways are so much more complex than my own. But, in the most amazing way, this verse tells us that we are already seated with Christ, our "*body of humble state*" is simply waiting to be transformed "*into conformity with the body of His glory*" (Phil. 3:21). There is no greater richness to boast of than the inheritance of our salvation. Hearkening back to James 1:5, though, it takes much wisdom to recognize this in the midst of a storm.

Read James 1:10-11 again. What is the rich man to glory in? _____

What do you suppose is the rich man's humiliation?

_____

_____

The rich man is used for so many negative illustrations in the Bible, that it would be easy to glance through these two verses and assume the same is happening here – perhaps, that the negative rich man is being contrasted to the downtrodden poor. But, that is not the case. The two men, although contrasted in their socio-economic state, are both Christians (remember the recipients were Jewish believers) being called on to see their value in an eternal, rather than earthly, sense.

Read Isaiah 40:6-8. Who is like grass that will fade away? _____

What endures forever?_____

The point of this illustration is not to emphasize the physical demise of the rich man. All

To glory means to boast; we are to boast in the things that God values.

We are already seated with Christ; there is nothing greater to boast of than the inheritance of our salvation.

We are to see our value in an eternal, not earthly, sense.

men are like the grass that withers, not only the rich. James uses this picture, rather, to point out the volatility of riches and the fact that the rich man can boast in his eternal inheritance in Jesus Christ without concerning himself with the potential sudden loss of his earthly wealth. Although this sudden loss would seem humiliating to the secular world, he is able to glory in the fact that in reality, he would lose nothing of any true value; his true identity is not in his wealth.

Both the rich and the poor need wisdom, faith, and maturity to see their lives in the way God is requesting. No matter our economic status, we are asked to do the same. It takes an entire change of perspective to see each moment of our lives with an eternal focus. However, with daily practice it can become a life-changing habit that will not only bring peace to our own lives, but to the lives of those around us who learn through our godly example.

Seeing each moment with an eternal focus will bring the peace of Christ into our lives and into the lives of those around us.

Read Colossians 3:1-3. What are we to seek? _____

Where are we to set our minds? _____

Where is our true life? _____

These verses are the recipe for our altered focus. They are the hot cocoa sitting on the hearth while the blizzard rages outside the window. It isn't easy, but our eyes can learn to focus on the blessings of the cocoa and the warm fire even when the storm rages on. It is in this place where we allow God to show us a peace that we never imagined possible, and which truly knows no description (Phil. 4:7). Remember, the peace Christ wants to give to us, is completely contrary to what the world would tell you to expect. But hear Jesus Himself as He reminds us, *"Peace I leave with you; my peace I give you. I do not give to you as the world gives. Do not let your hearts be troubled and do not be afraid"* (John 14:27).

Day Five - A Crown Called Life

Have you ever had to sheepishly look into your past and admit that something you had adamantly argued against was indeed wisdom after all – perhaps something your parents, a teacher, or a wise friend had tried to express that you previously refused to accept as true? I wonder how many moments James had like that after realizing the Brother he had once called a lunatic was really his Savior. How humbled he must have been time after time, as he grew in wisdom and realized that the One he had so often considered a fool, was God Himself; it was he who had been the fool all along. I can only imagine that his understanding of the concept behind today's focal verse was born of one of those humbling moments when the light of a truth he'd heard his Brother preach became clear.

We've all had to admit that something we had once argued against was indeed wisdom after all.

Read James 1:12 noting the word trial as you have before. Fill in the blank:

_____ is the man who perseveres under trial…

Read Matthew 5:3-11. Fill in the blanks:

v. 3 Blessed are the _____…

v. 4 Blessed are those who _____ …

v. 10 Blessed are those who have been _____…

v. 11 Blessed are _____ when men _____,

and _____, and say _____…

Strong's concordance defines the Greek word for the term blessed, *makários*, as happy, blessed, or fortunate. This same word is used in James 1:12 and in the beatitudes found in Matthew, listed above. No doubt, James would have thought his Brother was crazy as he heard Him proclaim these things. Do the above descriptions sound like situations that would induce happiness or, on their own, make one feel fortunate? Of course they don't, and neither James nor Jesus was implying they would.

makários – happy, blessed, or fortunate

Let's look more closely at the beatitudes and see how they tie in with our text in James.

Blessed are the:
Poor in spirit, gentle, merciful, pure in heart, peacemakers
Blessed are those who:
mourn, hunger and thirst for righteousness, have been persecuted for the sake of righteousness, are insulted, persecuted, and falsely accused on account of Me (Jesus).

Theirs is:
The kingdom of heaven (listed twice)
They shall:
Be comforted, inherit the earth, be satisfied, receive mercy, see God, be called the sons of God

I'm a very visual person, so I've used two separate columns in order to separate two themes in our minds. The beatitudes are not "cause and effect" statements. Look at the "blessed" column in the chart. Everything listed there describes characteristics and situations that are consistent with the Christian life. It is true that unbelievers will go through trials, but in this sermon (the Sermon on the Mount), Jesus was contrasting the humble Christian walk to the pious and self-righteous way of the Pharisees. "This sermon showed how a person who is in right relationship with God should conduct his life."[4] This way of life would sharply contrast the way of the world, and would therefore generate misunderstanding and persecution of followers of Christ, as it did for Christ Himself.

Now look at the right-hand column that lists the promises given to us. These give Christians the hope of their eternal inheritance beyond the hardship of their persecuted experience. In other words, Christian, you are blessed, fortunate, and can be genuinely happy even though you suffer in this life *now*, **BECAUSE** you will reap an eternal reward *later*. Christ was offering eternity to the masses. We tend to get so caught up in what seems to be the "trial" part of the beatitudes that we can miss the fact that this part of Scripture is not about the trials, but about the hope that lies ahead; hope that we are blessed enough to claim today! It's a passage of encouragement to get us through our trials by teaching us an eternal perspective, not a passage that demands delight in persecution or suffering. Plenty of Scripture assures us that we will have to take up our cross and endure hurt for the sake of Christ; I'm not suggesting that is not the case. What I am suggesting is that this passage describes the Christ-like humility of a Christian and then declares, "There is hope!" And oh how important hope is; Paul reminds us that greater faith in Christ and love for one another spring from our hope laid up for us in heaven (Col. 1:4-5).

Read Matthew 5:12. Rejoice, and be glad, for your reward in heaven is _____!

Admittedly, that was a bit of a rabbit trail! But, I think it lays the right foundation for today's verse of focus in James.

Read James 1:12. This time, read it using the corresponding word for blessed: fortunate.

According to this verse, why is the one who perseveres under trial considered fortunate?

_____

_____

There is great eternal promise in this verse, and we will soon get there and rejoice in it together, but first, we must focus on the phrase "*when he has been approved.*"

Let's clarify something important before moving on - this is not a stipulation for salvation. By grace you have been saved; it is Christ's blood that has been approved in order for you to receive this grace, there is nothing further you can do to deserve or attain it. This approval refers to a refining process, a progressive withstanding and endurance in the ongoing trials of life.

The Greek word for perseverance here, *hupomenó*, is a compound word comprised of "*hupo,*" meaning "under/by," and "*menó*" – "to remain, not flee, to abide." Together, it means "to stay behind, to await, to endure under the pressure/heat." Its meaning works in tandem

Christian, you are blessed, fortunate, and can be happy even while you suffer now, because of your eternal reward later.

The beatitudes offer encouragement in trials by teaching an eternal perspective; they do not demand that we delight in them.

hupomenó – to stay behind, to await, to remain, to endure under

---

4   John F. Walvoord and Roy B. Zuck, *The Bible Knowledge Commentary, NT edition*, p. 28

with the translation of the Greek word for approved, *dókimos*, which is translated "tested, tried, acceptable." This word is used elsewhere to describe the refining of precious metals and the testing of coins in order to prove them genuine. If we plug these definitions into the context of this verse, we can see that our testing allows us to be tried, and successful endurance gradually refines us, so that what is left (what "stays behind") is acceptable, genuine, and pure. The goal is an enduring steadfastness that proves itself in trial after trial. This hearkens back to Romans 5:4, where we saw that perseverance brings proven character, and proven character, hope.

We all endure in different ways. What does endurance look like to you?

_____

_____

dókimos – tested, tried, found acceptable

In trying to think of a tangible example of endurance, I could think of nothing better for a women's study than childbirth. The outcome is precious, but the process requires more than a little endurance. I'm sure if we had 20 different ladies try to describe 20 childbirth experiences, we would hear 20 different endurance methods. In my own experience, I needed quiet. I wasn't the type of labor patient who yelled, screamed, threw anyone out of the delivery room, or blamed any pain on my husband. However, I talked very little. I needed to be still and quiet to get through the pain. I was only 20 years old during my first labor experience; a labor that turned out to be very difficult. Due to financial restraints, unless my daughter or I was in physical danger, Cesarean section was not an option. As a result, I labored for two entire days and by the end of the second day, I couldn't stay awake even for the brief time between contractions. Family members took shifts staying with me so each could take breaks and rest. I could see the pain and concern in their eyes as they felt helpless watching me go through my trial; they didn't know what to say, and frankly, neither did I. We were quiet. I do remember after one long contraction toward the end, looking at my family and saying, "I want to go home…"

Endurance is like that. Yet, if we will still our hearts and quiet our souls while we endure our trials, it is possible to hear from God during them. It's funny how much louder I can hear His voice when I soften my own. His eyes are always looking on our pain, and unlike my helpless family, He is never helpless. He may not see it fitting to change the course of the trial as we would hope, but His everlasting arms are always available to hold us securely and bring us peace when there is no easy escape. There will even be times when we look to Him and cry, "I want to go Home…" He knows, He's anxious for us to be there as well, but for now He asks us to trust Him while we are being refined into His image. Our responsibility is to stay steadfast and keep our eyes on the outcome, our eternal hope.

While we may want to "go home," for now He asks us to remain and trust Him while He refines us into His image.

We've come to the end of a week-long look at trials, trials that will one day end in a crown.

Read James 1:12 one more time.

Once he has been approved, he will _____.

When the refining process is over, when all our enduring is done, we will come to an end beyond our most glorious dreams and receive the crown of life.

Read Revelation 2:10.

In this passage, the church of Smyrna was being asked to endure persecution that most of us can't even imagine. During a time when martyrs were being gruesomely tortured and killed because of their faith, the Lord asked them to endure until death, for they would receive the crown of life.

stéphanos – a crown of victory, honor, glory, or authority

The word used for this crown is *stéphanos,* and is traditionally thought of as the laurel wreath given to a victorious athlete. It can also apply to a crown worn on occasions such as feasts and weddings, a crown worn in authority, or victory, or one that symbolizes honor and glory. Regardless of whether one or all of these are implied in this passage, they all seem fitting for the beautiful eternity that awaits us. It is very easy to jump to the conclusion that this crown is literal, as are some other crowns referred to in Scripture. We are accustomed to thinking this as we have been told of crowns that we will lie at our Savior's feet. Yet, this crown is different. Unlike literal crowns with formal titles, this crown is literally the crown *of* life – in other words, our eternal life is this crown. Once we have endured, when our weary days are done, we will receive our crown – life – life free of sorrow, free of tears, and free of pain, life with our God. We will come to the end of our journey and have the opportunity to hear, "Well done, good and faithful servant." Be steadfast, dear sister, for your crown will be life.

When our weary days are done, we will receive a crown of life – life free of sorrow, tears and pain; an eternity with God.

It's so hard to think that way on a daily basis as the waves of life threaten to knock us down. This life crowds in and threatens to steal our focus; it happens so easily. Humor me for one minute longer and hold this paper up in front of you. Read a few lines from it entirely focusing your attention on the page in front of your face. Without altering your focus, notice that the things in the room outside of the paper are blurry. Now, keeping the paper in the same spot, raise your eyes and focus on something across the room that seemed blurry a moment ago while you focused on the paper. As it becomes clear, notice that the paper is now blurry. No matter how hard you try, it is simply impossible to achieve clear focus on both at one time. You must choose to focus on what is right in front of your face or on what is in the distance. Friend, our perspective is like that. When we set our gaze on the here and now, we cannot have an eternal perspective. What is in front of our face will crowd in on us and we will not be able to view it in the context of God's bigger picture. But, when we set our minds to have an eternal perspective, eternity becomes clearer as we take our eyes off of our situations and learn to focus on God's greater plan.

It is not possible to focus clearly on more than one thing at a time.

Read Ephesians 1:18a. I pray that the _____ may be enlightened.

This way of looking forward to what lies ahead and finding peace in it even during the darkest storms is about heart focus, and it never happens by chance. This takes training and practice; it's an intentional choice to look to God for how He can use our trials in our lives and in the lives of others. Our endurance not only refines our own lives, but becomes a large part of our testimony as well. As those around watch how we endure, we have an opportunity to reach them and bless the Lord. Our trials are not only useful to us once we reach the other side of them. Sometimes, right in the middle of our own storms, we can be the brightest light of hope to others as they go through storms of their own.

Read Philippians 4:5-8 below. Absorb these verses and meditate on them in the context of everything we've learned this week.

> *Let your gentleness be evident to all. The Lord is near. Do not be anxious about anything, but in everything, by prayer and petition, with thanksgiving, present your requests to God. And the peace of God, which transcends all understanding, will guard your hearts and your minds in Christ Jesus. Finally, brothers, whatever is true, whatever is noble, whatever is right, whatever is pure, whatever is lovely, whatever is admirable—if anything is excellent or praiseworthy—think about such things.*

Our ability to endure refines us and becomes a part of our testimony.

Take some time now to ask the Lord to help you to endure and to be your strength. Ask Him to give you an eternal perspective when this life doesn't make sense and to give you peace in the chaos. Be open with Him; He knows your every thought, tell Him what's on your mind and ask Him to open the eyes of your heart to truths that only He can bring. Be still and quiet; allow Him to speak.

_____

_____

_____

_____

_____

_____

_____

WEEK TWO: A TESTED AND TRIUMPHANT FAITH

Day One – The Blame Game

As we begin today, I would like to revisit the two definitions of the Greek word for trials mentioned on Day One of the first week. Looking back to page 2, fill in the blanks:

The Greek word *peirasmós,* used for the word "trial" in these passages, holds two meanings.

The first meaning refers to a _____ that challenges the _____

_____.

The second refers to _____that challenge one's

_____.

Today's verses use the second meaning. Read James 1:13-14.

The beginning of verse 13 includes something significant that we might miss upon first glance. It reads, *"Let no one say **when** he is tempted…"* (emphasis mine) In other words, we are **all** going to run into temptation, it's just a matter of when. 1 Corinthians 10:13 says, *"No temptation has overtaken you but such as is common to man…"* We are all susceptible to temptation; there is no one above any temptation, no matter his or her position in life.

You will notice that the portion of James, emphasizing the second meaning of "trials," follows immediately on the heels of the section that highlighted the type of trials that challenge the strength and integrity of one's faith. The trials we've studied in verses 2-12 are not born of temptation to sin; they are the hardships of life that inevitably come our way. God is able to allow and use these trials to test, refine, and strengthen our faith while maturing us in wisdom. There is no sin or malice in Him as He allows this; in the end, they are for our good, even while they seem so unbearable at the time. In our humanity, we naturally ask God why He allows these hardships which we feel inadequate to handle. Our same human nature can lead us to believe that we should question God concerning temptation.

Have you ever found yourself asking God why He would tempt you with something you feel unable to resist? Have you felt He was tempting you with a proverbial carrot? If so, explain:

_____

_____

Finish the sentence using James 1:13: *"Let no one say when he is tempted, 'I am being tempted by God'; for God cannot be tempted by evil, _____."*

We will all be tempted, it is just a matter of when.

Our human nature can lead us to question God about our temptations.

It is very important to keep the two meanings of the word *peirasmós* in context, for we now see that one can originate with God for our good, whereas the other never comes from the Lord. For a quick summary, we will boil the two definitions down to a few words. The first is a **testing** of faith; the second is a **temptation** to sin.

If temptation never comes from God, where do you think it comes from?

_____

Using James 1:14, fill in the blank: *"But, each one is tempted when he is* _____

_____*."*

Peirasmós – a testing of faith; or a temptation to sin

I don't know about you, but I find it much easier to think that there is something or someone whom I can blame my temptation on besides myself! We know that it isn't God, because we've just seen His Word tell us that very clearly. If it isn't God, then it must be something else, and one of our favorites to blame is Satan! But, here's the reality. Yes, Satan and his legions of demons are tempters; that is certain. However, this verse clearly tells us that often-times, Satan does not even have to enter the picture for our own sin nature to be tempted.

Apparently, we need to learn to take responsibility in the matter. To be responsible for anything, we need to understand it and be educated on the subject. So, let's break down the process of temptation in order to learn how to reasonably withstand it.

Satan does not have to enter the picture for our sin nature to be tempted.

All of humanity has been tempted from the dawn of time, so we might as well start at the beginning.

Read Genesis 3:1-7. Who tempted Eve? _____

We can all agree that Satan, himself, played an active role in this temptation. Looking closely, though, we see that there is more to the picture. The Greek word for entice used in James 1:14 is *deleázō*. It is a fishing term, used to describe the bait that lures in the catch. Satan was baiting Eve, but she wasn't tempted at first.

I'm assuming that Adam and Eve had seen this tree time and time again. We know from our reading that it was located in the center of the garden. Unless they lived in the suburbs of Eden, I'd imagine they passed it most every day as they walked the dogs. Obviously, I'm kidding, but the fact is, the "bait" of the tree had been there all along. Even when Satan first asked Eve about it, she apparently wasn't tempted by it.

deleázō – a fishing term describing bait that lures

There are things in this world that tempt some, but not others; not all bait looks the same to each of us. If you place a worm on a hook in front of a hungry fish, you've presented that fish with its greatest weakness and it's going to have trouble resisting. On the other hand, if you dangle a worm on a hook in front of my eyes, there is no way you're going to get me to put that worm in my mouth! I'm simply not going to be tempted. You may have baited me, but you didn't tempt me. I know that worms are not good for me to eat, and you would have to do a great deal of convincing to get me to believe otherwise!

Eve knew that the fruit of the tree of knowledge of good and evil was not good for her to eat. Not in the sense of its flavor or satisfaction, but because she knew her God had told her not to. At this point, she wasn't tempted by its presence in the garden, or by Satan bringing it up. She even explains to him why she doesn't intend to eat from it. It is at this point, though, that Satan sprinkles sugar on the bait and it appears different to her than it ever had before. Suddenly, Eve is tempted. But, what has caused that temptation to begin to burn within her? Yes, Satan provided the bait, yet in order for her to be tempted, a lust, a longing for what she didn't yet have, had to arouse her desire for acquiring it. According to James 1:14, "Each one (even Eve) is tempted when he is carried away and enticed by his **own** lust." As much as we would love to, we can't even blame the bait.

According to Genesis 3:6, when did Eve decide she wanted to eat from the tree?

_____

_____

Each is tempted by his own lust; we can't blame the bait.

That verse lists three reasons she desired to eat from the tree, all of which can be summarized in one statement: She suddenly saw it would bring her something she didn't have and she **decided** she wanted it. That's where temptation is conceived. There is bait all around us every day, but it isn't until we desire the bait and are carried away by **our own** lust that we are tempted. We are the ones who carry a great responsibility to guard our hearts against temptation. We may be tempted to blame the tempter or the bait, but no one can physically force lust to arise in our own being.

Understanding where actual temptation originates is important, but it is equally important to understand that temptation, in and of itself, is not a sin. We do need to guard ourselves from getting into situations where we know we will be easily tempted. But, this is because we want to prevent ourselves from succumbing to the temptation. If Eve had only been tempted, yet turned away from the tree just as she approached it, she would not have been in sin.

When we see something we don't have and decide we want it, temptation is conceived.

Read Matthew 4:1-10. Who was tempted in this situation?_____

I cannot begin to imagine the level at which Jesus was tempted. Honestly, my eyes well with tears as I consider it. Look back to the final paragraphs of Week One, Day Two and all we discussed that Christ didn't deserve. This was still another, and yet He willingly endured it for you and me.

We often use the old cliché "the devil made me do it," but the truth is, Satan has far greater targets to set his radar on than little ole me. If there is any influence tempting me outside of my own selfish desire, I'm sure one of his depraved minions is behind it and not Satan, himself. Jesus, though, was taken on by *"the commander of the powers in the unseen world"* (Eph. 2:2, NLT). Not only was Evil, himself, the tempter, he came to the desert with barrels fully loaded. He knew whom he was facing and he hated Him more than anything in heaven or on earth. He'd waited for this moment for thousands of years, and this was his chance for revenge. After 40 days of fasting, God incarnate was famished, starving for an earthly bite to eat, and endured perhaps the most intense season of temptation known to man. He knew who He was and what He could do, yet He resisted not only the temptation to succumb to the bait being spoken, but probably the temptation to throw Satan from the top of the temple as well!

Temptation, in and of itself, is not sin.

The temptation of Christ was not just meant to be a dramatic moment in the story line of the life of Jesus. The valuable lessons we can glean from it are endless. Among the most precious is the understanding of the love He showed for us while enduring it, as well as the compassion He now has due to His own understanding of the experience.

Read Hebrews 2:17-18. Because Christ suffered temptation, what is He able to do for those who are now tempted? _____

Read Hebrews 4:15.

What can our High Priest, Jesus, do in respect to our weakness? _____

How many things was He tempted in?_____

Are there any temptations you face that you feel you simply cannot withstand? _____

Christ has compassion for us due to His own experience with temptation.

We've all heard many times, "I just can't help myself;" we may have even said it ourselves. Upon asking our children why they aren't obeying what we've asked them to do, we may hear, "Because I can't!" when the truth is they have just chosen not to. We know what they are physically capable of; they have just entered into a battle of the wills. Temptation is like that. Sure, there are some temptations that are small and easily avoided, but we need to be honest here – there are some serious temptations out there that can all but blindside us! It's in these times we are likely to tell ourselves and God, "I can't! I can't withstand this! I can't help myself!"

There is as much temptation not to do the right thing as there is to do the wrong thing.

Temptation comes in all shapes and sizes; there is just as much temptation not to do the right thing, as there is to do the wrong thing. When we feel overwhelmed and defenseless against temptation, are we justified in meeting it with an attitude of, "This is just who I am. I can't change. I can't fight this?"

Read Romans 6:1-14.

Our relationship to God and our relationship to sin were both changed at the cross.

Wow, that's a mouthful; Romans is full of rich, heavy stuff! Let's look closely at the victory it proclaims for us as believers. These verses tell us that believers are dead to sin; **we died at the cross**. It wasn't only our relationship to God that changed at the cross; our relationship to sin was altered as well. Its power is dead in our lives; it is no longer the controlling factor. Verse 6 tells us that sin used to dominate us and we were enslaved by it, but verse 7 tells us that by being crucified with Christ we have been freed from it! This doesn't mean we are free from the desire for sin or the temptation toward it, it means that **we have been given the power to deny it**!! When we were unsaved, we were slaves to sin. We literally had an "excuse" to sin because it held us in bondage and we did not possess the power of Christ necessary to resist it. But, when we surrender our lives to the Lord and submit to a new Master, we have the power of the resurrection alive in us to conquer the patterns of sin in our lives and live in the freedom of the power of the cross. We now have a new life!

We possess His power, but how can we apply it in practical ways? I have multiple medical conditions that have demanded that I not drink caffeine. I remember when I first cut caffeine from my diet and I'll admit, I was cranky. I loved Dr. Pepper, drank it all the time. I remember purposefully avoiding the pop aisle of the grocery store from where it taunted me; upon just seeing it, my attitude would spiral down the drain. I also remember the day when a light bulb went off within me. I was well past any caffeine withdrawal, but I was still grumpy about missing my pop. I realized I was choosing to let the pop adversely affect my attitude simply because I wanted what I couldn't have. I was letting pop control my emotions because I was choosing to continue to be tempted by it. The next time I needed groceries, I intentionally walked straight to the pop aisle, stood myself square in front of a 12-pack of Dr. Pepper, pointed my finger at it, and in full voice, said, "You are not the boss of me!" That day, in my life at least, the Dr. died. Well, at least he lost his fizz. ☺

While this is admittedly a humorous example of a small temptation that was not directly sinful, I've found the use of the same technique effective in battling significant areas of sin and temptation in my life.

Read 2 Corinthians 5:17. Write it in the blank below:

_____

_____

To claim freedom from the domination of sin, we must KNOW that sin is powerless against us.

What old things are passed away? Our bondage to sin, our excuse to sin, our defeat at the hands of sin! What new has come? Power to face our worst temptations square in the eye and say, "YOU ARE NOT THE BOSS OF ME!" Three times in Romans 6, Paul uses the word "know" (vv.3,6,9). Repetition in Scripture is never coincidental; it's always to drive a point home. Paul recognizes that in order for the believer to claim his or her freedom from the domination of sin, they must KNOW that sin is powerless against them; otherwise they walk into the ring already defeated. When we say, "This is just who I am," he says, "KNOW that you are <u>not</u> who you were; you can walk in new life!" (v. 3-4). When we say, "I can't change," he says, "KNOW that you are no longer enslaved to sin, you <u>can</u> do this" (v. 6). When we say, "I can't fight this," he says, "KNOW that just as death has no mastery of Christ, sin has no mastery over you" (vv. 9,14). You are free; you are free, indeed. (John 8:36).

How we meet temptation will be determined by what we have resolved to do ahead of time.

Ladies, temptation is going to knock on our door; it always does. The way we meet it will be determined not only by what we know about our new life in Christ, but by what we have resolved ahead of time to do when we answer the door. Are we resolved and committed to meet it with, "You are not the boss of me," or have we conceded to defeat before it ever comes our way? If we are going to be resolved, we must have something greater we believe is worth fighting for. We must ask ourselves what is more important to us, the temporal satisfaction of getting hooked by the bait, which always leads to heartache, or the commitment we've made to our God who promises peace, even when what we temporarily deny brings us such pain. It's hard; there's no getting around that. But, when we seek a way out, He will provide. The physical tempting agent may not disappear, but when we cannot change the bait, we can ask God to change our mind, our heart, and our will. I've experienced the stronghold of fear that I would never escape the way in which temptation consumed me, and I've seen Him work miracles even in the midst of the storm. But, my heart had to be willing to lay down my own desires in order to accomplish His.

We must be willing to lay down our desires in order to accomplish His.

Fear and temptation are quite similar in their attack. They consume the mind and heart and squeeze out all reason. When both of my daughters had nightmares as little ones, they would come to me in the dark of the night and ask me to pray over them. They were consumed with fear and they needed to be reminded that they were safe. I would whisper prayers over them, asking their heavenly Father to bring them peace by replacing the thoughts that had flooded their minds with new thoughts; thoughts of His protection, thoughts of all of the ways He'd provided for them in the past, and thoughts of the way He wouldn't leave them now. I would ask Him to wrap His loving arms around them and give them a sense of having a beautiful bubble of protection around them, as He would peacefully guide them back to sleep. Most nights, they were back to sleep by the time I was finished praying. They needed to be reminded of what was real and who their "Daddy" was. Their fears weren't of something real, but they were consuming. Their heavenly Daddy was bigger than their fears, He was real, and He provided the stability they needed when their peace was lost.

If anything we are drawn toward is not pleasing to the Lord, our sin nature is playing us for the fool.

Temptation lures us toward something we convince ourselves is a source of real satisfaction – and much like fear – that can be consuming. Do we need to be reminded of what's real? If anything we are drawn to is not something pleasing to the Lord, we can rest assured that our sin nature is playing us for the fool as it tries to convince us otherwise. Do we need to remember who our "Daddy" is? We are accountable to Him to make the right choice, and out of **His strength**, He has given us the power necessary to withstand the temptation. Remember, being tempted itself is not a sin, but are we prepared to stand strong when temptation strikes or have we admitted defeat before the attack?

The power of sin was conquered in your life when you surrendered to Him.

Is there one or more temptation in your life that burdens you time and time again? Some of them may be a temptation to do wrong, others may be temptation to not do what you know is right. If so, you are not alone. Will you take time to ask the Lord to whisper new thoughts over you that remind you that you are a new creation because of Him and that you **have** been given the power to resist as the power of sin was conquered in your life when you surrendered to Him. Will you give Him your weaknesses and ask Him to show you the abundance of blessing awaiting you when you choose to turn from the old and move forward to the new?

_____

_____

_____

Day Two — One Breath at a Time

Personally, I could use a breath of fresh air. We've talked about some pretty heavy things over the last 6 days, and a light at the end of the tunnel would be a welcome relief. Fortunately, God gives us those lights time and time again in Scripture, an example of which we will see today. We need to finish looking at one more verse completing the process that originates with the temptations we spoke of yesterday. Then we will be able to contrast it with the light of God's hope. Stick with me through the darkness for a little bit longer and remember that the morning sun is always more radiant after the darkest nights.

When tempted, we have to make a choice; to turn from it or walk toward it.

Read James 1:13-15. We're backing up a bit in order to highlight the complete process of sin. Fill in the blanks according to these verses.

Each one is _____ when he is carried away by his _____,

when _____ has conceived, it gives birth to _____; and when _____

is accomplished, it brings forth_____.

Sin doesn't just happen, it's a process. Our desires tempt us and we have to make a choice. Are we going to turn from temptation or walk toward it? When we turn away, we employ the power of the resurrection to claim our new life in Christ, having been freed from the bondage of sin. When we walk toward it, which we all do in thought or action on a daily basis, we've given birth to sin, which brings forth death.

I don't want to get bogged down with the differences of opinion concerning what is meant by the "death" brought forth by sin. So, we will briefly touch on it and move on.

"Jewish Christians saw people as either traveling the path of life (walking with Christ by the Spirit) or the path of death (walking apart from Christ in the flesh). To be "dead" was often a description of the poor quality of life rather than the cessation of being."[5]

"Lust can lead to physical death in a believer, and it can lead to physical and spiritual death in a non-believer."[6]

Unrepented sin prevents us from living a surrendered and fulfilled life of service to God.

This death may be an eternal, spiritual death for the non-believer, a physical death for the believer who refuses to turn away from habitual, unrepented sin, or "death" which is symbolic of not living the "life" Christ intends for us. Regardless, we can see that its effect prevents us from being able to live a surrendered life, fulfilled by proper service to our God.

Let me draw a practical comparison between the sin and death described above and something we may all find easier to grasp. One thing I have found very therapeutic in my life is gardening. Not vegetable gardening – oh no, I grew up picking row after row, bucketful after bucketful of green beans, and I now get them from where God always intended me

---

5   Swindoll, *NT Insights,* p. 37

6   Thomas L. Constable, *Notes on James, 2010 Edition,* p. 15

to – the grocery store! ☺ However, every spring, after winter has killed off every sign of life and produced a barren wasteland, I love to plant new flowers in the soil of hope and watch them grow into beauty. I can't quite describe the joy that it brings me to see the color and birth of new life, especially after the darkness of winter. These new flowers almost breathe fresh air into my lungs as I hope for the beauty and joy of the upcoming spring and summer. Inevitably, as the year goes on, my schedule fills, and I don't have as much time as I would like to weed my flower beds. What starts out as one harmless weed, quickly multiplies into many. While I water, I'll bend down and pluck out the easy ones; you know, the ones that don't take much effort – the ones whose roots don't go too deep. Unfortunately, not only am I neglecting to pull the deeply-rooted weeds before they take over and choke out my entire garden, I'm also watering them. By the time I've let them go this far, it would take so much time and effort to get rid of them that I just let them go. This year, I was even foolish enough to think that one particular weed looked somewhat like a fern and decided to purposefully leave it. Within a month, it had transformed into a hideous monstrosity. You're way ahead of me here; I know I don't need to elaborate much further. Just like sin that leads to death, the weeds of the flower bed may not choke out every flower in the garden, but they are certainly keeping the garden from becoming the vision of splendor it could be.

Like weeds in a garden that choke out what we want to grow, sin prevents us from becoming what we could be for God.

Read Romans 7:15. What does Paul **not do**? _____

What does Paul **do**? _____

It was only the chapter before in Romans where Paul had declared that we are no longer captives to sin; that we have the power to overcome its mastery in our life. Here, Paul is showing his frustration with the **knowledge** that he has the power to resist temptation; yet, due to the sinful nature which constrains him while trapped in his physical body, he finds himself committing both the sins of doing what he shouldn't do, as well as not doing what he should.

Knowing that Paul shared this struggle gives me great relief. While it does not in any way give me the freedom to use my human nature as an excuse to sin, it does show me that I am not alone in the battle against my own flesh and blood. Paul was an amazing man of God, striving to live the most Christ-like life possible, and yet he identified with the never-ending war to do so this side of eternity. My goal needs to be the same as his, but I must not get bogged down when I fail.

You are not alone in the battle against your own flesh and blood. None of us can make it a full day on our own.

I've come to the point in my own life where I don't live one day at a time anymore. I now realize that I'm actually far too weak to make it a full day on my own. As I've often told those around me, I've come to living no more than one breath at a time. Let me try to explain by comparing this concept to a failed pattern of dieting. We often set a goal for when we will begin a diet plan, saying, "I'll start on Monday." Monday rolls around and we have a successful day; but if we stumble on Tuesday, we may give up for the rest of the week and decide to begin again the next Monday. We allow defeat to set in for the rest of the week, and after multiple cycles of the same defeat, we may not begin again at all. We so often tend to live in similar defeat in our Christian walk. We set our minds to standing against temptation and sin and when we fail, we surround ourselves with the prison walls of guilt and shame, convincing ourselves we are unworthy of the grace that says we can begin again. By living one breath at a time, I've learned that I can give Christ my current moment, my current breath, in full. When I do fall, He looks at me with grace-filled eyes saying, "Give me the next breath; we can do this together. You don't have to wait for a new day to enjoy a new beginning." In living this way, the power of defeat has no victory; mercies don't have to wait until morning.

Do you have a pattern of defeat in your life? Can you identify areas where you have allowed the weeds to choke out the life you know you were meant to live?

_____

_____

Are you willing today to begin removing the weeds, committing your next breath to moving toward new life and hope? _____

I can't tell you how much it breaks my heart when I hear a dear brother or sister in Christ comment on their own sin, stating that they've ruined everything, that their testimony is beyond repair. Precious friend, let me say something clearly – **that can never be!** Yes, our testimonies can be tarnished, but have you ever polished an old, tarnished set of silver dinnerware? Upon first glance, it looks unpleasant, but after time, effort, and tender-loving care, it gleams as if it were new. Not only does it appear new again, its beauty is much more attractive and astounding when we recall the condition from which it came. Temporarily tarnished, but never destroyed, our testimonies can not only be restored, both our successes and failures can become an integral part of who we are and how God can use us. He will use our failures, shortcomings, and seasons of defeat to reach people we never would have been able to relate to before, people who would have never been able to relate to us! We who have been forgiven much, have a greater capacity to understand and have compassion on others. Will you let Him use you? It is never, never too late…

What are the first 4 words of James 1:16? _____

We need to realize something very clearly. Our enemy, Satan, wants nothing more than for us to be deceived. He wants to deceive us into believing we must continue to walk in defeat, and in this verse specifically, we see that he wants us to be deceived concerning God's intentions toward us. The father of lies would have us believe that our temptations to sin come from God. If he can get us to fall for that lie, he can convince us that God is a tyrannical ruler enticing us to fail so that He can squash us like a bug. James now contrasts that lie with the reality of God's true intentions.

Read James 1:16-18.

Rather than temptation, what comes from God? _____

What characteristics of God are pointed out at the end of verse 17?

_____

Our God is the "Father of lights," the Creator of the heavenlies and all they contain; the sun, moon, and stars are at His bidding. Note the contrast James gives between the Creator and His creation. Unlike the constant moving of the cosmos, which manifests itself in shifting

When we fall, Christ simply asks for our next breath. His mercy need not wait until morning.

Our successes and failures become a part of the testimony of who we are and how God can use us.

Satan wants nothing more than for us to be deceived.

shadows and full eclipses, our God has no variation within Him. He is good and pure, and therefore He only desires what is good and pure for us. We do not serve a fickle God who reacts and responds to us with emotional shifting; we do not serve a God who tempts us with a desire to watch us fall.

Read Matthew 7:11.

This verse speaks to our mother's hearts, because we know how deeply we want what is best for our children. Yet, God in His holy perfection wants good for us on a much deeper level, because His love is not tainted, it is not moved, and it does not vary during the storm. This love does not keep us from trials, for a loving parent knows they must **allow** their children to fall as they learn to walk. However, that loving parent never intentionally trips their child in order to deliberately **cause** them to fall.

Because God is good and pure, what He desires for us is also good and pure.

As James concludes his defense of God on the issue concerning temptation, he wraps it up with a reminder of God's ultimate gift of goodness toward us, the message of truth.

Read Ephesians 1:13 and Colossians 1:5.

What is the message of truth?_____

According to James 1:18, fill in the blank.

In the _____ He brought us forth by the word of truth.

In His love, God allows us to fall, but He never trips us causing us to fall.

In other words, He initiated our salvation in the exercise of His will. God didn't have to create the heavens and the earth; but He wanted to, so He initiated it. He didn't have to create man; but He took the initiative to do so. Just as He had no obligation to create him, neither was He obligated to save him. But, because He loved him, He chose to, and He initiated the process that would cause His Son to die a grueling death on a cross. When we are tempted to blame Him for enticements He would never send our way, He wants to remind us that such evil is beyond Him and what He **did** choose to give us, was the best He had to give.

Ladies, you understand thankless sacrifice; some of you give more than it seems you even have to offer. You understand the pain of giving so much and having it questioned, or even ignored by others, whether by a child, a spouse, or a friend. I can't imagine the pain that must strike at the heart of God when we forget that He gave us everything He had to give, and then question whether or not He wants what's best for us.

Far from tempting us to sin, God chose first to create man, and then to save him.

According to verse 18, why did God choose to gift us with salvation?

_____

First fruits are often referred to as something superior in excellence – the choice fruit, picked fresh from the vine at the perfect time, rather than the one left rotting and neglected. The first fruits in Israel were used as sacred offerings to God. They were not only first in order, but first in honor.[7]

What a beautiful reminder of our position in Christ. In an effort to remind us that He loves

---

7   James B. Adamson, *The New International Commentary on the New Testament, The Epistle of James*, p. 77

us so much and gave us His very best, God also reminds us of what that fully entails. Being His first fruits, we have been given a position of honor and excellence in the Kingdom; never forget, you are a daughter of the King. You have been chosen and never neglected, loved and not discarded. You are the crowning achievement of His creation; the masterpiece of His hand. Some of us may even need to write that on our mirror to remind ourselves every morning. At the same time, even in our position of honor, our lives are to be a sacred offering to our God; they are not our own – He has bought them at a tremendous price (1 Cor. 6:20, 1 Cor. 7:23). He has chosen us, He delights in us, He has gifted us with eternal life with Him, and in return, we are to turn our lives over to Him as an offering of the best we have. He gave us His best and He asks the same of us in return.

We have been given a position of honor and excellence in God's Kingdom.

Take time today to thank God for His good and perfect gift of salvation that we so often take for granted. Perhaps spend time speaking with Him concerning times you may have questioned His love. Thank Him for His steadfast holiness that does not respond to us in variation or shifting shadows. Above all, thank Him that the reminder of His promise of love found in our passage today came after His description of a pattern of sin. Even knowing that we are going to continue to sin, He reminds us of His love, His choice to save us, and our place of honor in His eyes. We are never broken beyond repair, never tarnished beyond restoration; bask in His light and love right now. You need not wait for a new day.

He gave us His best and He asks the same of us in return.

Day Three — The Soil of the Heart

In our busy world, we greet each other with quick hellos and don't often take the time to sit and listen to one another's hearts. Our society has even come to the place where two people can pass by each other and say, "Hi, how are you?" and find it completely acceptable to proceed walking without waiting for an answer. Oftentimes, when opportunity is given for a response, it is simply a brief, "Fine," when the reality is, the status of their heart may be anything but fine. In the past few years, I've decided to sporadically stop my friends as our busy paths cross and ask, "How's your heart?" honestly desiring to hear their answer. We've become so accustomed to answering, "Fine," that, at times, I literally have to drag the answer out of them.

The status of our hearts determines what we will do with what we've already learned.

Today we're going to look at our hearts. For it is the status of the heart that determines what we choose to do with what we've already learned.

Read only the first three words of James 1:19. Write them here:_____

What did they know? What is James referring to that we know? They knew, as we do from vv 17-18, that Christians are the first fruits among His creation as a result of the good and perfect gift of salvation given to us. As first fruits, we are made to be excellence among His creation; however, first fruits were also sacrifices to God. Likewise, we are to be living sacrifices for Him; our lives are to be an offering for Him to use as He sees fit. James is now going to ask them to understand that the condition of their hearts must be analyzed in order to respond accordingly to what they know.

As first fruits we are both excellence among His creation, and living sacrifices for Him.

The rest of verse 19 tells us there is a contrast between what they *know* and what they still need to fully *understand*. Admittedly, when reading the next few verses, they seem a bit disjointed. They don't seem to reflect back to the previous thought, nor upon first glance, do they necessarily seem to blend with each other. But, there is a uniting word that runs a thread of purpose through them all, if we are willing and patient enough to find it.

Read James 1:18-22. Use one word to fill in the following three blanks:

What we are to do with the Word is the theme that binds these verses together.

James 1:18 – What were we brought forth by? _____

James 1:21 – What are we to receive? _____

James 1:22 – What are we to prove ourselves doers of? _____

What we are to do with the Word that has brought us forth is the binding theme that gives a sense of unity to these verses. As mentioned above, it seems that James has a sudden break in thought after declaring our position in Christ in verse 18. From there, he seems to elaborate on what nice characteristics Christians should strive to have. Yet, verses 19 through 21 don't seem to complement each other in that manner. Verses 19 and 20 seem to elaborate on anger, and while verse 21 begins with "therefore," a word that tells us it is referencing the previous thought, it then goes on to speak of *all* filthiness and all that remains of wickedness, not merely sinful anger.

There is an old saying when it comes to the word "therefore." Upon its occurrence, we must ask, "What is 'therefore' there for?" These verses begin by telling us that we **know** the Word of truth, **but** we need to have a proper response to it so we can **therefore** proceed to handle the Word in the way James further prescribes in this passage.

Based on the fact that we have been brought forth by the Word as a new creation, what three instructions do we find in verse 19?

_____

These verses are often used for life application in guarding the tongue and keeping our temper. The three instructions found in this verse hold great truth when it comes to those topics, but in its original context, the instructions apply to how we respond to the Word rather than how we respond to others. Verses are so often plucked out of their context in order to prove a point, that we lose the intent of the original message. Historically, these verses have fallen into that category. Because we are accustomed to hearing them taught as truths for personal relationships, seeing them in a different light will initially seem unusual, but stick with me and we will see it all pull together in the end.

When verses are taken out of context to prove a point, we often lose the intent of the original message.

Keeping the end in mind is so important when trying to understand these verses in context. Someone once said, "If you don't know where you're going, you'll get there every time." When planning a trip, we have to know our final destination before we can understand how to get there. Such is the case with verses 19-21. As we move forward, let's set our eyes first on the destination, then we'll plug in the practical tactics for getting there. First, fill in the next 4 words of James 1:21.

Therefore …in humility _____ .

dechomai - to take, receive, accept, welcome

The destination of verses 19-21 is for the believer to **humbly receive the Word implanted**. We have the saving knowledge spoken of in verse 18. We are now being asked to absorb its truths with a ready and humble heart. The word "receive" here is *dechomai,* which means "to take, receive, accept, welcome." The word "implanted" is used to describe how we are to receive God's Word in our lives and appears only here in Scripture. The Greek, *emphutos,* means "inborn or natural;" figuratively, it speaks of what is planted and hence natural. In other words, we are to welcome the Word of God in our lives in such a way that it becomes planted in our hearts; imbedded so deeply that all that grows from it is naturally glorifying to God.

emphutos – inborn or natural

Therefore, knowing that this is the intent of this section of verses, we can now go back and look at the preceding verses in the context of their end goal. In order for us to ever come to the place where we receive God's Word in such a way that we are not only accepting it, but welcoming it into our lives, the soil of our hearts has to be properly prepared for its planting.

We've already listed the three instructions given for properly receiving the Word, but now that we've identified their unifying goal, let's look at them one at a time.

According to verse 19, what is the first instruction for receiving the Word implanted?

_____

What do you think it means to be quick to hear?

_____

The word used in this verse for "quick" is *tachus,* which means "prompt, ready, swift." In order for us to adequately receive and absorb the Word of God in a manner that can effectively change our lives, we must be **ready** to hear it because we are eager to understand.

tachus – prompt, ready, swift

Don't you just love it when you're talking to someone and you can tell they are in a totally different world? They're not rude enough to walk off, but they're definitely not engaged in what you're saying either! We can all be prone to doing that once in a while. My own mind is usually in so many places at once, that I literally have to remind myself to focus on what others are saying instead of getting distracted. Our children can be great examples of this. I homeschooled my girls for 6 years, and more often than not, they would "listen" to my teaching with eyes glazed over and no concentration. On the other hand, when it was time for me to tell them our plans for a fun vacation, or something that they were excited about, I had their full attention with their eyes locked into mine. They were eager to hear every detail, anxious to learn how it was going to affect their own lives, and quick to share their news with others. The latter is the kind of hearing we are called to in this verse – a quickness to listen and a readiness to absorb rather than forget.

Read Matthew 13:1-23. According to verses 14-15, why did they hear but never understand?

_____

When approaching the Word of God, we are to have a quickness to listen and a readiness to absorb.

According to verse 15, what would God do for them if they would only listen?

_____

Verses 20-21 explain the seeds that landed on the rocky places. What happened to them?

_____

According to verse 23, who represents the seed that fell on good soil?

_____

What sort of a crop does this seed produce?

Greet the Word with eager anticipation of truth you need to hear.

_____

We have a God who is so anxious for us to listen to Him, because the seeds He desires to plant in our hearts will bring forth a harvest of fruit for Him and abundant peace and joy for us. It is our decision, though. Will we read through Scripture as if we are reading the dictionary, glazed over and uninterested? Or will we greet the Word with eager anticipation for truth we need to hear? Will we still our own minds enough to listen, or stay distracted with our own pleasures and worries - always hearing but never understanding? It is ultimately up to us. But, just as it was with my own children in school, when testing time comes, the measure of our listening is always revealed.

According to James 1:19, what is the second instruction for receiving the Word implanted?

_____

No matter how you slice it, it is impossible to listen while the sound of your own voice drowns out the voice of the one speaking. The heart cannot be still enough to hear the voice of God while the tongue is unhinged. We cannot learn and grow if we cannot hear God; we cannot hear Him if we will not be quiet. Remember, the desire of a wise man is to grow in more wisdom. The wise bite their tongues in order to allow for that.

What is the third instruction for receiving the Word implanted, found in verse 19?

_____

As we are still and listen to the Word, allowing it to shape our lives, it will convict us. God's Word shows us a perfect standard, and as the light of that standard shines on us, it will reveal areas in our lives that we need to correct. We must not respond with defensiveness and anger toward what we hear.

When you are in a situation where something personal or dear to you is being questioned, what is your first inclination?

_____

To hear the voice of God, we must silence our own.

Did you say it was to sit quietly and listen, or did your answer reflect more of a natural tendency to defend yourself? If we are perfectly honest, we will admit that it is human nature to want to defend ourselves. Because of that reality, when God's Word is the catalyst for conviction, we can, at times, want to turn away from it, defending our right to proceed as we wish, rather than heeding what we've read. Some may tend to avoid a certain passage of Scripture because it makes them uncomfortable, while others may try to twist the meaning of a passage to give them license to do as they choose rather than conform their will to the Lord's leading. Lastly, as verse 19 says, some may respond in outright anger, offended by the Word of God and desiring to hold on to their "rights" to live as they choose.

Verse 19 says that we are to be slow to this sort of defensive anger. Why? (verse 20)

_____

It is human nature to want to defend ourselves when God's Word brings conviction.

This verse is one of the examples of why it is so important to see these instructions in the light of their context. If we don't understand what kind of anger is being addressed here, it would appear that of all sin universally known to man, James chose anger to point out as not meeting God's righteousness. True, it doesn't, but neither does any other sin. In its proper context, we can now see that the righteousness of God cannot be achieved in a believer who has a defensive anger against the convicting Word of God.

Read Romans 12:2. Do not be conformed to this world, but be _____

by the _____ of your mind.

The righteousness of God cannot be achieved if we have a defensive anger against His convicting Word.

We absolutely cannot achieve the righteousness that God desired us to strive for when He "brought us forth by the word of truth" if we keep our defenses high and refuse to allow the Word to transform and renew our minds. God's righteousness here does not refer to the righteous part of His character, but to the way of life that He requires of us. This righteousness will become ours, if we genuinely accept His Word.[8]

_____

8   Adamson, *NICNT, James,* p. 80

We have finally made it full circle back to our word "therefore!" Hopefully, all of the puzzle pieces fit together now, and you can see how the beginning of this verse fits perfectly with everything we've discussed today.

Read verse 21. What are we to put aside? _____

If we are quick and eager to hear God's Word, slow to speak our own mind, and slow to defend our sinful nature in anger against Scripture, we put ourselves in a position to submissively follow James' next directions – namely, to surrender to the Lord everything that remains in our sinful nature. This is definitely not easy; it's a daily process of surrender and a constant battle against our inborn antagonist, pride. That is why special emphasis is put on **how** we are to receive the Word in the following section of verse 21.

Surrender to the Lord is a daily process and a constant battle against our pride.

In _____ receive the word implanted.

There's no getting around it, asking the Lord to identify every area of sin in your life and allowing Him to ask you to change what He reveals requires extreme humility. But, placing yourself under the mighty hand of God is the safest and most blessed place you can ever hope to be.

What do James 4:10 and 1 Peter 5:6 promise the humble?

_____

The safest and most blessed place to be is under the mighty hand of God.

Our circle around these verses has brought us back to our hearts. The question we are left with is whether or not our heart is in a place where we will allow it to be still, quiet, and humble enough to receive the Word implanted in the way in which God is asking us. As we conclude our day, I'd like to revisit the Greek words used for "receive" and "implanted." *Dechomai* not only meant to receive, but to accept and welcome. *Emphutos* gave the image of one thing being imbedded so deeply that something else grows from it naturally. "The soil of the heart must be hospitable, if the seed of the Word is to grow."[9] How's your heart? Do you greet God's Word with a welcoming eagerness for it to transform your life or with drudgery? Are you allowing what you take in from the Word to transform you, to become so deeply imbedded in your heart that what grows from it is a natural overflow? So, how's your heart?

"The soil of the heart must be hospitable, if the seed of the Word is to grow."

_____

_____

_____

_____

_____

_____

_____

_____

9   Ibid., p. 81

Day Four – The Woman in the Mirror

We left off yesterday right in the middle of James 1:21.

Fill in the blank: Therefore, putting aside all filthiness and all that remains of wickedness, in humility receive the word implanted, _____.

For the benefit of review, who were the recipients of this book? _____

Because we know they were Christians, we know that James was not presenting them with the plan of salvation for "saving their souls." He had already established that they were a kind of first fruits among God's creation. His instruction to them to receive the word implanted was an exhortation to allow the Word of God to grow them into the type of mature Christian who permits Scripture to mold his or her heart when the Word has convicted them. If the putting off of sin and the receiving of the Word implanted is not his way of explaining salvation, then we are left asking why it is followed with the clause *"which is able to save your souls."* The term *"save your souls"* is not a term used anywhere in the New Testament to describe a conversion to Christianity.[10] Rather, "by obeying God's Word, the believer can save his life, himself, from the consequences of sin."[11] Our eternal security is certain; we need not worry about losing our salvation. Neither do we need to fear that this passage puts conditions on our salvation. Yet, it does tell us that there are consequences, both good and bad, in this life, based on how we respond to the Word on a daily basis.

"Save your souls" refers to saving oneself from the consequences of sin by avoiding sin in the first place.

The next verse could easily be the theme verse for the entire book of James. As we saw on Day One, James' greatest focus was on **demonstrating** one's faith through an outpouring of observable evidence.

Read James 1:22.

If we have humbled ourselves and received the word implanted in our hearts, what should naturally happen as a result?

_____

Again, James begins another verse with the word "but." What do you suppose he is contrasting from the previous verses?

One's faith should be accompanied by an outpouring of evidence.

_____

_____

James has given us very important instructions for the way in which we **must** prepare our hearts to effectively hear from, and respond to, God and His Word. Yet, this next verse, in essence, says, "But, don't stop there!" I was born and raised in Missouri, which is called

---

10   Idem, *The Gospel Under Siege,* p. 24

11   Constable, *Notes on James,* p. 19

the "Show-Me State." In many ways, the book of James is the "show-me book" of the Bible. The emphasis of his entire book is to establish truth that the reader already knew, as well as give new guidance and direction for the Christian walk, all of which he sums up with, "You understand the gospel, now show me."

Using verse 22, fill in the blank: But prove yourselves doers of the Word,

_____.

paralogizomai – to cheat or deceive by false reasoning

I don't know if any of you can relate to having a stubborn child, but I certainly can. Upon having been given clear directions on how to accomplish a task, one of my daughters would often look at me and say, "Well, that's not how I do it." Even if it was something as concrete as how to add 2+2, it was more satisfying to her to argue than it was to comply. She had heard me and I knew she understood, yet she deluded herself into thinking that having her own way was going to bring her more satisfaction than complying with an absolute truth. In reality, most times it caused her more frustration and pain due to consequences than the argument was worth, yet she stood her ground.

We often do that as Christians. We hear the Word, we understand the Word, and yet we look at God and choose to say, "That's not how I do it." When we do so, we have deluded ourselves. The Greek word for delude is *paralogizomai,* which means "to cheat or deceive by false reasoning." How often must God shake His head in wonder, knowing that what He has chosen for us is so much better than any plans we could devise ourselves. Yet, our pride deludes us into thinking that ignoring the Word and going our own way will somehow lead to satisfaction. This fits the description of the man portrayed in our next few verses.

Warning: Objects in the mirror are reflections – of YOU!

Read James 1:22-24.

The one who hears, but does not "do" is compared to what kind of man?

_____

_____

From the context, what kind of man do you suppose he saw in the mirror before he turned away?

God's Word is a mirror for our souls.

_____

This verse isn't describing someone who looks in the mirror, sees perfection, and then quickly forgets how beautiful they are after turning away. This is a person who sees the imperfection of their reflection, realizes the changes they need to make, but forgets as soon as they walk away.

Read Hebrews 4:12-13.

The Word of God is like a mirror for our souls. If read openly and honestly, it will cut to the heart of our thoughts and intentions and lay bare our innermost being to the eyes of the Lord. For those of us who go to it with the desire to grow, it lays us bare before our own eyes like a mirror that does not lie. At this point, we have a decision to make. Are we going to turn away from our reflection and forget what we've seen, or are we going to begin addressing what we see by applying what we've heard from the Word?

We **are** to hear the Word, but we are also to seek to hear it in such a way that we crave it like we crave air to breathe or food to eat. To hear the Word in the way we're asked here is to absorb it so that it becomes such a part of us that it saturates our very being. Hearing without the intention of living out what we've heard is merely hearing without listening. Knowledge that goes in one ear and out the other does no good.

Upon walking into any bookstore, we find aisle after aisle of self-help books on nearly every topic imaginable. Many of us read them as if they are the solution to our problems, yet don't understand why our lives aren't changed by the time we've turned the final page. Oftentimes, instead of going to the effort of implementing the changes in our lives that the books suggest, we simply find another book, as if it will have the magic "easy button" that the previous one obviously didn't possess. Many times, Scripture is approached the same way. We may "give it a try," reading it to see if it will really make the difference in our lives that so many tell us it will. But if we don't see an instant change through a purely academic reading of the text, we may assume that it just doesn't "work" for us.

We are to crave God's Word like we do air and food.

Read James 1:25. Fill in the blank:

The one who _____ at the perfect law, the law of liberty,

and _____, not having become a _____

but an _____, this man will be blessed in what he does.

We must approach the Word as a tool that the Lord can effectively use in our lives, but the tool will not be forced upon us. The word used for the **intent** way we are to look upon God's Word is a compound word derived from the two words *para*, meaning "from beside or by the side of," and *kuptó*, meaning "to bend, stoop down, or bow the head." Together, *parakuptó* means "to stoop sideways to look at." This makes me think of visits we may make to the zoo, where a particular animal we came to see is just beyond the line of natural sight. We may stand on our tiptoes, crane our necks in every direction, or stoop down to peer through a tight spot just to get a glimpse. We don't go to the zoo to simply read the placards outside each animal cage. We go looking for an up-close encounter with something that is outside of our everyday experience. The animals are there for us to see, but when they're not right out in the open, we must decide whether or not the benefit of finding them is worth our effort.

parakuptó – to stoop sideways to examine

This brings us to our intent. Why do we come to the Word? Is it to check it off of our "to do" list because we are told we should be spending time in it, or do we approach it with an eager desire for it to open our eyes to truths we've not yet known? Do we hope to allow it to change our lives, or do we glance through it, hoping there won't be anything that makes us uncomfortable? When it does show us something within ourselves that needs to change, will we actually make the change? If we do, what is our motive for doing so? For some, there is academic enjoyment in reading the Word, combined with a sense of superiority, as personal flaws are peeled away one by one in order to attain a higher level of "righteousness." Such was the goal of the Pharisees; they went to the Word regularly, but it was for their own self-exaltation. They were hearers of the Word, and they appeared to be "doers" of the Word, but with wrong motives. They did not absorb the Word correctly, as we'll see.

In Matthew, we find several "woes" Jesus speaks over the Pharisees. Read a sampling of them here: Matthew 23:23-28.

These verses emphasize the fact that the "cleaning up" the Pharisees were doing was for the benefit of their outward appearance and not intended to be a changing of the heart. They were hearing the Word and doing **something** with it, but boosting one's own piety was never the intention of the law.

Reread Matthew 23:23. What three things had the Pharisees neglected while they instead put great emphasis on their tithing?

When the Word requires a change, do you make it? If so, what's your motive?

_____

This passage doesn't condemn tithing, but it does condemn the Pharisee who only focused on acts of self-righteousness. Tithing is an act that can be done by oneself, for one's own glory. Justice, mercy, and faithfulness are actions learned by the Word that benefit others and often call for self-sacrifice. Absorption of the gospel is meant to change more than our actions; it's meant to change our hearts in such a way that it overflows from us and, in turn, benefits others in a way that draws them to the gospel. If we are selfish in our Christian walk, allowing Scripture to only impact our own lives, we are not fully living out the Word. We have not become effectual doers and we, therefore, have not allowed the gospel to change our hearts in the way it intends.

Jesus put great emphasis on "doing" the Word. Read Luke 6:47-49.

To whom did Jesus liken the man who listens to His words and puts them to practice?

_____

To whom did He liken the man who hears His words but does not practice them?

_____

Absorbing God's Word is meant to change our hearts first, then our actions.

I'd like to revisit our Greek word for the intent way in which we are to look at the Word. *Para* meant "from beside or by the side of." The meaning of this word actually stresses a closeness that implies intimate participation. In other words, the one who looks intently at the Word is one who stoops down, cranes her neck, or does whatever she can to closely observe the Word that she is already intimately abiding in. When she looks into the mirror of the Word, it is not for a quick glance to see if she has any broccoli stuck in her teeth or to make sure her hair is still in place. She studies it and absorbs it until it is so much a part of her that she can't look away from it. It has become the foundation of her life; without it, she knows that there is no hope.

For many of us, it's nearly impossible to read the above verses in Luke without thinking of the children's song about the wise man who built his house upon the rock and the foolish man who built his house upon the sand. From the mouths of babes comes the lesson concerning what will happen to each of us when the storms of life assail. As life squeezes us, what comes forth will be evidence of what we have chosen to absorb. Those who hear the Word and yet walk away will have no firm foundation to stand on and will more easily crumble under the burden of this life. On the other hand, those who allow themselves to be changed by their encounter with it will have the ability to stand firm on their foundation of the Word and the work it has done in their lives.

When we make the implanting of the Word the priority of our lives, putting ourselves in whatever position necessary in order to see its truths, we will see our lives transform before our very eyes and what we've **heard** will naturally become what we **do**. Just like the animals at the zoo that we have to reposition ourselves to see, we must put forth whatever effort necessary to see the Word for the powerful tool it is meant to be in changing our hearts and lives. What extra effort might you be willing to make today in order to make yourself more available to its changing power? I'd like to look at our Greek word *parakuptó* one last time. *Kuptó* was the portion of this word that emphasized the need to reposition ourselves in order to intently focus on the Word. The positions included in its meaning were not only to bend or stoop down, but to bow the head. Might I suggest that in order to begin seeing the changing power of the perfect Word in our lives, we must first begin with a humbly-bowed head and an honest prayer? Would you offer the Lord whatever might be hindering you from placing full priority on not only hearing, but also "doing" the Word as a natural outpouring from your life?

To receive God's Word with humility, begin by bowing your head and knee to Him.

_____

_____

_____

_____

_____

_____

Day Five – A Life of Worship

We've made it to the end of Chapter One and have seen that it takes great faith to endure trials and temptations in the manner we are required to. We've learned that our faith is strengthened by an evolving relationship with the Word of God, which helps us grow in grace and wisdom as it deepens in our hearts. From this deep-seated implanting of the Word comes a natural growth of action, as we begin to "do" the Word.

James chose a sin of the tongue to represent a lack of sincerity in one's religion.

What does "doing" the Word look like to you?

_____

_____

Read James 1:26-27.

Immediately, James shows us what "doing" the Word does not look like.

According to verse 26, whose religion is worthless?

_____

James spends a great deal of time looking at the dangers of the unbridled tongue in Chapter 3, so we will not camp here for long now. But, it is undoubtedly important to note that of all of the sins he could have pointed out as evidence for a lack of sincerity in one's religion, he chose a sin of the tongue. Whether the rampantly running tongue is drowning out the sound of the Word as it needs to speak personally to our own hearts, or carelessly carrying on in pride or selfishness with others, it is a hindrance to the productivity the Word needs to accomplish in our lives.

Read Luke 6:45. From what does the mouth speak?

_____

Hypocrisy – when our actions don't match our words.

We read previously about the Pharisees and their misguided self-righteousness. James 1:26 speaks of vain religion; the Greek renders a sense of "piety denoting the scrupulous observance of religious exercises – in action or words – …performed in the guise of devout religion."[12] Even in the "show" of their religion, the hearts of the Pharisees were revealed as their hypocrisy was made evident by actions that did not match their words. They spoke openly of their own religious superiority, while freely pointing out the faults and shortcomings of others, censuring and strangling them with legalism. "When we hear people ready to speak of the faults of others, that they themselves may seem the wiser and better, this is a sign that they have but a vain religion."[13]

The Greek word for religion used twice in this passage is *thréskeia*, which refers to worship

---

12   Adamson, *NICNT, James,* p 85

13   Matthew Henry, *Matthew Henry's Commentary in One Volume,* p. 1932

expressed in ritual acts. So, when James talks about their "religion," he is really speaking to them concerning the sincerity of their worship. He warns that knowing the Word, speaking academic knowledge of the Word, and yet having no evidence of an overflow of the Word in one's life is nothing more than vain worship and deception of one's own heart.

Read Matthew 6:1-8.

Although the Jewish leaders sought to give the appearance of worshiping through charitable acts and lofty prayers, Jesus saw the intent of their hearts and questioned the sincerity of their religion.

What is your own personal definition of worship?

_____

_____

thréskeia – worship expressed in ritual acts

Time spent in music and praise within a church service is often labeled the "time of worship." Worship can be thought of emotionally when one comments on a particular song that really "gets them worshiping." But, to limit the meaning of worship in this way is to grossly limit the understanding of how we are to daily relate to our Lord. Worship occurs **any** time we put focus onto God and off ourselves. When we give our God priority in any moment, we are worshiping Him. Music in no way has to be involved, although we can certainly worship our God through song. The emphasis is the intent and focus of the heart. Worship is an outpouring of selflessness in obedience to God in order to honor Him simply because He is worthy of honor. We are called to live a lifetime of worship, not to merely enter into worship in the sanctuary of a church one day a week.

When we give God priority in any moment, we are worshiping Him.

According to James 1:27, what is pure and undefiled religion (worship)?

_____

_____

Interestingly enough, not one single translation of this verse, defining what God accepts as pure and undefiled religion, mentions singing. Our religion is not a set of rules; our worship is not a book of hymns. We are to have an ongoing and "ongrowing" relationship with the Father who is worthy of the devotion of our every moment; our every breath. When we wake up in the morning and choose to surrender our actions of the day to the Lord rather than focusing on what we think will bring us personal satisfaction, we are committing ourselves to worship. When we have our own plans, yet choose to alter them in order to help someone in need, because that is what the Word in us has conformed our hearts to do, we are choosing to worship. When we are in the midst of a trial and the world would tell us to turn our backs on God, yet we give Him a sacrifice of praise while our hearts are breaking, we are choosing to worship.

Our religion is not a set of rules; our worship is not a book of hymns.

Pure and undefiled religion in the manner described above is clearly evident in a person's life, for the type of mindset that leads to these actions would never come from our own human nature; it is only possible through the indwelling power of the Holy Spirit. For to sacrifice self – our time, energy, desires, opinions, and expectations – is unique to the life sold out to serving the Lord. Yes, we are to **reach up** to God in verbal worship, proclaiming His holiness, sovereignty, power, and provision, but James makes it clear to us that this sort of worship is only acceptable to God when it flows from the heart of one who is also **reaching out** in order to lavish love upon his neighbor. "Worship is empty and idle unless it sends a man out to love God by loving his fellow men."[14]

Although Scripture points out quite clearly that God does have a heart that cares for the orphan and the widow, this is not an exclusive list of requirements for attaining an "ideal level" of Christianity. In the context of James, it is important to note that these two social concerns were prominent within the 1st century church. But, we can look at them as two examples of living in the trenches with our hands reaching to the sick, our hearts ministering to the downtrodden, and our eyes weeping with the wounded, all of which would include, but not be limited to, the orphans and widows.

It may seem easy to set aside a few hours on Sunday to devote to God and His people. It may be a little harder to carve out time to commit to Him every day in prayer and Bible study. But if our religion is to be pure and undefiled in God's eyes, our worship must go beyond these personally-enriching worship activities and translate into actions that benefit others. Our worship must not have an "on / off" switch.

When you come in contact with others throughout your day who need someone to talk to, an extra hand with a project, or an extended word of encouragement, do you think of it as an opportunity or an inconvenience? What is your initial, honest response?

_____

_____

It is in **these** moments where we are given opportunity to prove ourselves "doers" of the implanted Word. It is at these times when the overflow of the heart shows its true colors. It is during these opportunities that we can bless the Lord with the worship of our lives, giving evidence of the work we are allowing Him to do in us.

There is almost nothing as precious to a parent as when our children finally show an understanding of a difficult life truth that we have been desperately trying to convey to them. Words can hardly describe the moment we see them **act** on the truth that we've doubted they've really even heard. I wonder sometimes if that is how God feels with us. He's given us His Word, told us over and over to reach out to those in need, and yet we often get so wrapped up in our lives that we forget that one of the most significant avenues for obedience to Him lies in reaching out to others. I wonder how much it blesses His heart when He can finally gaze down on us as we put someone else's needs in front of our own and say, "I taught her that. I've been working on this lesson for quite some time now. I'm so proud of her; she listened." That, my friend, honors God, and in honoring Him in this way, we worship.

It's not easy to focus on the needs of others in our society. There is such an emphasis on making sure everything is done quickly, conveniently, efficiently, and proficiently. Marketing

We are to reach up to God in verbal worship and reach out in love to our neighbor in practical worship.

Our worship should not have an "on / off" switch.

Society tells us to focus on "Number One;" yet God thinks differently.

---

14   William Barclay, *The Letters of James and Peter*, p. 62

and ad agencies make sure their commercials convey the message that the needs of the consumer should be put first; we all need to look out for "Number One." Yet, the Lord tells us a different story.

Read Matthew 25:34-46.

Describe how seriously God takes reaching out to those in need.

_____

_____

Again, these acts of mercy toward others are not stipulations for salvation, but a tree is known by its fruit. We all need to seriously search our hearts and ask ourselves if the fruit of our lives is demonstrating the salvation we profess.

aspilos – without spot or defilement

What is the final description of pure religion in James 1:27 and what does it mean?

_____

What did James 1:18 call us? _____

First fruits are holy and set apart for a holy purpose. Not only does pure and undefiled religion reach out to those in need, it also strives to be unstained by the world. The one who seeks to set her heart on God, sets her mind to living her life in a way that does not compromise the standard which the Lord sets before her. But, maintaining this steadfast character does not happen on its own; it takes concerted effort to live a life that resolves to be set apart for the gospel. In no way does this imply that Christians should live their lives excluding all contact with non-Christians, for we are directly commanded to go into **all** the world with the gospel (Matt. 28:19-20). It does, though, recall a reference to the "double-minded man" of James 1:8, who wants to trust God's will, but refuses to give up his own. Giving up our own will is hard business; we are naturally drawn to selfish desires. However, using the Greek word *aspilos,* which means "without spot or defilement," James asks us here to live a life above reproach, unstained by all that the world deems desirable, yet God rejects for our own good.

In order to live this sort of life, we have to guard our hearts and minds, for again, it is not innate to our human nature. Not too long ago, I was driving on an old country road and noticed the most peculiar thing. There was a large home sitting quite a distance from the road surrounded by many acres of land. With no fence in place, the land was openly accessible from the road and yet, the driveway itself was guarded by a large, iron gate which was firmly bolted shut. I understood that this was most likely an effort to keep uninvited traffic from using the driveway, but I found myself chuckling as the stand-alone gate, without a fence, seemed such insignificant protection for the house, as it was still left vulnerable on every side. Like this house, we stand vulnerable to the intrusion of sin in our lives if we do not allow the Word of God to stand guard in **every area**. We cannot live like the double-minded man, unstable in all his ways. For the areas of our lives that we cling to are the chinks in our armor that the enemy will use to take us down. We may have a gate over our driveway, but by leaving ourselves unguarded in any area, we are inviting trouble. The world is prone to

If we leave ourselves unguarded in any area, we are inviting trouble.

stain the soul; it is hard to live within it and have to deal with it while remaining undefiled by it, but this must be our constant endeavor.[15]

To what areas of your life do James 1:26-27 speak? Does the way your worship **appears** match what your worship **does**? Are you living a lifestyle of worship or is worship something you choose to turn off and on depending on the day of the week? Does your worship include loving on those who God loves, even the "unlovable?" Are you able to live a life of worship that is uninterrupted by the intrusion of the "stains of the world" due to unguarded areas in your life? Take time today to journal a conversation with the Lord concerning these things. Be honest with Him; He already knows your heart. He longs for us to worship Him in Spirit and in truth (John 4:24); the truth of who He is, and the truth of who we are. Remember, it is only when we allow ourselves to be fully honest with our own hearts that He can do the greatest work in and through us.

Does the way your worship appears match what your worship does?

_____

_____

_____

_____

_____

_____

_____

_____

_____

15   Henry, *Commentary in One...*, p. 1932

WEEK THREE: AN ACTIVE AND LOVING FAITH

Day One – The Price of Partiality

One particular period in my life that no one could ever pay me enough to revisit would be junior high. Let's face it, junior high girls can be down-right mean, and if you're not one of the mean ones, you're likely one of the recipients of their hurtful ways. I'm pretty sure that there are secret classes given during the summer between 6th and 7th grade on how to give looks that can kill and how to crush someone's spirit in a matter of seconds.

Faith in Christ and personal favoritism cannot coexist.

As much as I would like to believe that this is limited to junior high, our next passage of Scripture shows that although we may grow up and out of a junior high mentality, our predisposition toward hurtful, cliquish discrimination may not altogether disappear. We may have only learned to polish it up, making it look more sophisticated and refined.

Read James 2:1-7.

Right off the bat, James uses three contrasting phrases within one sentence that simply cannot coexist: my brethren, faith in our Lord Jesus Christ, and personal favoritism. By calling them brethren, he reaffirms their position as Christians, which establishes a sense of accountability in the matter. He then reminds them of their faith in the Lord Jesus Christ, the high and lifted up exalted name above all names, who lowered Himself so far as to become a poor man. There is irony on both sides of this coin. On one side, they were discriminating against the very kind of man their Savior had become in order to save their own souls. On the other, that Savior was and is the King of Kings and Lord of Lords who judges all of mankind according to His righteousness and we all stand lowly and poor in comparison. A helpless beggar should have no right to discriminate against another beggar, and this is how we all come to the cross.

Just as the poor in spirit should be sensitive to those equally poor in spirit, it would also seem that a feeling of camaraderie would naturally bond those who are burdened with the weight of literal poverty. That was apparently not the case in this early church.

Even those who should have a sensitivity to others are susceptible to prejudice.

Read Acts 11:27-30. What did Agabus prophecy was coming? _____

Not only were these early Christians enduring fierce persecution, they were suffering the effects of worldwide famine. Let us be reminded that these were not churches you would see on TV every Sunday morning. These congregations were persecuted by Rome for being Jewish, despised by the Jews for being Christian, and were suffering the hardships of famine. You would think that in such a setting, there would be tenderness for each other's burdens. But no, we see here that even those who should have a sensitivity to others, born from their own marriage to suffering, were susceptible to the blindness of prejudice.

What contrasting treatment to the rich versus the poor did James give in his example?

_____

_____

Oh how my heart breaks at the vision of the one who walked into the "sanctuary," equally persecuted and starving, looking for solace and comfort from those who were said to have a message of hope, and yet because of his haggard appearance, was asked to sit on the floor. It may seem easy for us to look at this example and think, "I would never do that to someone!" But, let's consider the rest of the picture.

Do the poor find sanctuary and hope among us?

Why do you think the rich man was given preferential treatment?

_____

_____

The rich had discriminated against them, robbed them of their land, dragged them into court, and blasphemed the name of their God! The Greek word for oppression used in verse 6 is *katadunasteuo*, which means "to overpower or treat harshly." It also speaks of denying someone the higher position or blessing they should enjoy, literally tyrannizing them. It would seem ludicrous to show them favoritism when it was at their very hands that the Christian suffered. Yet, this is precisely the type of action James is chastising.

katadunasteuo – to deny someone their rightful high position or blessing by overpowering, treating harshly, or tyrannizing them

According to James 2:4, what did these Christians have?_____

When something seems entirely illogical, it is helpful to consider the possible motive behind the action. Perhaps they were fearful of the rich man. They'd suffered at his hands; might giving him preferential treatment have lessened the severity of his future oppression? He was rich and they were poor; could the rich man have possibly benefitted the congregation financially if he found their treatment of him appealing? No matter their motive, James tells us it was inherently evil, although I'm certain they would have felt it justified. Imagine with me for a moment. These rich people have your life in their hands, they hold the power over whether or not you have a home to live in, food to eat, or a means of income, and all you're doing is giving them a special spot in the sanctuary in order to perhaps lessen your burden. It's potentially life and death, your own and your family's. It seems reasonable - is it really that big of a deal?

Christ associated with those we may tend to avoid.

In order to answer that question, I'd like to look at several examples Christ gave us. As you read each of the following passages, ask yourself, "To whom did Christ give the priority of His time?" List each name or description of the person by their corresponding Scripture reference in the **first** blanks. Instructions for the 2nd and 3rd blanks will follow.

John 4:7-29 _____ , _____ , _____ .

The woman at the well was a "questionable character" for Jesus to associate with on many levels. The Jews did not associate with Samaritans whatsoever, and of all possible Samaritans for Jesus to choose to be seen with in public, He chose one that even her own people most likely labeled as "trash." Some of the descriptions I am going to use today may make us wince;

they certainly do me. We think to ourselves, "Oh, I would never call anyone trash!" and you are correct, most of us would never say such a thing. However, would she be on your list of people you would seek to make contact with if she entered your sanctuary on any given Sunday? Why is that? On the **second** blank by her description, write "the questionable."

Mark 5:1-20_____, _____, _____.

Strong enough to break through shackles, insane enough to scream among the tombs night and day, and wild enough to gash himself with stones, this demon-possessed man was the epitome of "scary." I can imagine that no one went near him for fear of their lives. I'm sure that he was the talk of the town, shunned by all who lived in the vicinity; certainly they all wished that he would just go away, perhaps even going so far as to wish that he would die so his existence would stop inconveniencing their lives. However, whom they saw as horrifying, Christ looked on with love. We read those words with gratefulness for the work that Christ did in the life of this man, but how would you feel if you found him sitting in your pew next week? Why is that? On the **second** blank by his description, write "the scary."

Those we may see as horrifying or scary, Christ looks on with love.

Luke 18:35-43_____, _____, _____.

For us to actually run into a literal demoniac would be an extremely unusual occurrence, although we do cross paths with people who scare us. We may not come in contact with a large number of blind beggars either, but he provides for us today an example of something we come in contact with, or perhaps avoid, on a regular basis, "the awkward." Sitting on the corner of the street, the beggar was an eyesore who cluttered up the view, and truthfully, he never shut up. Those who had to go in his direction might have walked on the other side of the street, hoping he wouldn't come in contact with them that day. Or perhaps they'd learned the skill of looking straight forward as they passed, pretending they didn't even see him. When Jesus came by and he cried out to Him, they hushed him and tried to put him back in his place. "You be quiet and sit there on the ground, don't bother Jesus… and don't bother us, either." The truth is, he doesn't have to be a beggar or a leper to make us feel awkward. She can be the woman at church that we know will talk for an hour if we make contact (and we just don't have time for that). He is the man in the pew near us that smells different, looks peculiar, or just acts unusual. Do we make a special effort to spend as much time loving on them as we do others we've looked forward to seeing when we get to church? Why is that? On the **second** blank by his description, write "the awkward."

Do we pretend we don't see those who make us feel uncomfortable?

Mark 2:1-5,11-12_____, _____, _____.

How do we deal with others who interrupt or inconvenience us?

I mean, really, how rude. They were already crammed tightly into a hot room trying to hear Jesus speak and suddenly roof material is crumbling onto their heads, and this group of disrespectful friends had the audacity to interrupt the assembly in order to lower one man down on a pallet! Couldn't they see Jesus was teaching and they were trying to learn? We may not exactly shun them, but how put out do we get with the parent who lets the baby cry through the entire church service, the class member who interrupts with input that we don't feel applies to the lesson, or the one that takes thirty minutes to give a prayer request about her Great Aunt Zelda's dog's cousin's pet squirrel twice removed? Obviously, these are gross exaggerations, but I believe the concept behind these examples is common enough that we all understand. Why is that? On the **second** blank by his description, write "the rude."

Mark 14:66-72_____, _____, _____.

He's been zealous, a die-hard leader for the Lord, yet you just watched him fall. He had seen the example of Judas, who also failed. Should Peter end his life as well? Coming back to the other disciples was going to be humiliating; he had been so bold when he said he'd never do such a thing, and yet he did. Will they accept him? Should he even try? He's no stranger to us; if we're honest with ourselves, we see him in the mirror. But, when we see him in the congregation, do we greet him with grace, or do we condemn him because he let us down? Do we shower him with love, or do we avoid him because, although we're glad he's come back, we're not sure what to say? Or do we possibly fear what others may say if they see us associating with him? Why is that? On the **second** blank by his description, write "the failure."

The list of those we may find ourselves avoiding could obviously go on and on. However, for time and space constraints, we'll stop here. From each example, it is apparent that Jesus spent most of His time lavishing His love and grace on those who were far from perfect. Those we may tend to discount, Christ counts as highly-valuable. But, the question we were addressing was whether or not it's really that big of a deal to show preferential treatment to those who enter our sanctuary who might be of some benefit to us, especially in the case of potential life and death, as was the case in James 2. That question can be answered with another question. What's the cost? What price does the poor man have to pay at the expense of elevating the rich man? What price would all of the above examples have had to pay had Jesus spent all of His time with the Jewish leaders? What price would the entire Kingdom of God have to pay if we did not have the testimony of the miracles done in their lives?

We've labeled each of the characters above with words that sting my eyes with tears, for I relate to every one. I am the failure, I've been the rude. In my own awkwardness, I often fear making others uncomfortable, and I have just as much capacity for being the questionable and the scary as anyone else who walks this earth. But, because Jesus came to save the sick and not just reach an elite few, He was able to rescue me, a dark and desolate sinner.

What's the cost of partiality within our churches? Life. Life is available for those who are searching for hope, but we have to be willing to share it with any and all. If Jesus hadn't come to spend his time among the broken, we wouldn't have the hope of their testimonies to call upon in our own broken lives. Most of us, no doubt, would feel hopeless knowing that we cannot measure up to some standard that we simply can't obtain had He only ministered to the elite. Jesus showed us the restoration from deep sin in order to show us in His Word that we, too, no matter how low we are, can be fully-restored.

On the **third** blank after every description, go back and write "restored."

The cost of partiality is to send the message to a broken soul that their life is not worthy of being restored and the ripple effects of that message are catastrophic. Every example above was not only restored, but went on to proclaim their story to all who would listen. Jesus left His "comfort zone" of heaven and came to dwell among us who were all hopelessly lost. Are we willing to leave our own comfort zones and extend love to all we come in contact with,

When others fail, do we extend grace or condemnation to them?

Those we may tend to discount, Christ counts as valuable.

No matter how low we are, we can be fully restored!

realizing that many of the most amazing testimonies begin in the most unlikely places and we may have a part in that?

It is impossible for us to show this kind of selfless love to others without first humbly seeing ourselves as their equal. It is only when we realize our own former hopelessness, that we become sensitive to the fact that we needed the hope of Christ as much as they do. When we truly realize where we've come from and are overcome with gratitude because He was willing to restore us, we want nothing more than for others to experience the same hope and relief that our own restoration brought us.

Showing partiality can send a message that another's soul is not worthy of restoration.

Read the passage below (even if you have it memorized, read it fresh today). Fill in your own name, a label of some sort that applies to your own life without Christ, and finally fill in the last blank with "restored."

John 3:16. _____, _____, _____.

Thank Him today that He showed no partiality when extending His love to you, and ask Him to give you a tenderness of spirit to do the same for all others you come in contact with. Praise You, Jesus, for Your amazing love.

When we remember our own hopelessness, we will be passionate about sharing the hope of Christ with others.

_____

_____

_____

_____

_____

_____

Day Two – Lavish Love

For his visual learners, James uses a word picture to illustrate his point about partiality in verses 1 through 7. In verses 8 and 9, he summarizes his point in two concise statements, just in case the emphasis of the illustration didn't make it across to everyone! In a pointblank manner, he states both the positive and the negative aspects of the situation. If you do "this," you do well, if you do "that," you don't.

The "royal law" is to love your neighbor as yourself.

Read James 2:8-9.

What are his readers doing well if they do?

_____

If they don't, what are they committing? _____

James 2:8 calls the command to "love your neighbor as yourself" the royal law. Why do you suppose that is?

_____

Read Romans 13:8-10.

How are all of the commandments summed up?

_____

The royal law is a repetitive theme throughout Scripture. It was originally stated in the Old Testament (Lev. 19), but Christ, as well as other New Testament writers, reaffirmed its importance many times, not only restating it, but adding gravity to its meaning. *Basilikós* means "royal; to be connected with a king." This law is royal as it was decreed by the King of Kings, demands a level of obedience due to the King by his subjects who will inherit the Kingdom, and it is considered the king of all laws concerning human relationships. As the above passage in Romans points out, all laws are summarized within this one command. Not even the greatest command to love the Lord with all of your heart, soul, and mind can be fulfilled exclusive of the royal law, for to love God in full, is to obey Him in full. Full obedience to Him cannot be accomplished without showing His love to others.

basilikós - royal; to be connected with a king

Fill in the blank: Love your neighbor as _____.

What is it to love oneself?

_____

_____

It might be easier to define what self-love is not.

Read Philippians 2:3.

This verse dispels any misconceptions concerning the level at which we are to love ourselves. "*Love your neighbor as yourself*" does not imply that we are to have a vain conceit of ourselves and that we should strive to love others that much as well. In fact, it instructs us to regard others as more important than ourselves.

"Self-love" as the world defines it, is actually "self-demise." We are constantly fed the lie that whatever "feels" good will make us happy. Yet, we are shown time and time again in Scripture that instant gratification brings us nothing but sorrow in the end.

Read Matthew 26:14-16, 47-50; and 27:3-5.

We are to regard others as more important than ourselves.

Granted, the example of Judas is extreme, but it is a picture of the downward spiral our selfishness can lead to. Between our own sin nature and the fact that the enemy knows our greatest weaknesses to enticingly whisper in our ear, selfishness that may begin very small, can snowball out of control. When small self-indulgences do not lead to any immediate consequences, we can become desensitized to the fact that there is anything wrong with them. But, as we become addicted to the drug-like effect of their temporary fulfillment, the desire for more and more grows until it's out of control. Judas' greed, fed by a desire to feed his self-love, didn't start where it ended; he let it grow until it consumed him.

Let's consider a practical example:

A small desire for having something new leads to its purchase and a sense of satisfaction. While there is usually nothing wrong with a single purchase, this may lead to a desire for more, and the temporary fulfillment felt from making a new purchase may give way to a constant drive to acquire excess. While the world would tell us not to deny ourselves that pleasure and to find any way to make it happen; in the end, we may find ourselves drowning in debt, wondering how we ever got there, and wishing we could get out.

The world's sense of self-love can consume us and end in self-hate.

Ironically, Judas' self-love ended in self-hate. Satan does that to us. He convinces us that we **need** what we **want** until we can't see straight. We allow ourselves to become consumed as we feed our love for ourselves and then he drops us, leaving us feeling helpless to get out of the situation we find ourselves in. This pattern can be applied to every single sin; no fire begins as a raging inferno. The need to feed self-love in the way the world would prescribe will ultimately lead us all to self-loathing. This is not what Scripture is implying by loving yourself.

We are, though, created with an innate sense of self-love that is critical to our human existence. This is a fundamental love of self that protects our life and health out of natural reaction, that finds joy as good comes our way, and mourns when we are hurting. It nurtures survival as we learn to forgive ourselves and it desires for us to learn and grow. This inborn love of self is what we are asked to freely share with our neighbor.

We were created with an innate self-love critical to our survival.

This type of love for our neighbor is not a tolerance beyond their faults, but an actual love for who God has created them to be. It is a love that seeks what is best for another, just as we would do for ourselves. **It is a love that puts ourselves in the place of others in order**

to understand them and love them more deeply. This love will not give up on them when they fail, and will ultimately spare no expense to ensure that they have the opportunity to know the Savior.

When taken seriously, that sort of love is difficult to share on a daily basis with even those we care about the most. Does God limit whom this sort of love is to be lavished upon?

Read Matthew 5:43-48.

Who are we to love? _____

Love for our neighbor goes beyond tolerating their faults.

Let's redefine the word "enemy." You are to love those who burden you, hurt you, stress you out, cause you pain, or consistently bring you sorrow. As you read those words, are there specific people in your life who come to mind? In thinking about being commanded to love them in the way described above, what is your first reaction?

_____

_____

We tend to read passages like this light-heartedly. But, when Christ told those gathered to love those who persecuted them, it wasn't a light command. When we gloss over the depth of its meaning, we are unconsciously belittling the level of love the martyrs were being asked to give to those who were taking their lives, the level of forgiveness a mother is asked to have for someone who has harmed her child, the level of grace asked of a wife who's been left helpless, a friend who's been betrayed.

Our "enemies" include those who burden and hurt us, cause us stress and sorrow.

It may be tempting, at this point, to think that this request is just too much for us, that there are some we simply cannot love, and could never forgive. But, let's look again at the example of Christ, whom we are asked to be like in every way.

Yesterday, we looked at a list of people with whom Christ chose to spend His time. They might have seemed "unlovable" to others, but none sought to do Him actual harm. Today, though, we've already looked at the example of Judas, the man who sold Him right into the hands of the executioners. Jesus had loved him all along, just as He had His other disciples. When Jesus washed the feet of the disciples at the Last Supper, He did not skip the feet of Judas, even knowing what was to come. Looking back to the example of proper self-love, even when we are at our worst, we innately care for ourselves. In loving others as ourselves, we continue to love them at their worst, just as Jesus did for Judas.

Loving others as ourselves involves loving them at their worst.

Read Luke 22:47-51.

In verse 51, what did Jesus do for the very man who came to do Him harm?

_____

The man whom Peter couldn't imagine looking on in love during that moment, was loved, touched, and healed by the One who shows us how to truly love our neighbor. This amazing example of love not only shows us **how** to love our enemy, but **when**. Jesus didn't wait to see if he would come and ask forgiveness, He loved Him right there and then, whether it was reciprocated or not.

Read Luke 23:33-38.

During the ultimate act of love, what did Jesus request of His Father for those who

were executing Him? _____

He not only asked for the forgiveness of those present, but for you and me.

Look to the sentence in bold at the bottom of page 57 to fill in the blank:

True, selfless love is a love that _____

in order to understand them and love them more deeply.

Love is to be given freely; whether it is reciprocated or not.

When we are tempted to think that the kind of love we are asked to give to all we come in contact with, whether they seem deserving or not, is more than anyone should be expected to give, we need look no further than the cross. In an effort to put Himself in our place, to be tempted and tried as a human as we would be, He came to show us how deep His love truly goes. I wonder, as He looks at us and sees how little of ourselves we are willing to sacrifice in order to show love, if He shakes His head, remembering all He sacrificed in order to teach us true love. Are we ready to learn? Will we humble ourselves and follow His example?

Read Romans 12:9-21.

Here we find a beautiful recipe for loving our neighbor as ourselves. When our time comes to an end today, use these verses in a time of prayer, asking the Lord for the strength, grace, and wisdom needed to love in each way described throughout this passage.

Loving others as ourselves requires great strength, grace, and wisdom.

As you pray, consider these things: Our verses in James today are based on an emphasis in partiality. They tell us that the royal law, love your neighbor as yourself, cannot coincide with partiality in any way. But, this royal law does not end with a simple lesson on showing favoritism. It challenges us to extend our willingness to love, and it encourages us to search our hearts and question our motives for when and where we choose to show love. Are our decisions concerning our extended love based on how they will affect ourselves, or the good it will do for others? Is your personal interaction with others based more on what they can do for you or how you can serve them? If others have no apparent benefit to us, will we take the time for them? The recipients of the book of James made a fuss over the rich man and neglected the poor. Today I ask, who is worth the "fuss?" Where is the line between those who are worthy of our love and those who aren't? If we're honest with Scripture, we must admit, there should be no line. We all stand equal at the foot of the cross. No one's sin is more worthy of punishment than mine; no one deserves grace any less than I do. If God in His perfection can find a way to put Himself in my place in order to show me love, I must do no less for everyone He places in my path. Help us, Lord, to learn to innately desire what is best for others in the same way we do for ourselves.

We all stand equal at the foot of the cross.

Day Three – The Law of Liberty

Yesterday we left off with loving our neighbor as ourselves without showing partiality. James 2:9 tells us that if we do show partiality, we are committing sin. What does the rest of verse 9 tell us?

…you are committing sin and are _____ .

The Ten Commandments, as well as the many other Jewish laws, were collectively known as "the law."

To understand this portion of James, we need to delve into some good, old-fashioned theology. Don't run! If you're a Christian, what we will look at today is at the core of your faith. Stay with me and we will be refreshed by a reminder of God's glorious mercy by the time we finish.

Read James 2:9-11.

When you hear the word "law" in the Bible, what do you think of?

_____

Some of you may have said the Ten Commandments, others might have made reference to the hundreds of ceremonial Old Testament laws the Jews were required to live by found in the first five books of the Bible, also known as the Torah. Either way, you would be correct. The Ten Commandments, as well as the many other Jewish laws, were collectively known as "The Law."

What do you think was the point of the law?

_____

When we think of our own laws, we know that they are given to us in order to promote structure and safety. The Old Testament Law, no doubt, was practical in this manner as well, but God's intent in giving it to man was far more than imparting a set of safety guidelines. In fact, the law did the exact opposite of providing safety, at least in the eternal sense.

The primary purpose of the law is to show us our sin.

Read Romans 7:7. What did the law reveal to man? _____

The fundamental purpose of the law was to show man his sin. A toddler doesn't know not to stick his finger in a light socket until someone tells him not to. It is at this point, that he must choose whether or not to obey or disobey what he has been taught. The law didn't create the sin; like the light socket, sin was already there and was inherently dangerous. But, the law did shed light on the fact that there was a right and wrong decision surrounding the light socket.

Read Romans 3:19-20.

The book of Romans tells us that God gave us the law, which shows us our sin, and at the same time, reminds us that keeping that law in its entirety is completely impossible. Why in the world would God want to reveal the fact that we have constant decisions to make between right and wrong concerning the law, and then turn around and tell us that there is absolutely no way we can fully succeed? Why give us a law that condemns us to failure?

In your opinion, does this seem unfair, making the law evil and vindictive? _____

The law, itself, is not evil. In fact, it is perfect. The fact that it is so perfect is what makes it unattainable. **The Old Testament Law revealed the character of God and set His perfect standard for living**. This standard is so high that even our thoughts of covetousness cause us to fall short of obeying it.

According to Galatians 3:10, what is the word used for the man who cannot follow **everything** required in the law? _____

Ouch! From my birth, until the day I die, if I cannot follow every single standard required by the law of God, 100% of the time, I'm cursed.

What are we cursed to? Romans 6:23? _____

No, we will not drop dead the moment we sin; well, not usually at least. But, we are cursed by the law to an eternal death, separated from God in hell, by committing only one infraction of the law. Seems pretty hopeless, doesn't it? That is **exactly** what God wants us to see by showing us His perfect standard. He needs for us to understand that there is no way that we can attain perfect submission to the law, no matter how hard we try. It is only when we realize this hopelessness that we become desperate to realize THE hope He has to offer us.

Read Romans 5:1-2.

Is there any way that we can have peace with God and hope in our eternity even though we are unable to achieve the standard of the law?_____

Through whom do we obtain that peace and hope? _____

Romans 3:24-25 tells us that even though the law condemns us to death, we can be **justified** through faith in Jesus Christ. To be justified, *dikaioó*, is a judicial term meaning "to declare righteous." It sounds the echo of the gavel in a courtroom after the verdict "not guilty" has been declared by God, Himself. But, how can we be declared "not guilty" if the law condemned us to death, and we know we've fallen short of meeting its requirements?

Many translations remove some of the key words in this passage that we need to look at, so a literal translation is provided below:

> ...being **justified** as a gift by His grace through the **redemption**, which is in Christ Jesus; whom God displayed publicly as a **propitiation** in His blood through faith. *Romans 3:24-25a*

We've seen that God justifies us, but how was He able to do that? Does He just decide one day to go easy on us if we will tell Him that we'll do our best? No, it is absolutely impossible for God to look on sin, and when there is sin in our life that hasn't been "paid" for, He cannot look on us. This is the foundation of our faith, the cornerstone of our salvation. God

The law revealed the character of God and set His perfect standard for living.

The hopelessness of ever fulfilling the entire law perfectly makes us desperate for the ONLY hope we have.

dikaioó - a judicial term meaning to declare righteous

is only able to justify those who have been **redeemed** by the death of Jesus Christ on the cross. Redemption, *apolutrósis*, means "a release effected by payment of ransom; deliverance." When you redeem a coupon, the value stated upon its face is accepted as cash by the merchant, being applied toward payment in full; once redeemed, you owe no other amount toward the purchase. The **ONLY** way the debt incurred from breaking the law could be paid was with a perfect, spotless, blameless sacrifice; a requirement that only Jesus Christ could pay in full. His payment for our ransom became our deliverance out of the debt that would have cost us our lives.

apolutrósis – a release effected by payment of ransom; deliverance

What was required by the law is called **propitiation**. The word, *hilastérion*, describes "a sin offering, by which the wrath of a deity shall be appeased." In other words, propitiation is the appeasement of God's just and holy wrath through Christ's worthy sacrifice. His perfect life and sacrificial death appeased the perfect law and allowed Him to redeem **any** of us who would choose His gift by placing our faith in the adequacy of what He did on the cross. Once we accept Him as our Savior, when we commit an infraction against the law and Satan accuses us before our God, He looks at him and says, "It's been paid in full once and for all! Step aside. You have no argument against this one; case dismissed." HALLELUJAH!!

hilastérion – a sin offering, by which the wrath of a deity is appeased

Phew! In case you were wondering, we are still studying James! Let's see how this applies to our current passage. Read James 2:9-11 again.

Based on what we've seen concerning the strictness of the law, what does verse 10 mean?

Christ's perfect life and death appeased the perfect law.

_____

In the context of these verses concerning partiality, this verse tells us that even the "little" sin of favoritism condemns us under the law. One sin, no matter how trivial it may seem, is all it takes for us to entirely violate the whole law, which mandates our need of a Savior. But, we know that James was speaking to Christians. Why would he need to tell them this if they were no longer condemned by the law?

Read James 2:12.

God justifies man. Christ redeems man. Christ propitiates God.

James needed to remind his readers of the gravity of the sentence they were saved from in order to appreciate the way they were to live their lives in response to that salvation. This verse gives the command to speak and act as those who are judged by the law of liberty. This leaves us with two dangling questions: 1) What is the law of liberty? and 2) Why are we still judged by a law when we've established that our sentence has been paid in full and the case against us in court has been closed?

Following Christ's death, God's character and His standard did not change.

Christ came to fulfill the law, and He did just that. We are no longer condemned by the law, yet the law itself never disappeared. God's character didn't change; His standard did not lower. We are still to live as if He expects such a standard. **Our freedom is not from the expectation of the law, but from the fear of the penalty of its infraction.** We are judged under a law for which arrangements have already been made to satisfy. We have the liberty to live at peace with this law, for it cannot condemn us with a penalty that Christ has already paid.

Does our liberty give us license to sin because we need not fear the death penalty of the law anymore?

_____

Read Galatians 5:13.

Our emancipation from the penalty of the law does not give us liberty to sin, only liberty to live outside of the fear of its eternal wrath. Knowing this, we are to live our lives with an acknowledgment of the debt that was paid in order to secure such a freedom, while we strive to meet God's standard. We do so not out of a bondage of negative slavery to the law, but from an indebted gratitude for the mercy He bestowed on us. We are to realize the magnitude of the penalty taken from us and understand what an ultimate act of mercy was required to remove that penalty.

We are still judged, "tried" by a judgment tempered by mercy. God's attitude toward sin is unrelenting, but his attitude toward sinners saved by grace is abundant in mercy. Understanding where we stand in relation to that mercy should make us sensitive to sharing it with others. For he who seeks mercy, must show mercy.

Read James 2:13 and Matthew 18:21-35.

Although this parable has specific reference to forgiveness, it speaks of God's heart of mercy and His intolerance toward our lack of the same. The cross paints the ultimate picture of mercy triumphing over judgment. God's mercy teaches us to be merciful.

How does James 2:13 say the one who shows no mercy will be judged?_____

The ultimate price was paid in order to make a way for us to live righteously. At the heart of righteous living is loving others and living mercifully with them. When we choose not to, we are judged accordingly. We will not lose our salvation, but we will reap consequences in this life and this passage tells us they will be merciless.

Read James 2:12 again.

The verbs "act" and "do" are preceded by the adverb "so," or *houtós,* to stress their importance and put emphasis on their fulfillment in the present tense. If you have a teenage child who is acting like a two year-old, you may need to remind them that they are no longer a toddler and follow it with, "**So**, act your age!" James has done just that. He has reminded his readers that partiality is a grave sin, in that it violates the royal law. He has further illustrated the law that all Christians were once cursed by. In doing this, he has established that if all were once condemned by the law and only the work of Christ could change that status, no one should think of themselves more highly than another, for nothing they did secured their own salvation. By having a humble assessment of oneself in this manner, mercy should triumph and partiality should be a thing of the past.

Granted, today was a bit "off the beaten trail." But, I believe that some days it is vital to our ongoing faith to be reminded of the absolute hopelessness we were saved from. After a while, we Christians tend to take our salvation for granted; we often gloss over the severity of what

Freedom from the penalty of the law does not give us liberty to sin; but we can live without the fear of the law's eternal wrath.

If we want to receive mercy, we must extend mercy to others.

houtós – an adverb that means "in this manner"

Occasionally we need to be reminded of what we've been saved from.

we've been saved from and in doing so, we belittle what had to be done in order to avert our punishment. Today, would you take the next few moments to humbly come before your heavenly Father and thank Him for saving your life? Thank Him for His perfect law, which showed you your desperate need for a Savior and for His willingness to give His Son to be that Savior, even though it cost Christ everything. Ask Him to teach your heart the same mercy that He was willing to show you and to remind you of that mercy in the moments when you need to show it, and not only during your time of prayer. Thank Him for the cross that shows us that although we walk in a fallen world that wears us down, not only did mercy triumph over judgment on Calvary, but it will continue to do so until the day of completion, when all sin will pass away and we will bask in His perfection and glory. Oh glorious day!

_____

_____

_____

_____

_____

_____

_____

_____

Day Four – Passion in Action

As we begin today, let's review something we learned from Chapter 1. In Week 2, we established that James 1:22 could be the theme verse for the entire book of James. Write it below:

_____

If James could have chosen a modern-day logo and motto for his book, they likely would have been a "swoosh" and "Just Do It." Throughout the entire book, he demands action that demonstrates faith. It's almost like he's touched on it before, been hinting around about it ever since, and just can't seem to hold it in any longer. In this next section, he fully lays out his frustration concerning dormant faith. These verses likely made the original readers squirm a little in their comfortable seats. If we're honest with ourselves, it should do the same for us. For it was a call to action, and that call rings just as loudly today as it did 2000 years ago.

James provided a call to action 2000 years ago that still rings loudly today.

Read James 2:14.

Eek!! Wait a minute! Ephesians 2:8-9 tell us that we are saved by faith alone and that works of righteousness have no bearing on our salvation. In the books of Romans and Galatians, Paul argues emphatically that salvation is through faith in Jesus Christ alone. The entire Old Testament pointed to salvation through faith in the coming Messiah and the entire New Testament confirms it. What in the world could James mean? Ladies, if you learn nothing else from this study, I want you to go away from it with this very firm truth that I first stated on Day One: Scripture **never** contradicts itself. Scripture **always** interprets Scripture and **context is king**. If there is a passage of Scripture that seems confusing while standing on its own, other Scripture will explain and support it. When it comes to interpreting anything within Scripture, its context must be considered.

By calling them brethren throughout, James established the fact that the recipients were those who claimed to have an understanding of a saving knowledge of Christ. Yet because of their actions, or lack thereof, he's calling their faith into question. James isn't writing these words in order to shed doubt on the fact that true faith can save a man; he's calling the recipients out concerning the sincerity of what they are calling "faith!"

Scripture never contradicts itself. Scripture always interprets Scripture and context is king.

Sometimes the littlest words in a sentence are the most important; they can go unnoticed, and yet hold two valuable notions together, as glue does between two objects.

In the final portion of James 2:14, what does James ask his readers?

_____

The word "that" is integral to the meaning of this passage. Within the structure of this verse in the original Greek, the word "that" is implied with "faith," yet unfortunately, some (though very few) translations have left it out.[16] When "that" is left out, the question reads, "Can faith save him?" which gives the impression that true faith is not enough to save. This was not James' intention at all. He does, though, intend to question the professed faith that produces no works, a faith that is a matter of speech but results in no action. By next giving a tangible illustration, James proves his point.

Read James 2:15-17.

Following on the heels of James' teaching concerning partiality against the poor, he uses a word picture with similar imagery. Although there is practical application to be found in the illustration, he is not intending it to be a lesson in kindness toward the needy. This is a visual image of the point he is trying to make concerning the type of faith he is concerned about.

Good intentions without followup actions are inadequate and worthless.

How useful was the good advice given to the brother in need?_____

It was good advice. It sounded great and it spoke of what was necessary for the one in need. But, the advice by itself, was useless and inadequate because there was no follow-up action that proved the sincerity of the advisor. This insincerity is at the heart of James' concern. It illustrates the insincere faith that is not followed by life-changing action. In verse 17, James says that this faith, by itself, is dead.

When you see the words "dead faith," what impression does it give you?

_____

When the Greek word for dead, *nekros*, is used in this context, it means "useless, inactive, inert." This type of faith is unproductive and ineffective. But, what exactly does that mean? Let's look at the next few verses and see if they shed a little more light on the meaning.

Read James 2:18-20.

Verse 18 is an example of a diatribe often used in New Testament letters where the author needs to make a point by inserting an imaginary objector into the "conversation." This objector is made to appear as if he is arguing with James so that James can, in turn, respond with a rebuttal.

What does this objector seem to be arguing?

nekros – useless, inactive, inert

_____

Obviously, James saw a need for inserting this objector's opinion. He must have gotten wind that this was the kind of argument being given within the churches in order to defend their lack of "faith follow through." This objector inserts his opinion by stating that, "Some have faith, whereas some do works, and that's just fine." James responds to this with a resounding, "No way!"

Within verse 19, we see the kind of "faith" that causes James concern.

What did James acknowledge that they believed? _____

---

16   Moo, TNTC, *James*, p. 114

Deuteronomy 6:4 says, "Hear, O Israel! The Lord is our God, the Lord is one!"

This passage of Scripture is known as the *Shema* and is a part of the Jewish confession of his faith. This is their way of proclaiming their monotheism, acknowledging that there is one, and only one, God. James tells us in verse 19 that the demons share this same academic understanding of a monotheistic God. The demons don't struggle with choosing which religion they think is accurate. They've seen our God, they know He's real, and they tremble. But, this intellectual assent has not brought them salvation. James simply illustrates here that an academic acknowledgement of who our Lord is does not produce a saving faith.

The demons have seen our God, they know He is real, and they tremble.

James is obviously concerned with the fact that his readers claim to have faith in God, but are apparently giving no evidence of this in their lives. Again, we know that he has consistently called the recipients of his letter "brethren," but as in every church, there were likely those who were living their faith and those who had merely made a verbal profession of faith without any obvious commitment.

Verse 20 begins with a poignant question. What is it?

kenos – means empty

_____

You foolish fellow, are you willing to recognize that something is wrong in your life? The word used for "foolish" here is *kenos*, meaning empty. He is asking those who are claiming to have an understanding of something to recognize that they don't; that their understanding has been truly empty! This can be so hard, especially when it concerns something we've been confidently advertising that we know. He's asking some of these church members to humble themselves enough to admit that their insincere faith is, indeed, insincere.

What word does he use to describe this faith at the end of verse 20? _____

argos – inactive, idle, lazy, thoughtless, unprofitable, injurious

This word comes from the Greek word *argos*, meaning "inactive, idle, lazy, thoughtless, unprofitable, injurious." How profound. A useless faith is obviously inactive, but it is also injurious.

How could a false faith be injurious?

_____

In its inactivity, an insincere faith does injury not only to the person who possesses it, but to the rest of the Kingdom of God. In their own lives, people holding onto a false faith have fooled themselves into thinking that a mere confession of who God is, a confession equal to that of a demon, is all that is required for salvation. This is, indeed, unprofitable and injurious to them in the eternal sense, as such a profession does not save. As for the rest of the Kingdom, those who call themselves Christians, yet live a life that says otherwise, do great detriment to those around them. As the world looks on, we are judged by our actions, not by our professions. We do injury to others who may base their decisions concerning their acceptance or denial of the cross of Christ on the works that they see us do (or not do).

Others may base their decision to accept or deny Christ on the works they see (or don't see) us do.

In yesterday's homework, we saw James call the churches to action. In the same way that we may tell our kids, "Act your age," he is telling his readers, "Act your faith." As we read these verses, we need to ask ourselves the same questions James was challenging the first century church to ask themselves. "If you say you're a Christian, are you acting like it?" "If you aren't acting like it, why do you say you're a Christian?" I've stated it before in this study and I'll certainly state it again: Our salvation is secure for eternity from the moment of our sincere acceptance of Jesus Christ as our Lord and Savior. That is not up for debate. Yet James poses the question – "Is your faith sincere?" Was it merely a verbal assent to the reality that there is a God or was it a proclamation of faith in a Savior worthy of active obedience?

Our salvation is secure for eternity from the moment of our sincere acceptance of Christ as Savior and Lord.

There is a beautiful praise song named "The Power of the Cross." Its chorus follows:

The power of the cross is moving in my life,
'cause the power of Your blood has saved me.
The power of the cross still draws me to Your side,
'cause the power of Your love has changed me.
Oh, let my life be lost in the power of the cross.

Paul focuses on the root of salvation, while James focuses on its fruit.

James wants to know if the power of the cross is actively moving in these church members' lives. Was their commitment to the Savior sincere enough that they allowed the power of His love to **change** them? Was their faith authentic if it wasn't manifesting itself in action? No, James is not disagreeing with Paul concerning salvation through faith alone, but he is asserting that a faith that never acts, may not have been sincere in the first place. Paul focuses on the **root** of salvation, whereas James focuses on the **fruit** of salvation.

Read James 2:21-24.

dikaioó – to declare righteous, or to show to be righteous

James supports his position with the example of Abraham. When does he say that Abraham was justified? _____

We discussed yesterday that we are justified, declared righteous, or "not guilty," as in a court of law, at the moment of our salvation. Paul teaches that, and James supports it, yet James speaks of justification differently within this passage. There are two meanings for the Greek word used for "justification" in Scripture. *Dikaioó* can mean "to declare righteous," as we've seen, or "to show to be righteous" as we will see today.

Read Genesis 15:6.

God declares us righteous in His sight, while we show ourselves to be righteous to others by our deeds.

This is where Abraham was first declared righteous, or justified, solely due to his faith and trust in God. No action occurred at this moment; he was proclaimed righteous in the sight of God because of the deep-seated faith he had that was going to change his life.

James 2:21 tells us that Abraham was justified when he offered up Isaac many years later (Gen. 22). It was at this time that he was justified in the sense that he "showed himself to be righteous," in the sight of man. The first event had an emphasis on God's perspective of Abraham; the second, on man's perspective of him.

This is the passage that I referenced on Day One that Martin Luther got hung up on, arguing that Paul and James were in disagreement. However, a close study of the text shows that they are not. "Paul wants to make clear that one 'gets into' God's kingdom only by faith; James insists that God requires works from those who are 'in.'"[17]

teleioó – to complete, accomplish, make perfect

According to James 2:22, fill in the blanks: *You see that faith was* _____

_____, *and as a result of the works,* _____.

By using Abraham, James gives an example of a faith that is not useless but is working in tandem with obedient actions. As two inseparable entities, faith and works were working together in order to achieve a goal of spiritual maturity in Abraham's life. We've already studied a form of the Greek word, *teleioó,* used here for "perfected." It was the word in Week One, Day Two that spoke of implied perfection toward a given end; a maturity in order to fulfill a task. It speaks of something accomplished; a completion. Abraham's faith and works completed each other, and because of his works, there was no doubt of the sincerity of the faith in his life.

James spent a great deal of time in Chapter Two reprimanding the recipients of this letter. Apparently their actions were not matching their profession of faith and for that, he called into question the sincerity of their faith. Some of us need to ask ourselves if we would fall into the category that some of the original readers no doubt fell in to. Have we made a sincere profession of faith, or have we simply made an academic acknowledgement of God? If you are certain about the sincerity of your profession of faith, would the world recognize you as a Christian based on the fruit they see through your actions? Abraham demonstrated his faith to the world through his actions and not through a private, unspoken, undemonstrated faith. Our actions always match our passions. What do your actions say you're passionate about? Do your actions say you're passionate about your faith?

Our actions match our passions. Do your actions demonstrate you're passionate about your faith?

17   Ibid., p. 114

Day Five – A Life of Surrender

Yesterday we saw that a faith that never demonstrates itself is useless; faith is not to be a one-time declaration, but an ongoing lifestyle. If it is sincere, it should change our actions, our focus, our choices, and our very life. James used two illustrations of a working faith. The first was Abraham, who demonstrated his faith when he offered Isaac as a sacrifice to the Lord, even when the outcome seemed hopeless.

Read James 2:20-24.

If our faith is sincere, it will affect every aspect of our life.

The example of Abraham shows us that we are justified by the type of faith that can't help but demonstrate itself in complementary works. It's not about the value of the work, but the value of the faith that produces the work. At the risk of being redundant, I want to reiterate that we are saved by faith and faith alone. When verse 24 says that man is not justified by faith alone, it is speaking of an insincere faith that has done nothing to change the life of the one who claims to have it. No work of our own can replace or add to what Christ did on the cross in order to get us "more saved." The emphasis on Abraham's "work" of offering Isaac demonstrates that his faith was sincere and that his trust in the God of his salvation was complete.

Would you say that your faith is consistently demonstrated by your actions? Would others agree? _____

Read James 2:25.

All of my commentaries have much to say on James 2:14-26. They go to great lengths to prove that James and Paul did not contradict each other; they spend ample time elaborating on Abraham's justification and the amazing faith that he showed through his obedient action. When they come to verse 25, their message boils down to, "…and Rahab did a good job, too." Personally, I think it's significant that out of all the figures God could have chosen to inspire James to use as an example alongside Abraham, He chose Rahab.

Why do you think God selected Rahab? Note your initial thoughts here.

_____

Rahab is often treated as an "afterthought" in this passage; however, God must have chosen her for a reason.

Read Joshua 2:1-21; 6:1-5, 16-17, 20-25.

The context of our passage in James focuses on something similar in the lives of Abraham and Rahab. But, I'd like to take a moment to focus on their dissimilarities. Abraham was, and is, an icon in the Bible. Particularly in the Jewish faith, he is held in extremely high regard. We as Christians like to ask, "What would Jesus do?" No doubt, children growing up in the Jewish faith are held to a standard according to an example set by Abraham. Abraham was willing to leave everything behind to follow God, he was willing to trust that God was going to do the impossible and give him a son in his old age, and he was willing to sacrifice that son. The list goes on. Although we do have examples of his imperfection, he is held in such high regard that his standard seems almost unattainable. If we're honest with ourselves, if asked whether or not we would be willing to go to the extent that he did in preparing to sacrifice Isaac, most of us would have to admit that we might draw the line there. Abraham was a model of working faith and no doubt deserves to be regarded with high esteem. But, as with many iconic figures, we tend to dismiss the possibility within ourselves of ever being capable of matching such a standard. I find it quite comforting that when God and James decided to give us examples of faith in action, they chose two people on such far ends of the human moral spectrum that we can all find ourselves somewhere in between.

How was Rahab referred to in the passage in Joshua? Rahab the _____

It is hard to imagine two more dissimilar people than Abraham and Rahab. But did they have something in common?

Whereas Abraham was the poster child for everything good to the Jews, Rahab was the questionable harlot. I find it interesting that James chose to use her as an example of extreme faith following his chastisement of the churches for showing partiality within their fellowship. Certainly, Rahab would have been looked down upon and cast aside because of her sinful lifestyle. But, once again, God establishes the fact that He can, and will, be glorified by any willing vessel who has faith enough to entrust their life to His hands.

Unlike Abraham, whose example might have seemed unattainable, Rahab was the underdog. I wonder if Jewish children would sit eagerly as they listened to her story told again, cheering for the unlikely hero in a story where grace and mercy provided a glorious second chance. If God could use a harlot, maybe he could use them as well!

Rahab shows us that God can, and will, be glorified by any willing vessel who entrusts their life to His hands.

Have you ever felt too ashamed, too guilty, too "anything" to be used by God? _____

How does the example of Rahab speak to your heart? _____

_____

When held to the example of Abraham's near-sacrifice of Isaac, it may be easy to throw up our hands and resolve that we will never measure up to such a faith. But Rahab, who seemed ordinary, or even hopeless, can help us to see that a life-changing faith can be realized by anyone willing to fully trust in God.

God knew that Rahab's heart was available and ready to help; so He created an opportunity for her to act.

What did Rahab do in the story of Joshua and the battle of Jericho?

_____

Thank God, He doesn't typecast in this story called life! He will, and does, use anyone whose heart will sincerely recognize Him for who He is. In all of Jericho, the spies could have chosen anywhere to go, but God led them to "Rahab the harlot", "for God knew where they had a friend, though they did not."[18] He knew her heart was available and ready to help, so He created the opportunity for her to be used.

Are you available for God's use today as Rahab was?

We live in a fast-paced society that thrives on activity and stress. When God asks, are you too busy to take the time to answer with a "yes?" Are you too busy to even hear Him ask? Be very honest with yourself and God in this moment. Is your heart available for God's use today?

_____

18   Henry, *Commentary in One...*, p. 212

According to Joshua 2:3, who sent word to Rahab demanding the spies?_____

Rahab was daring in her faith, so much so that she was committing treason. I think it is significant to note that this was quite possibly a new faith for Rahab. We don't know exactly when she chose to surrender her life to this God of the Israelites, but she certainly hadn't been raised in the teaching of the law as the Israelites were. She had only heard about the greatness of their God. Joshua 2:10 tells us that the inhabitants of Jericho had heard of the Israelite's deliverance from Egypt across the Red Sea and other ways that their God had provided for them in victory. With no visual proof for herself, she had chosen to put faith in this God that she had only heard of. Verse nine records her telling the spies, "*I **know** that the Lord has given you the land…*" (emphasis mine). Rahab's faith acted out of confidence in a God her eyes had never seen tangible evidence of. There is great irony here, as the Israelites had been wandering in the wilderness for 40 years because those who **had seen** God's miraculous provisions had doubted, and were denied entrance to the Promised Land.

Rahab's faith acted in confidence in a God she had not seen.

Must God continuously "prove Himself" to you before you will trust and obey Him?

Why or why not? _____

Rahab had the threatening hands of death around her throat no matter what she chose. If she betrayed her king and country, she risked death at their hands. If she betrayed God, she would surely die with the rest of the city. Rahab recognized the God who stood above all manmade laws and chose to obey Him rather than men. Her faith in this crucial moment demonstrated more than academic knowledge of God.

Rahab's faith was demonstrated through her choices.

In this, Rahab's faith was demonstrated through her choices. She knew why the spies were there and she knew that helping them might cost her life, but she recognized that this God was the One who was worth both living and dying for. If she lived, it would now be for His glory. If she died, it would be for the same. Her choice demonstrated confidence in God's nature, character, and reliability; her action made this apparent. Her choice was to obey; she simply could do no other.

What do your own choices demonstrate about our faith? - Your choices of time use? - Your choices in crisis? - Your everyday choices?

Many times our obedience to God must precede our understanding of His ways.

_____

_____

Rahab's choice gave evidence that she had total reliance on the One who was able to provide. Our desired knee-jerk reaction is to become one that says, "I don't know what God is doing in this situation, but I know His character and I will trust Him. I choose to act on that trust." Those actions affirm our sincere faith.

We've discovered that Rahab was an unlikely hero, and we are grateful that God gave us those examples in Scripture to give us hope when we feel hopeless. I appreciate immensely that He was willing to put her name beside Abraham's in order to give us another example of true faith. But, as I searched the Scriptures wondering why it was that James chose Rahab out of all of the other faithful figures available, I couldn't keep my eyes off of one particular verse. I'd like to now focus on some items that I believe tie Rahab, Abraham, and Christ together in a beautiful way that only God could orchestrate.

Abraham and Rahab were both valiant in the examples of faith given in James 2, but why were those two particular events chosen over some of the other amazing miracles of faith provided in the Bible? Why were their two stories ideal for using as examples of sincere, saving faith? While James never tells us why he selected them, there seems to be a common theme in their courageous acts of faith that may connect them.

Read Joshua 2:14a which follows Rahab's request for provision and deliverance:

So the men said to her, "Our life for yours…"

In both Abraham and Rahab's examples, lives were being offered in obedience to God, and in both, deliverance from death was made available due to a demonstrated faith.

Abraham was willing to trade Isaac's life for obedience to God, having faith that one way or another God would work it out for good and continue to keep His promises. God had promised that Abraham would have descendants with numbers like the sands of the sea and the stars of the sky (Gen 15). To sacrifice Isaac was to threaten that promise, yet Abraham had seen God's miracles before and trusted that He would provide again.

God was willing to provide the blood of a ram to trade for Isaac's life when Abraham had shown great faith; the blood of one stood in place of another.

Rahab was willing to trade her life for obedience to God, having faith that one way or another God would work it out for good and continue to be the God she'd heard of and placed her trust in.

Read Exodus 11:1,4-6 and 12:21-24

What similarities do you see between the Passover described in Exodus and the story of Rahab? _____

_____

Abraham and Rahab both offered lives in obedience to God; deliverance was made available due to demonstrated faith.

In the story of Jericho, God instructed Rahab to display a scarlet cord in her window and remain within her house. In an act of great obedience that demonstrated her faith in God's adequate provision, she followed His specific instructions, and as a result, He protected her and all those gathered in her home just as He had promised. With striking similarity, God provided the same protection to all those gathered inside the Israelite homes displaying blood on their doorposts when the death angel passed by in Egypt. The blood on the doorposts in Egypt provided immediate protection, pointed toward, and showed their faith in, a future provision of salvation.

Abraham and Rahab both had faith that God would adequately provide a way of escape; their actions demonstrated this faith in God's provision.

In both their cases, God had given specific instructions for Abraham and Rahab to follow; He gave them choices to make. If they followed His plans in obedient, surrendered faith,

He offered a means for their deliverance. **Because of their faith that was ready and willing to act based on their trust in God's reliable character, God provided a life-saving way of escape**. This willingness to trade one's life for faith in God is what symbolizes the deep faith God and James were trying to describe earlier in James 2, a faith that realizes the debt paid on our behalf, the life traded for our own. Today, God continues to offer a means of deliverance - His Son. What was true with Abraham and Rahab is true today; a sincere, obedient faith that acts is still required. On the cross, Christ was willing to say, "My life for yours." There was no provision for His own escape. He was, and is, God's provision for our escape; He is our ram, our scarlet cord, the blood on our doorpost, our spotless Lamb.

Sometimes I wonder if that means anything to us anymore? Rahab acted in faith because of the small amount she'd heard concerning the God of Israel. We have every miracle in the Bible, even the clear gospel, which Rahab had no clue about. We haven't just heard a rumor of this great God, we have thousands of years of evidence of His worthiness of our service. Are we willing to trade our lives for His, to give our lives for service to Him? Are we willing to trade our life in for a life that shows faith in our every action, decision, choice, and priority? When we tell God that we "give Him our lives," what do we mean? Have those words become so cliché that we've forgotten their meaning? Is He the focus of our lives or just the focus of our extra time, should we happen to come up with any? Do we fit Him in after everything else, or is He our passion that everything else comes in second place to? Can we say we'd give up our lives for Him if we can't give up our time to spend in His Word, at His feet in prayer, or loving on His people?

We've asked if our faith is sincere. Now let's ask how deep it is. Is it deep enough to commit to Him our time, priorities, and passions, trusting Him to do more in, and with, our lives than we could have done holding onto them for ourselves?

It can be tempting to say that this type of faith can't be expected of just anyone, and certainly not too quickly. But, Rahab shows us differently on both fronts. She was likely a babe in her faith, and yet a giant in her obedience. I stand amazed as I consider the act of risking her life for the God she had only heard of. I'm both humbled and challenged by her example. We also cannot believe that she was simply a woman of such high character that this sort of action came easily for her. No, we know that her past character was questionable, but what a beautiful example of God's grace that is ready to clean the slate and use the willing vessel. A tarnished life was cleaned and restored in order to be used mightily...amazing grace, how sweet the sound. In fact, her life shows us that the greatness of sin has no bearing on the great impact God can still have on a surrendered life. Mercy is always available to the repentant, and it is mercy that is shown through the life of the forgiven as they walk forward in faith.

Thank Him for the mercy He has shown you and ask Him what He would like to do with your redeemed life. It is now His – He bought you at a great price.

On the cross, Christ said, "My life for yours." In response, are we willing to surrender our lives for His?

Rahab shows us that even "babes in Christ" can demonstrate tremendous faith and obedience.

WEEK FOUR: A CONTROLLED AND GENTLE FAITH

Day One – The Teaching Life

We've all heard the saying, "Put your money where your mouth is." James has spent a great deal of time emphasizing the necessity of "putting your action where your faith is." He has given a few practical examples of ways to do this, such as walking faithfully through trials and dealing with one another without partiality. He is now going to give instruction concerning an area of the Christian walk where we can all use improvement – the use of our tongue. There is nothing that reveals the intent of the heart louder than the tongue.

James warned about teaching God's Word due to the greater judgment involved.

Read James 3:1.

What is the warning given in verse one? _____

What is the reason given for the warning? _____

First, it is important to point out that James is not discouraging his brothers and sisters in Christ from speaking boldly concerning the gospel of Christ, for we are all called to go into the world in order to make disciples (Matthew 28:19). He is, rather, warning them about seeking a position teaching the Word within the church because of the greater judgment they will face.

didaskalos – instructor, a teacher, a master

We're going to employ our "context is king" rule for interpreting Scripture at this point and focus on the historical context of the passage. The Greek word, *didaskalos*, means "instructor, a teacher, a master." It is necessary for us to remember that this first century church was still influenced by the way they had previously conducted their religion as Jews in the past. Rabbis had been their teachers and were held in extremely high regard; *rhabbi*, in fact, means "my master, my teacher." The teacher who had taken the place of the rabbi was now respected highly, as were the apostles and prophets (1 Cor. 12:28). These teachers were responsible for relaying Christian doctrine, and this position came with much prestige, especially in areas marked by illiteracy. These teachers held great responsibility in their hands; they were sometimes the only means by which the Word was conveyed and were considered the "be all and end all" of its interpretation. For this reason, James gives a strict warning about volunteering for this position.

rhabbi – my master, my teacher

What are some of the temptations in teaching that these men could have found themselves up against?

_____

_____

Read Matthew 23:8.

Jesus instructed His disciples not to allow anyone to call them Rabbi, for they only had one Master and were not to seek that glory for themselves. This is the distinction James is seeking to convey. While he does not want those who are spiritually-gifted in teaching (Rom. 12:7) to shirk their responsibility to answer the call to teach, he is warning them of the dangers of pride in that position. Even the meaning of rabbi, my master, implies greatness; it wouldn't take much for that title to go to one's head.

Now please read the verses preceding Jesus' warning: Matthew 23:4-7.

A teacher may be tempted to take credit away from God.

These teachers battled pride. Their position of authority and respect gave them a feeling of piety that they could easily lord over the heads of the people. They would certainly be tempted to revel in their high places of honor at functions, would take pleasure in the unquestioning service of their followers, and would probably take great pride in any apparent advancement of their students. Instead of giving God glory and credit for what He has accomplished in someone else's life, a teacher is susceptible to falling into the temptation of taking that credit away from God. The statement, "She learned everything she knows from me," is an example of this sort of pride. The glory should belong to neither the teacher nor the student, but to God alone.

The teacher of God's Word is accountable for their influence on others – good and bad.

As the teacher's knowledge of the Word would be highly respected, they would, no doubt, be tempted to take pride in their level of insight. As their self-confidence grew, they may have taken liberties with their "right of insight," falling into the danger of twisting Scripture for their own purposes. Instead of admitting they may not have known an answer to a deep theological question, making something up would have been an option that would feed their pride and protect their ego. If they desired more subordination from those "beneath" them, translating Scripture in such a way that would demand this would be a simple way to make it happen. In this way, false teachers were capable of not only twisting minor details, but also the entire Christian religion for those who would blindly follow.

It is due to this extreme responsibility that the teacher of God's Word is under a stricter judgment. They are accountable for their influence on others, their ability to both nurture and harm. All of the temptations listed above for those teaching in the early church apply to those teaching in this day and age. Humble teachers will bless others and receive blessing from God; those who teach with pride and with selfish motives will have to answer to God for their actions.

Read Acts 15:24.

What had these false teachers done by what they had said?

The fallen teacher gives his students cause to doubt God's Word.

_____

Confusion leads to chaos and Satan loves nothing more than causing chaos in a local body of believers. He also delights in inviting judgment on those who teach. If he is able to publicly destroy a teacher of God's Word, he can more easily get his hands on the students. The fallen teacher gives them cause to doubt.

For example, by pressing the topic of circumcision in the early church, false teachers troubled the minds of their followers, which led to confusion. The task of rightly dividing the Word of God should make every teacher live his or her life with a great deal of fear and trembling at the responsibility. By carelessly throwing out their own interpretations and mandates, these false teachers harmed the very students who trusted them, making their duty as teachers entirely counter-productive. Teachers of God's Word cannot base their leadership on their own speculation, opinions, or agendas. The ripple effect within the Kingdom of God following this sort of action is huge. The attitude behind teaching is of the utmost importance. God needs teachers to be tools in His hands; He doesn't need for them to think they are holding the tools that should be shaping others. Teachers are to be shaped by God and in turn, teach what God has shown them and allow God to shape others through the Holy Spirit. Teachers bear an awesome responsibility for nurturing people in the faith; this is to be done with great love and care. There is no room for selfishness and pride.

Read James 3:2.

As stated earlier, we **all** stumble; we are **all** susceptible to sin, especially the sin of the tongue. The teacher has just been singled out as a specific example of one who bears great responsibility, and now his warning is narrowed down by specifying the agent he can do the most damage with, the tongue. The teacher of God's Word is a constant public example and the teaching, with his tongue, has the ability to affect many. This holds him to a higher standard. The teacher's tongue can be used for great good or great devastation, and he possesses the possibility for causing either daily. The negative "loose tongue" of a teacher gives the impression to his followers that they can follow his example of unbridled speaking; the negative impact leads to an elevated level of destruction.

James 3:2 makes a transition from the "teacher" to "all," but the word "for" at the beginning of the verse implies that he is still referring back to the previous thought. Therefore, the message of this verse applies to the teacher as well as everyone else. Before we jump away from the topic of teachers, though, I find it important to point out that this verse does not imply an "easy button" for those who are not officially employed as teachers. Before anyone says, "Phew, I don't have the gift of teaching, I'm glad none of this lesson applies to me," let's think about a broader application.

Yes, James was specifically speaking to those who might fall into the dangerous temptation of pride surrounding the prestige that came with the role of teaching within the church at that time. But, we can apply the truths to our everyday lives in a very practical manner as well. Unless you live in a complete bubble, your words and actions are teaching someone somewhere. My mom always told me that no matter how old I was, someone younger was always watching me – and she was right.

I have a niece who is seven years younger than my oldest daughter and has always thought that "big Cousin Cassidy" is the coolest thing in the world. Yet, Cassidy didn't realize the influence she had on her younger, impressionable cousin. One day in the car, when my niece was pretty little, she and her mommy were having a discussion about her favorite colors, as moms and toddlers often do. No matter what her mommy said, she was determined to hate the color green; it was icky and that's all there was to it. Suddenly, her mom had an idea and

Teachers cannot use their position to teach their own speculation, opinions, or agendas.

The tongue can be used for great good or great destruction.

piped up with, "Cassidy's favorite color is green." Without hesitation, from the back seat of the car, her voice belted out the words, "I LOVE GREEN!"

My point is this - someone is always looking up to us, and most times, we probably have no idea that they are. Our lives, through spoken words as well as unspoken actions, are sending messages, and whether we like to admit it or not, we are always teaching. We hold a great responsibility to live a life pleasing to the Lord, so that "students" looking on will be pointed to Him and not turned away from the faith. Those younger in their faith are looking to those who are more seasoned. Others may be looking to your example in both good times and bad. Children watch other kids' parents to see how they relate. Teenagers look up to college kids, children to the teens. The list could continue indefinitely, but the universal truth is that our lives teach. The prevailing questions are, "What am I teaching? And to whom?"

The universal truth is that our lives teach!

I suppose the most practical example of this may be the parent-child relationship. How many of us, as adults, have caught ourselves sounding just like one of our parents (and usually at a time when we wish we hadn't)? Even without trying, we, as children, learned their mannerisms and subtle characteristics through our time observing them. Likewise, our own children study us. What messages are we conveying to them? What characteristics of our own do we hope they do or do not pick up?

You may not be your child's schoolteacher, but your life is certainly teaching them by example. What are some positive characteristics that you hope they pick up on?

_____

_____

What are some negative areas you pray that they don't?

_____

_____

Are you willing to make changes to teach them something different?

Your life is teaching your children by example; what are they learning?

That question is not intended to make anyone feel guilty. In fact, we all know that none of us lead perfect lives and we each have room for improvement. Yet, I think it is important for us to consider that type of question and answer it honestly, for when we gloss by these topics without thoroughly examining our hearts, we can be tempted to ignore any potential problems that may need addressing. As I examined my own heart, I asked myself a series of questions. We will end with them today; honestly ask yourselves the same. I will word the questions with an emphasis on our influence over our children, but these questions go beyond our parental persuasion. As you reflect on these questions, don't only consider the answer for the way you influence your children, but for the others who are observing your life from day to day as well: coworkers, friends, family, acquaintances, fellow church members, strangers at the store...

-Am I living a life of faith that tells my children that God is #1 in my life, or that He is a side note?

-Do my habits tell my kids that church is optional or do they see that everything else is optional, and time set apart for God is not?

-Do my kids see God in and through my life, or do they feel vindicated in their own sin because I do "it," too?

-Do they see that my actions from Monday through Saturday match my actions on Sunday when I'm at church?

-Is "Christian" my "stage name" on Sunday or the true description of my heart?

-Am I teaching my kids to be honest in their dealings?

-Do they hear me say one thing to one person and another thing to the next?

-Do I teach them, through my actions, to live a life above reproach or to "get by" by fudging the truth here and there?

-Do I respond to hard situations in my life in a manner that I hope they will mirror?

-Do they see testimony of forgiveness and peace or conflict and strife in me?

-Have I taught them humility by admitting when I am wrong, or pride by defending what I shouldn't?

-Am I teaching them the fruit of the Spirit by my actions and not just my words? Do they recognize in me: love, joy, peace, patience, kindness, goodness, faithfulness, gentleness, and self-control?

-Would my children be able to accurately describe Christ to their friends by describing me?

-Have I shown them how to live an active faith or have I trained them in how to give my faith lip service?

Read Hebrews 5:12.

Are we taking time to learn and grow in the Word?

Jesus warned about pride in one's status as teacher, but also commissioned everyone to go into all the world. James warns about the high standard set for those who attempt to teach the Word, but Hebrews chastises those who stay "baby Christians" when they should be learning enough to teach others. Obviously, there is a healthy balance to be found. Are we taking the time to learn and grow in the Word so that we are prepared to give an answer for our faith (1 Pet. 3:15)? Are we teaching others through our actions of faithfulness, or are we settled into a busy life that leaves that job to others whom we deem "official teachers?"

Will you ask the Lord, today, to open your eyes to areas of conviction where He desires to make changes in your life in order to make you a better teacher to those who are watching and listening? Ask Him to reveal areas where growth is needed and then commit to making those changes. Change can be hard, even scary, but remember, we live one breath at a time. When in one breath we fail, we begin fresh with the next and He is there with new mercy to start again. Ask Him to speak to your heart, open your heart to hear His answers, be still and listen, and journal the stirring He brings below.

We need God's help to make changes in order to be a better teacher to those who are watching and listening. Will you ask Him for it?

Day Two – Taming the Tongue

Oh, be careful little mouth what you say.
Oh, be careful little mouth what you say.
For the Father up above is looking down in love.
Oh, be careful little mouth what you say.

If we can control our tongue, we can control our entire body.

Many of us recognize that children's song from our own childhood. It's such a simple song for preschoolers. Sweet little hand actions are accompanied by a simple melody, with lyrics easy enough for a toddler to master. But, from the mouths of babes comes a message concerning one of the most challenging tasks known to man – controlling the tongue.

The teacher has been warned in James 3:1. His primary tool for teaching is his tongue and James clarifies in verse two that with the tongue, we **all** stumble. We know from the context of our study, that James has been talking about what it is to have sincere faith. He is now preparing to elaborate on practical, everyday ways to demonstrate it.

Read James 3:2-5a.

Apparently, the tongue is at the pinnacle of our temptation, for if we can learn to control it, we can control our entire body.

Read James 1:26.

If anyone thinks himself to be _____, and yet does not _____

_____, but deceives _____, this man's

_____ is _____.

We studied this passage on Week Two, Day Five. On that day, we discovered that this man's "religion" is his worship and that worship is an "outpouring of selflessness in obedience to God in order to honor Him simply because He is worthy of honor." Our active faith is a life of worship. We have seen the word "perfect" appear multiple times already in our study. Each time, it has referred to a fulfillment or completion, a maturity in order to fulfill a task. Again, we find *téleios* (perfect) in James 3:2. As our understanding of what James has meant about a sincere faith has grown, we are now able to apply *téleios* better. Sincere faith is evidenced by active obedience, and active obedience is genuine worship, which we could define as consistently putting God ahead of ourselves. Sacrificing self for God in a consistent manner leads to maturity and wisdom, which makes us *téleios* – full grown, complete, and thoroughly disciplined. James 3:2 tells us that a thoroughly-disciplined Christian possesses a bridled tongue. We all stumble in many ways, but the effort to control the tongue is a worthy cause, for it will affect our entire lives, not just one part.

Sincere faith is marked by active obedience.

To support his emphasis on the power of the tongue, James gives two word pictures: a horse's bit and a ship's rudder. We will look at two main points concerning these illustrations; namely, the impact each has on determining the direction of something else and the relatively small size of each in comparison to the "beast" it directs.

The bit for the horse, and the rudder for the ship, are both used to guide a "beast" in whatever direction it is to go. Likewise, the tongue defines the direction we allow ourselves to turn, which can impact how others perceive us and affect how we are received. How we are received directly affects whether we can or cannot be used by God. Someone who turns others away due to their uncontrolled tongue cannot be an effective tool in God's hands. Instead, our speech should be seasoned with salt that creates a thirst for God in others (Col. 4:6).

Do you think the way you speak allows God to use you effectively?_____

Our speech can determine the direction of our lives.

James didn't necessarily intend to mean this, but I find it interesting that both the bit and the rudder are in concealed areas when in use. The bit is deep in the horse's mouth and the rudder is under water. Both are hidden out of view, but each is working for the benefit of the one in control. God placed our hands and feet in the open to be used freely for His work, yet He placed our tongues in an enclosed spot where we can readily bite them. The bit and rudder are best used when diligently working toward their positive purpose and in their proper place. When hanging in the barn, out in the open, the bit does the horse no good. In fact, it rusts. When it is in use, it determines the direction of the horse, but only when attached to reins that are held by a skilled rider. In James' illustrations, we are the horse, we are the ship, and the tongue (bit and rudder) may control our lives positively or negatively. Both have potential to lead their beast into safety or disaster; both the horse and ship can be used for great good or great destruction. The questions are: Who is holding the reins? Who is at the helm? Are you or is God? A horse cannot effectively hold its own reins; a ship cannot steer itself. Similarly, we cannot control our tongue on our own; it is a God-sized task.

Verse 5 compares the tiny tongue to the body it controls. By stating that the tongue "boasts of great things," it would be easy to assume that it is speaking of prideful boasts that a person can make using their tongue. Keeping with the context of the examples, though, we are able to see that James is still speaking metaphorically about the tongue. As the small bit can boast of the power it has over the horse, the tongue boasts of the control it has on our lives. The fact that the tongue does control the direction of our lives can be either positive or negative.

What are some very positive ways our words can be used?

_____

_____

Controlling the tongue is a God-sized task.

What are some very negative ways our words can be used?

_____

_____

Never underestimate the power of the spoken word. James is about to delve deeply into the negative impact it can have. However, let's first take a moment to appreciate its potential for good. Communication is vital to our human existence. If we all walked around in complete silence, we would all be suspiciously wondering what everyone else was thinking! God gave us our tongues to speak, He just wants us to keep them in check.

Read Proverbs 16:24 and Ephesians 4:29.

Make no mistake about it, the words you convey to others can be life-saving and "bone-healing." We live in a world that is judgmental and harsh; a warm encouraging word in a cold, cruel world is an amazing gift from God. Never take for granted the value of a kind word; it's like honey for the soul. As you walk through your day, if you think of something kind about those you encounter, tell them. Harsh words can crush a spirit, silence is nearly impossible to interpret, but a kind word is seldom misunderstood. Never assume those around you have had their fill of kind words and encouragement; I don't believe there is such a thing.

Think of someone right now who you could extend an encouraging word to and make it a point to do so today. Making an effort to share encouraging words on a daily basis will not only bless others immensely, but will bring personal blessing to you as well.

Read Colossians 3:17.

Absolutely everything, all of our deeds, and all of our words, are to bring God glory. We were created for no greater reason than to worship God and bring Him glory. It must disappoint Him greatly when we use the most powerful tool He gave us in ways that do anything other than that. We have the potential to bring others to Christ with our spoken words. Like a warhorse and a battleship, we have the opportunity to fight against Satan in the battle he continues to wage against God and His people (Eph. 6). Our tongues, equipped with the Sword of the Gospel are our greatest weapons. As we walk through our days, we need to keep in mind that we are indeed in the midst of a battle and must constantly ask ourselves for which army the weapon of our tongue is fighting. Remember, the tongue guides us in our direction. We must be on the alert not to allow it to guide us into the enemy camp.

Read James 3:5-8.

James has gone from two neutral examples of small things that have big impact, to a very negative illustration of a tiny thing that can cause vast destruction.

What does James compare our tongues to in verse 6? _____

It only takes one spark to set ablaze a beautiful forest of trees that took hundreds of years to grow. One false rumor can destroy the testimony of another person in a matter of days or destroy a vibrant church before they even know what hit them. One snide remark can crush the spirit of someone whom God has been working to build up for use in His Kingdom, causing them to doubt the progress He's made in them. One fit of rage can unleash words that never should have been spoken, but will never be forgotten. Although each fire may die down, their damage is catastrophic.

I find it interesting that we use our tongues so carelessly when they hold such potential for great danger. We've all seen TV shows where ticking bombs are handled with the most calculated care possible due to their potential to destroy lives. Our tongues should be handled no differently, for their power can do the same. We ought to constantly consider our tongues

Never underestimate the power of the spoken word.

Harsh words can crush a spirit, and silence is impossible to interpret, but a kind word is seldom misunderstood.

All of our deeds and all of our words are to bring glory to God.

as undiffused bombs, capable of devastation, and carefully count the potential cost before each thing we say. A diffused bomb poses no threat of danger. Biting our tongue will diffuse destruction, whereas igniting it when we shouldn't will harm not only others, but ourselves.

Give an example of something you wish you could go back and "unsay."

_____

_____

Most of us learn the need for biting the tongue the hard way.

Unfortunately, I have so many of those times that I can't begin to count them. I have learned the need for biting my tongue the hard way. Unfortunately, I think that's the case for most of us, or we wouldn't find such consistently firm instructions about it in Scripture. "Nothing seems to trip a believer more than a dangling tongue."[19] Wouldn't it be embarrassing if you possessed a tongue that hung out so far that you could literally trip on it? If I had such a tongue, I'd do whatever possible to keep it hidden; to prevent it from bringing me embarrassment and humiliation. Of course, we don't have a tongue that literally reaches the ground; however, because our speech can trip up our entire lives, we should take great care to control all we say so as to avoid our own humiliation.

Our tongues are the outlets for our hearts, which long to be heard.

Why, then, if we realize the dangers of its misuse, is it so terribly hard to control our speech? Our tongues are the outlet for our hearts, and our hearts long to be heard. We were born with a nature that believes we have a fundamental right to be heard. When babies want to eat, they make themselves heard. When toddlers don't get their way, they make themselves heard. No one has to teach us this skill; it's innate within us. As we grow older, we may not scream when we're hungry or fight for our right to the toys in the nursery, but we do still consider it our "right" to be heard. "I have the right to express my opinion." "My feelings need to be heard." "I need to give them a piece of my mind!" "I *have* to defend myself!" "If no one can seem to get things right, I'm going to tell them how it's really done." "That person is out of line, and if no one else is going to tell them, I will!" Or maybe worst of all, "I just can't hold this in, I *have* to tell *someone*!" Oh, the dangerous "spark" that lies within those sentences and so many more like them.

One fit of rage can unleash words that should never have been spoken, but will never be forgotten.

C.S. Lewis' land of Narnia contains so many illustrations of life's lessons. Those books are family favorites in our house, and certain quotes from them can be said in order to get a point across quickly with no explanation needed. In *The Horse and His Boy*, one of the children tries to speak with Aslan, the Lion, concerning the business of someone else. His reply was simply, "I am telling you your story, not hers. I tell no one any story but his own." "It's not your story" are four words that are heard in our household on a regular basis when someone tries to nose their way into a situation that does not involve them. May I challenge you to hide these words in your heart and call on them when you are tempted to interject your opinion into a story that is not your own? Friend, our two cents that we feel is worth a million dollars, may land us and others in great debt if they're spent where they don't belong. Most of the time, it is best to simply concern ourselves only with **our** story.

It is best to concern ourselves only with our story.

The range of sins that can be committed with our words is so vast that there is no way we

---

19   Walvoord and Zuck, *BKC NT,* p. 827

can cover them in a short study. From the harm they can cause when used in a rage, to the devastation they can bring to an innocent party slandered, to every hurt in between, their potential is incalculable. The next few verses tell us why.

Read James 3:6 again.

The tongue is the very world of iniquity. In other words, the full range of sin can use the tongue for its outlet. The tongue opens up the entire can of sinful worms. It is the tool of bitterness, envy, and pride. Without it, a person might harbor sinful feelings, but they won't drag others into it if they remain silent.

Read Matthew 15:11, 18-19. What makes a man unclean?

_____

The full range of sin can use the tongue for its outlet.

What comes from our tongue makes us unclean and reveals that which is unclean within our hearts. The next portion of James 3:6 supports this. *"The tongue is set among our members,"* or *"is the part of our body,"* that defiles our whole person. The word used here for defile is *spiloó,* which means "stain." We've already been told in James 1:27 that pure and undefiled religion (worship) is *"to keep oneself unstained by the world."* James has been painting an entire picture of someone with sincere faith who is willing to act on it and mature in it in order to live a life of worship pleasing to the Lord. The unrestrained tongue can "spiritually stain" the entire person, causing detriment in the progress toward spiritual maturity. On the other hand, the practice of holding one's tongue builds a reliance on God and an endurance in our faith. The whole body can be drawn into sin by the tongue, whereas the whole body can be rescued from sin by the control of the same.

spiloó – stain

Not only does verse 6 say that the tongue can negatively stain our entire lives, but it goes on to say that it furthermore sets the course of our lives. Simply stated, our tongues determine our course which directly relates back to the illustration of the horse and the ship. Even more frightening is the fact that this life's rudder, with its destructive potential, comes directly from hell.

geenna – a reference to Gehenna and the Hinnon Valley

The word used for hell in this verse is *geenna,* meaning Gehenna. Gehenna referred to the Hinnom Valley south of Jerusalem where, in the Old Testament, the Jews had sacrificed their children to Molech (Jer. 7:31). In New Testament times, this valley had become the dumping site for putrefying refuse that was burned with constant fire. Because of the hideous association with this valley, Jesus often used it as a word picture to describe the ever-burning fires of hell.

How does it make you feel to think that your negative words are set on fire by hell?

_____

I grew up in the country, where we had a barrel for burning all of our paper trash. I love that smell to this day, and the smell of a bonfire can't be beat, either. However, Gehenna referred to a valley that emitted nothing better than a nauseating stench; there were definitely no s'mores being roasted over this fire! Our hearts are heard through our tongues, and all those who hear our words "smell" whether what is inside is sweet or rotten. When you walk into a house where dinner is being prepared, you're likely to have one of two possible reactions. 1) "Mmm, what's cooking?" or 2) "Ugh, what's burning?" When others hear the message of your heart expressed through your tongue, will they be pleased with what's cooking, or will they be turned away by what's burning? What do you smell like today?

What does Proverbs 16:27 say a worthless man's words are like? _____

Remember Gehenna as the source of gossip, lies, rage, slander, complaining, cursing, boasting, etc., the next time you feel there are words "burning within you" that you just have to let out. The source of that "burning" is hell, plain and simple. When I was reminded in this reading that the Valley of Hinnom had been a place of child sacrifice for the Jews, I was struck with distain. How could they do such a thing and call themselves "children of God?" But, our words can so easily assassinate the character of another person. We hold life-giving and life-taking power in our mouths (Pro. 18:21).

Our words can assassinate another person.

Both of my daughters play volleyball. When learning to serve the ball, I had to teach both of them to stop, focus, get set, and then serve. Otherwise, they would walk right up to the line and swing their arm at the ball without preparation, which usually didn't produce good results. Before we speak, we need to stop and think. I often ask myself, before I speak or act, "What do I want this situation to look like five years from now? Does this have the potential to be a day I regret?" If I think my words might harm, I often choose to hold them realizing the potential long-term ramifications. We need to do everything possible not to run ahead with our words haphazardly. A fool rushes in with many words, but wisdom is found in the bitten tongue.

A fool rushes in with many words, but the wise hold their tongue.

James 3:7-8 simply elaborate on the difficulty of taming a tongue that is fueled by hell. The end of verse eight says the tongue is full of deadly poison, giving the picture of a venomous snake ready with his deadly strike (Rom. 3:13; Ps. 140:3). A few words before this, the tongue is called a restless evil. This is why it is so difficult to tame; it is restless, constantly tempted by the fire within that is fueled by our sin nature. No wonder taming the tongue is a God-sized task. We say we just *can't* hold in our rage, we just *have* to let out our frustrations, we just *need* to express our opinion, it's *impossible* not to, we just can't… It's true, *we* can't, but we serve a God who can. Recently my husband reminded me that our God is the God of the impossible. He said, "It only stands to reason that if He created the Red Sea and all the natural laws that keep it in place, He can also part the same sea." No one can tame the tongue, but the God of the impossible can give us the strength to hold it and use it for His good. Will we let Him?

We serve a God who can do the impossible; including helping us hold our tongue.

When someone borrows one of our tools out of the garage and forgets to return it to us, we can't use it for the reason we intended. You, and your tongue, are intended to be tools in God's garage to be used for His glory. Are you available to Him, or are your tools "out on loan," being used for some other purpose?

Day Three – What Goes in is What Comes Out

The letter James wrote to the churches contains running themes. He never completely dropped an idea, but, like a turning wheel, each element keeps coming back up, allowing James to elaborate on it and deepen the level of understanding with each pass. One thing we can be certain of by this point is that he is thoroughly annoyed with double-mindedness. In Chapter One, James calls out the double-minded man, labeling him unstable and wavering. Such a man is not to expect anything from the Lord because he asks God for wisdom, yet refuses to let go of his own desires. In Chapter Two, double-mindedness is revealed in one who claims to have faith but shows no evidence of it. Now, in Chapter Three, the tongue, itself, is portrayed as double-minded and rebuked for speaking one way toward the Lord and another way toward man.

James contains running themes that keep coming back up.

Read James 3:9-12.

What does verse nine accuse the tongue of doing?

_____

What does the end of verse nine point out about the people we "curse?"

_____

kataraomai – to curse, doom, wish evil upon

Blessing God was seen as the highest form of speech to the devout Jew, whereas cursing was the lowest. To curse, *kataraomai,* someone in the ancient world was "to desire that they be cut off from God and experience eternal punishment,"[20] literally, to damn them. To wish such a thing on man, God's highest creation who was made in His image, is deplorable. Yet, cursing does not have to be this extreme. Soon, James will confront his readers concerning conflict, and his current comment about cursing could have been in reference to slanders and disputes. We do not have to wish a negative eternity on someone to make their earthly life miserable with our words. Either way, James emphatically tells us that we cannot both bless God and curse man. In fact, the language he uses in verse 10 is the strongest possible in the Greek. Our modern translations of verse ten lose the impact, but when you read the words *"these things ought not to be this way,"* picture a very frustrated pastor, pointing his finger at a congregation full of backbiting gossips and shouting, "This is just WRONG! So, STOP IT RIGHT NOW!"

The character of our heart is revealed by our words.

James is apparently very fed up with inconsistency in the church. He is calling for consistent faith, consistent action, consistent obedience, and consistent speech. The double-minded person may be able to fool their fellow Christians in the other areas that James addressed, but the tongue will always give them away. The character of the heart is shown through our words. As stated before, verse 9 doesn't have to strictly apply to the most extreme form of cursing. Christians can be found blessing God in one moment and cursing man in another

---

20   Moo p. 133

in very subtle ways. Consider this possibility. One day, I am joyfully practicing a song to sing for special music at church. I'm praising God in song and having my own personal moment of worship. Suddenly, my child walks into the room and has "the nerve" to interrupt me. With a huff, I stop singing and ask, "What now? Can't you see I'm busy?" Ugh; while I did not specifically "curse" at them, I did send a message that I wished they weren't around and my ugly words became a means of harm rather than blessing. Unfortunately, we do that sort of thing frequently. We teach our children to play nice and yet we turn around and gossip about a friend. We stick a Christian emblem on the back of our car and yell at someone when they cut us off in traffic. We treat everyone at church like gold and yell at our spouse as soon as we get in the car to come home. My friends, "these things ought not to be this way!"

Describe areas in your life where you may feel susceptible to this bad habit.

When our hearts and minds are set on God and His Word, our speech will honor God and edify others.

_____

_____

The heart is "telling." If our speech consistently brings honor to God and edifies others, it gives evidence that our hearts and minds are set on God and His Word. If, however, we are consistently found talking out of both sides of our mouths, our tongues have revealed the true "double" state of our hearts.

Read Psalm 119:11.

"I have hidden Your Word in my heart that _____." (NIV)

tsaphan – to treasure up

Yes, the tongue seems to be the unstoppable villain, but we are clearly given the silver bullet for its defeat in this passage.

Read James 3:11-12.

James uses rhetorical questions to support his point that two opposite things cannot possibly come from a single source. Our heart is the source for what comes from our tongue; therefore, whatever comes out of our mouth reveals the heart's true nature. Jeremiah 15:16 says that Jeremiah **ate** the Word of God and it became **the** joy and delight of his heart. I'm not suggesting that we eat our Bibles, but we are to metaphorically devour the Word because it provides life-giving nourishment beyond what any food has to offer. We are to breathe in His Word as if it were our very breath. The Hebrew word for "hidden" in Psalm 119:11 is *tsaphan*, meaning to "treasure up." We are to store up and treasure God's Word as if it is our most valuable possession. We are not only to treasure it in the sense of holding it dearly due to its great value; we are to consider it our treasure from which we find our supply for life. His Word is to be our supply for our own provision and for feeding others. As we feed on it, we will in turn be able to feed others. As we inhale and exhale it, the smell of it will be sweet on our breath as **His** words flow from **our** mouths. If the Word, hidden in our heart, is the source from which we speak, we will not be double-minded in our speech and we will keep from sinning with our tongue.

Our breath will always be sweet if His words flow from our mouths.

Read Matthew 6:21. Are you spending enough time in the Word of God that it is the treasury from which you draw all of your speech? _____

What goes into your heart is what comes out of your mouth. Whatever a sponge absorbs, is what will ooze out of it when squeezed. If you are taking in the Word, the Word will come out. But, in this world, the Word is not a popular thing to take in. We will spend countless hours absorbing numerous other things in the name of entertainment, while God's Word collects dust on the shelf and maybe gets opened once a week. Is it any wonder why we struggle so with controlling our words, if we continue to pollute the stream flowing through our hearts with contaminated water? It's bound to taint us.

What do you spend the majority of your free time doing?

_____

With what are you filling your heart and mind?

Because we so freely toss words around daily, we may forget that they are revealing our heart to others at all times. We may be showing things we never intended others to see. Isn't it so embarrassing when you're wearing a dress and someone has to tell you that your slip is showing? How much more embarrassing would it be if we all told each other, upon every "slip" of the tongue that, "Your heart is showing." Our hearts tell all, just like our kids in Sunday School who tell every one of our family secrets during prayer request time! Be careful little tongue what you say, indeed.

What does your tongue say about your own heart?

_____

Do you primarily seek to hear or to be heard?

Does your tongue say that your heart is selfish, quick-tempered, prideful, or greedy? We don't have to sound blatantly sinful for our tongues to get us into trouble. Do we dominate every conversation, giving the impression that we are the only one in the room who matters; or do we allow others to speak and share their hearts as well? Do we interrupt, giving the impression that what others have to say isn't important? Are we condescending? Do we always make sure we build ourselves up in public, sometimes at the cost of tearing others down? Do we twist the truth just enough to give a good impression, to get ourselves out of trouble, or to have the most impressive story? Are we critical concerning things that truly aren't important? Do we point out others' errors in order to give ourselves an air of superiority? Do we vent our own frustrations freely, not realizing that we may be weighing others down too much? Are we a constant source of grumbling and negativity, making others weary? Do we make inappropriate jokes? Are racist comments tolerated in our conversations? Do we speak our immediate feelings, or do we consider the long-term potential for damage?

"Challenge your tongue" by questioning your words before you speak.

I don't know anyone who can pass the test presented in that list. The tongue constantly challenges us. Because that is true, we need to "challenge our tongue" by consistently asking several questions before we speak: Are the words necessary? Are they going to build someone else up, or could they potentially tear them down? Are they going to honor God, or are they going to show that your heart isn't as fully His as you would like to think? If all of our words are to be God-glorifying, then each of these questions should be answered in the positive. If they cannot be, we need to learn to bite our tongues. When we choose not to bite them, we need to check our hearts to see if our "slip" is showing and a correction needs to be made.

Read 1 Corinthians 13:1.

If my words are not seasoned with love, what are they as good as?_____

I have a bad habit of never turning my cell phone off. I charge it every night and leave the power on. Because of this, sometimes it acts up and reminds me that it needs a chance to reboot. Recently, it randomly began making noises during the night for no reason. It was causing me serious frustration as it kept making obnoxious noises when I needed to be sleeping! It wasn't alerting me of anything worthwhile; it was doing as much good as a clanging cymbal in the middle of the night! My phone does me great good most of the time, but when it begins making racket at inconvenient times due to a malfunction that isn't consistent with its intended purpose, it's simply a nuisance. By asking ourselves if our words are necessary before we say them, we are doing constant quality control, ensuring that our tongues are speaking words that are consistent with the purpose for which God created them and not just making racket at inopportune times.

Are your words sweet music to others or clanging gongs?

Read Colossian 3:23.

Whatever you do, do it with all your heart as if it were for the _____.

If we would remember that everything we say and do to others is equal to saying or doing it to the Lord, we might tend to weigh our speech and actions more carefully beforehand. Where do we want our relationships to be with the Lord? The way we use our words with others will directly correlate with how we help or hinder our relationship with Him. We cannot move forward and backward in a relationship at the same time, and the way we use our tongues affects the direction of that movement.

Would we use our words so carelessly if speaking directly to Christ?

Let's be honest. Would we use our words as carelessly as we do if we were speaking directly to the Lord? Words can, and do, hurt more than sticks and stones, and their bruises last far longer. If you tear open a feather pillow outside on a windy day, the probability of re-gathering all of the feathers in order to put them back inside the pillow and restore it is zero. Our words are no different. The damage is done once they've left our mouths, and we've potentially loaded more baggage onto someone's back than they were ever intended to bear. If we wouldn't do such a thing directly to the Lord, we need to think harder before doing it to those who were created in His image.

On the other hand, we are to bless the Lord and bless others as well. If we are inhaling the Word of God, our exhaled breath will be life-giving. God desires for us to infuse life into others through encouraging words. There are those who are feeling suffocated by life, and we may be the source of fresh air that God uses to help them begin inhaling again. You know what it has meant to you when such an encourager has crossed your path; will you choose today to become a source of fresh air for all you meet?

Who can you encourage with your words today?

Describe a time when someone encouraged you with words. _____

_____

Take time to thank the Lord for those encouraging words and ask Him to give you the opportunity to extend the blessing of encouragement to someone else today.

Day Four – The Power in "Prautes"

There are two very different types of wisdom – godly and worldly.

As he did with the topic of the tongue, James has touched on wisdom a few times and now comes back to elaborate on it. As we're going to study, there are two types of wisdom with two diabolically-different sources – God and the world. We will see, as we complete Chapter Three today and tomorrow, that James jumps back and forth between the two types of wisdom as he writes.

Within the context, we see that James went into great detail showing that our speech reveals our heart and that good and bad cannot both come from a single source (James 3:11-12). We find in the following verses, that the true nature of the source is shown in both word and deed.

Read James 3:13.

What is the first question James asks after his emphasis on the tongue?

_____

It takes wisdom, understanding and discipline to manage our speech.

Following his teaching on the state of the heart, James seems to throw this question out as a challenge. He asks who **claims** to be wise, and follows it immediately with a challenge that says, "Okay; then prove it." Much like his argument concerning a true demonstration of faith, James is now looking for tangible proof of proclaimed wisdom. It takes **wisdom** to bite the tongue and it takes wisdom to use it carefully when we choose to speak. It takes **understanding** to *realize* the need to both bite it and use it carefully. It takes great **discipline** to act on wisdom and understanding, as one produces the good works James is describing.

According to James 3:13, how does one show that he has wisdom and understanding?

_____

In Scripture, gentleness and meekness never imply weakness, but a willingness to submit to God's authority.

Demonstrations of true wisdom and understanding are always associated with certain qualities. Notice it doesn't say, "Let him show his wisdom through grand speeches, through teaching the hardest concepts, through elaborate prayers, or through having the most education, etc." No, he is to show, or demonstrate, his wisdom and understanding through good behavior. But, this behavior isn't fueled by lofty knowledge; the pure source of this wise behavior is of all things, gentleness.

Oftentimes, gentleness gets a bad reputation. We may think of gentle people as weak pushovers; those who can't, or won't, stand up for themselves. Yet, in Scripture, gentleness and meekness never imply weakness. Instead, they describe a strength of character that intentionally refuses to utilize the power available to them and chooses to place oneself under God's authority.

Read Matthew 11:29. How did Jesus describe Himself? _____

Fill in the blank: *"Take my yoke upon you and _____ from Me."*

I don't know about you, but every time I've read that verse or heard it taught, I've placed the emphasis on the fact that Jesus was telling the people that His burden was lighter than the burden of their sin and that His yoke would provide them peace and rest. That is completely true, but I haven't put enough emphasis on the significance of what lies in the middle of that passage! It is there that He said, *"**Learn from Me**, for I am **gentle** and **humble of heart**."* (emphasis mine) Why is it significant that we learn from His gentleness and humility in the context of this verse? Hold that thought; we'll come back to it! ☺

Read James 3:14-16.

James has told them to show wisdom through gentleness, but then he elaborates on what gentle wisdom is **not** before he expounds on what it **is**. Verse 14 is another verse where the subject and predicate are switched. It may make it easier to understand if we flip the sentence and read it this way:

> *"Do not be arrogant and lie against the truth if you have bitter jealousy and selfish ambition in your heart."*

The word **arrogant** in this verse is *katakauchaomai,* which means "to exult over, to boast against." It expresses the thought of "over-exalting one thing at the expense of another which results in wrong conclusions;" it downgrades truth "by boasting with a sense of false superiority."[21] In this context, it exalts one's self-proclaimed wisdom over the truth of God's own.

katakauchaomai – to exult over, to boast against; over-exalting one thing at the expense of another

The word for **jealousy** here is *zelos,* which means "to have warmth of feeling for or against; to be zealous or jealous." It is actually a neutral word that must be translated by using the surrounding context. Its root, *ze,* "literally means 'hot enough to boil.' It is metaphorically used of 'burning anger, love, zeal.'"[22] It is a bubbling passion for or against something. In James 3, it could be both, as it is a passion for one's own selfish desires, as well as a passion against the truth it boasts over.

zelos – to to be zealous or jealous; burning anger, love, zeal

The word used for **selfish ambition** in verse 14 is *eritheia,* which means "rivalry, self-seeking." It "places self-interest ahead of what the Lord declares right, or what is good for others."[23] Recall that in James 1:14-16, the process of sin begins with lust, which is every sort of selfish ambition. So, the grasp of sin on a person's heart drives him to boast of his own wisdom, which lies against God's truth.

eritheia – rivalry, self-seeking

By putting these words together, we can see that the wisdom fueled by a heart of zealous and selfish ambition exalts self, misrepresents the truth of God, and does not reflect His true wisdom. In verses 11 and 12, James spoke about the heart as the source for words, expounding on the fact that impure words cannot come from a pure heart. In that same vein, he is now stating that gentle wisdom cannot come from a heart full of selfish ambition. Therefore, the one whose heart is selfish and impure needs to stop himself before presenting his opinion as wisdom from God. We are not to boast against (lie against) the truth when our wisdom is tainted by the sin we hold dear.

Gentle wisdom cannot come from a heart full of selfishness.

---

21   Gary Hill, Helpsbible.com, http://strongsnumbers.com/greek/2620.htm

22   Gary Hill, Helpsbible.com, http://strongsnumbers.com/greek/2205.htm

23   Gary Hill, Helpsbible.com, http://strongsnumbers.com/greek/2052.htm

What might you be holding on to in your heart that taints your wisdom, and therefore misrepresents God and lies against His truth?

_____

James 3:15 begins with the words "this wisdom" which begs the question, "What wisdom?" Here, James is describing intellectual wisdom; wisdom that a person claims to have based on their life experience, education, or opinions. But, it does not reflect God's truth, which all things must be measured against, and so it is not the gentle wisdom God desires for us. We see this sort of wisdom all the time; our world is inundated with it. Talk show hosts and hostesses who are great humanitarians sway the masses with their "wise" words, yet they do so at the expense of the absolute truths in God's Word. Writers of books, magazines, journals, and blogs freely "bless" us with their wisdom of the ages, but so many of them don't use God's truth as the standard for their opinions. It may sound good, logical, and appealing, but Satan works in crafty ways, and we must **know** the Word of God in order to recognize faulty wisdom when we hear it.

Intellectual wisdom is based on human experience, education, or opinion.

What alternate sources of wisdom, as referred to above, have you seen sway those around you? Have you been swayed by them as well? If so, how? _____

_____

Unfortunately, we can even hear this sort of wisdom in our Christian circles. "Zeal for the Lord lies all too closely to a selfishly motivated, harsh and violent fanaticism."[24] In other words, we can be so fanatical about our Christian opinions and traditions that we fail to weigh them against the truth of God's Word. Or we can be tempted to twist the meaning of Scripture in order to support our dogmatic opinions. Some, seeking to appear lofty in their Christian knowledge, will say any number of things to demean others in order to lift themselves up. These are just some of the ways we misrepresent God (lie against the truth) which may drive others away from Him while we claim to speak in the name of His wisdom. This zeal is not from the Lord and it does not display wisdom in gentleness. Because of this, James says, "Don't boast in it, don't push it onto others, and don't say it's of the Lord!" It's really his very polite way of saying, "If what you're saying does not agree completely with the truth of God, keep your trap shut!"

If our motives and understanding are not supported completely by God's truth and the gentleness of wisdom, they are earthly and evil.

We truly must check our motives and our understanding. If they are not entirely supported by truth and the gentleness of wisdom, then they are earthly, natural, and demonic. Such wisdom creates disorder, and promotes every evil thing (v. 15-16). It is for these reasons that we are judged strictly concerning what we say and what we teach. If we claim His name as a Christian, we represent God; therefore, we must be ever so cautious.

Based on the wisdom you share with others, would those around you see a family resemblance to your heavenly Father in you? Why or why not? _____

_____

Now, let's get back to Jesus! In Matthew 11:29, we saw that He said, *"Learn from me, for I*

---

24   Moo, *TNTC, James*, p. 137

am gentle and humble of heart." We will learn more tomorrow about the gentleness of wisdom, but today we will get a basis for the fundamental difference between it and the worldly wisdom we've just discussed.

Gentleness, in James 3:13, is *prautés*, meaning "mildness, gentleness, meekness, humility." In Matthew 11:29, the word for gentle, *praus*, means "meekness, mildness, gentleness." Both of these words share the root word, *pra*, which is difficult to translate – there is no English equivalent word. It means more than meek. It expresses a gentle strength, a power that displays itself through restraint.

In non-biblical Greek literature, the word *prautés* was commonly used to describe a horse that has been broken. Such a horse is capable of extreme power and has the ability to use his strength to intimidate those around or to cause them harm. He is fully capable of showing off his potential, but because he has been broken, he has learned a new strength of character and obedience. He has nothing to prove and is now motivated to accommodate his rider in selflessness rather than selfishness. While his physical strength has not been compromised, his character is strengthened immensely through self-discipline and submission to a worthy rider. On the other hand, a wild stallion that wants to establish himself as the strongest in a herd, flaunts his strength with the desire to intimidate and pays no attention to the damage he may cause to anything in his path. He cares for nothing outside of himself and his position within the group.

prautés – mildness, gentleness, meekness, humility
pra – a gentle strength; power displayed through restraint

Jesus was the epitome of *prautés*. He was God incarnate, yet He bridled His omnipotent power because He had nothing to prove, only a mission to accomplish. Mockers could say what they wanted to Him; He felt no need to vindicate Himself or stroke His own ego. If anyone has ever had the right to flaunt their wisdom, or throw their weight around, it was Jesus while He was on this earth. But, He didn't. Instead, He told us to learn *prautés* from Him, and IF we would, we would find rest for our souls.

Jesus was the epitome of prautés.

How might learning strength under restraint bring rest to our souls? _____

_____

Read Matthew 11:28-30.

In verse 28, Jesus speaks to those who are burdened and heavy-laden. This burden is understood to be the weight of sin in a person's life. He's saying, "Come to me, all of you who are so burdened with the weight of your sin that you long to escape its grasp."

Sin taints our opinions, promotes evil, and leads to chaos not wisdom.

In James 3:14-16, we explored the grasp of sin on one's heart. Sin's hold taints our opinions, fooling us into thinking our opinions are wise when they may be entirely unwise. Sin promotes perpetual evil in our lives which leads to chaos. Sin may seem harmless or even fun for a while, but ask anyone who has let it go too far, and they will tell you what a burden it can become. Once it snowballs into something out of control, the chaos and confusion are consuming, suffocating one's heart while it desperately tries to gasp for air. As verse 16 says, where selfish ambition exists, there is disorder and every evil thing. Wisdom cannot come from such confusion.

As you know, all sin is not outwardly blatant. Many sins simply have to do with our selfish mindsets. We can become consumed with thoughts of what would please us, what angers us, what affects us, etc., all of those thoughts are driven by selfish ambition. When consumed with "self," our opinions are tainted and our egos cannot seem to find a way to swallow our pride. Because of this, we are constantly tormented, or at the least, frustrated and unsettled with life.

Jesus invited us to take off the yoke of sin, the selfish ambition that brings constant inner struggle. Instead, we need to learn that only *prautés* – an ego under control, power under restraint – will bring us the rest we long for. Christians have the opportunity to live a life of peace even in the midst of storms (as we saw in James 1). We know we are on God's winning team, and we know that He holds us in His hands. Therefore, we don't have to spend our lives striving to prove ourselves. We, like the powerful but trained horse, can know our full potential, yet walk in peace while we submit to God. We can choose to be like the gentle horse - a massive force to be reckoned with. He walks peacefully and when he runs, it's under powerful self-control. The other alternative is to resemble the wild stallion. He's skittish, jumpy, dangerous, aggressive, and never at peace. Jesus invites us to learn His Word, learn His ways, and find His peace. In that peace, our minds will grow calm and the inner torment will quiet. When we're quiet, when we resist selfish ambition, we will be able to grow in true wisdom - the wisdom of gentleness.

Only prautés, modeled and taught by Jesus, will bring real rest.

I've previously asked how your heart is. What about your mind? Do you struggle with a constant battle of the mind? Do you long for peace but feel you are always fighting for, or with, something? How's your mind?

The gentleness of wisdom does not seek its own glory or recognition.

_____

_____

James 3:13 says your wisdom will be evident through your good behavior and deeds in gentleness. Remember, what we have to say means little if not matched with what we have to show. The one who spouts great knowledge of the Bible and yet bulldozes over people in his path, is not showing gentle wisdom. The one who gives eloquent answers and recites elaborate prayers, yet makes others feel small and inferior is not exhibiting the gentleness of wisdom. Wisdom does not seek its own glory or recognition. If what we exude is not loving, graceful and mercy-filled, we are misrepresenting our God. Our job is to display His true character in order to draw others in. When our motives seek to draw others to **us**, or to vindicate ourselves, it is **our** sinful character we are displaying and we are therefore distracting them from the true character of God.

We may be the only view of God some people will ever see.

Have you heard people say that they don't want to be a Christian because Christians are all hypocrites? Even those who live a righteous and upstanding Christian walk need to be ever so careful not to give off an air of piety, but of gentleness and an ego under control. We are the only impression of God that some will ever see.

If you were the only Christian a person ever knew, would they see the true character of God? Why or why not? _____

_____

When I was all of 18 years old and wise beyond my years (cough, choke), a new, unsaved kid my same age came to church camp with our youth group. All week long, he and I had discussions about salvation, but he was never sold on the idea. On one of the final evenings, he came to me and told me that he'd talked to the camp pastor for a long time that afternoon and had just gotten saved. He looked at me and said, "Funny, he said all the same things you said, but it was different coming from him." At the time I was offended and crushed, thinking he was just being rude. But, looking back, I'm sure I would be embarrassed if I could replay a video of our conversations. I'm afraid I came across with a "know-it-all" air; I was probably condescending, and I was most likely wearing my "holier-than-thou" badge. Oh, how I cringe just thinking about it. Praise the Lord, there was a camp pastor who was an amazing speaker as well as a seasoned counselor who knew how to use the gentleness of wisdom in order to convey God's love when I did not.

The presence or absence of wisdom's gentleness determines if others will hear our words.

What wisdom are you conveying through your life? Is it from above or earthly? Whatever consumes your heart, will form your opinions and become your wisdom. What is your wisdom based on at this point in your life? Is it true wisdom, intellectual knowledge, or tainted opinion? Are your opinions based on your feelings or on God's Word? What is your heart consumed with that it boasts of outwardly? Is it riddled with sin, gasping for air and reprieve? If so, Jesus says, "Learn from Me…" Is your heart "sold out" for the Lord but still carrying an air of pride? To you, Jesus says, "Learn from Me…" Jesus had everything to prove, but sought to prove nothing aside from what His Father had sent Him to do and say. Even in this, He says, "Learn from Me…"

Are your opinions based on your feelings or on the Word of God?

Tomorrow we will look at the specific aspects of what makes wisdom gentle, but for today, pray that the Lord will teach you and that He will help you to open your heart to learn from Him and Him alone. Below, ask Him to show you the peace that comes from not barreling forward with opinions and self-proclaimed wisdom in every matter, but to be like the tamed horse, full of potential power, yet peaceful and under control. Whose control is your mind under today? Ask Him to clear your mind of every misconceived notion, and replace them with His truth. Ask Him to help you learn His gentleness and humility.

If Jesus were in the room next to you and He said, "Come, learn from me…" could you tell Him no?

_____

_____

_____

_____

_____

_____

Day Five — The Gentleness of Wisdom

Yesterday we learned that true, godly wisdom cannot come from a heart or mind that is tainted with selfish ambition. Instead, it must come from the pure source of a godly mindset. We saw that the mind cluttered with sin is too chaotic and tormented to be still enough to absorb the true gentleness of wisdom.

Before we dive into the practical aspects of how to live out gentle wisdom, let's look at a few verses that prove our need to have a peaceful mind in order to clearly process true wisdom.

The mind cluttered with sin is too chaotic to absorb the gentleness of wisdom.

Read Isaiah 26:3. What will be provided for the one whose mind is steadfast in his

trust of the Lord? _____

Read Psalm 119:165. Great _____ have they who love God's law, and nothing can make them stumble.

Read John 14:27. Our minds need not be troubled, anxious, and confused with sin, as

Jesus offers us _____.

Read Philippians 4:5-9.

Our gentle spirit needs to be obvious to all.

These verses are an amazing summary of so many things that James has said. Verse 5 tells us that our gentle spirit needs to be obvious to all. In other words, the peace that God gives us should show through our actions which demonstrate our faith to the world. Verse 6 reminds us of the way James has instructed us not to panic in our trials. Instead, we go to the Father with our concerns, not allowing our spirits to become anxious and troubled, because we trust that He is near.

What does verse 7 say that the peace of God will do for our hearts? _____

Our hearts that are so easily troubled in a fallen world, and our minds that are so easily swayed by selfish ambition, are guarded by the peace of God for those of us who **choose** to consistently set our hearts and minds on Him. Verse eight follows that line of reasoning with an exhortation to focus our mind and dwell on only that which is pure and of the Lord.

God desperately wants us to demonstrate His love to a dying world.

According to verse 9, how is God referred to? _____

He is our God of peace; Jesus is the Prince of Peace. We cannot escape the fact that God desires for us to know peace. I don't believe it is simply because He wants us to enjoy a life of peacefulness, free of stress. He never promises such a thing; in fact, He promises that this life will be filled with trials. He needs us to have peace in our hearts and minds so that we can properly process the wisdom He wants us to possess without having it tainted by the confusion of sin. If our minds are set on Him, and not cluttered with sin and strife, we can effectively show His character through our actions. He desperately needs for us to do so in order to demonstrate His love to a dying world. However, when our minds are torn and confused with our own selfish ambitions, we not only confuse ourselves, but we can also confuse others as they seek to find God in our actions.

Read James 3:17-18. The wisdom from above is pure, peaceable, gentle, reasonable, full of mercy and good fruits, unwavering, and without hypocrisy. We'll look at each in turn.

The wisdom from above is first _____.

After describing worldly wisdom that is tainted by sin, James begins his description of godly wisdom by noting that first and foremost, it is pure. It is free from the confusion of sin, free from any selfish motives, incapable of promoting anything evil. The Greek word used for "pure" here is *hagnos*, meaning "free from ceremonial defilement; holy, sacred." It speaks of a purity inside and out, to the center of one's being. It has no guilt, nor anything condemnable mixed within it.

First, and foremost, godly wisdom is pure.

Wow, right off the bat we can all see that none of us will be able to attain that sort of wisdom on our own. Our minds **must** be set on Him in order to hear Him speak His wisdom to us so that we might, in turn, live it out, sharing it with others.

Are your heart and mind places of purity where God's wisdom can be received? _____

hagnos – free from ceremonial defilement; holy, sacred

After purity, wisdom is then _____.

Peace is woven throughout our passage on the gentleness of true wisdom today. Not only does God need our hearts to be a place of peace in order to properly process wisdom, but once we receive this wisdom, its outpouring should promote peace. It promotes peaceful relationships with others and with God. We will not be quick to judge, argue, or belittle others when true wisdom is extended peaceably.

Peaceable wisdom seeks to remove animosity. Its goal is to produce healing and understanding in order to convey the truth and love of God. A person with a pure and peace-filled heart never pursues an agenda of his own, but seeks to promote only the truth that directly reflects the Word of God.

Godly wisdom promotes peace and removes animosity.

Peaceable wisdom is beautifully interwoven with the next two descriptions.

Following peaceable, wisdom is _____ and _____.

The following truth is one that literally changed my life when I came to understand it and allowed it to become a filter for all my thoughts and opinions.

"Why is wisdom *peaceable*? Because it is also *gentle* and *open to reason*. To be *gentle (epieikés)* is to be kind, willing to yield, unwilling to 'exact strict claims.' The person who is *open to reason (eupeithes)* is one, literally, who is 'easily persuaded' – not in the sense of a weak, credulous gullibility, but in the sense of a willing deference to others when unalterable theological or moral principles are **not** involved."[25] (emphasis mine)

Wisdom is peaceable because it is gentle and open to reason.

Yesterday, we covered the way that impure wisdom lies against the truth and misrepresents God. When we hear comments like that, our natural tendency is to assume it is talking about "extreme" sin. But, sin manifests itself in even the tiniest ways that can sneak up on us and cloud our judgment. Let's set aside the "extreme" sins for a while and consider some "minor" situations where tainted wisdom might cause ripples of discord.

Above, we saw that the word gentle, in James 3:17, speaks of being kind, willing to yield,

---

25   Moo, *TNTC, James,* p. 140.

unwilling "to exact strict claims." This is different than the word for gentleness that we studied yesterday (*prautés*), although it works hand in hand. *Epieikés* refers to being equitable and staying true to the "**spirit** of the law" by relaxing overly strict standards that seek to fulfill the "**letter** of the law."

Christians can exact strict claims on one another without realizing that we aren't acting in gentleness. Depending on our culture, we often grow into certain traditions that we come to hold as dogmatic truths. Because we expect others to adhere to our same "Christian beliefs," we tend to become judgmental when they may not adhere to them as well. To give an example, many years ago my husband walked into a church building on a Sunday evening wearing a baseball cap. One elderly woman quickly reprimanded him for his disrespect and demanded he take it off. Her upbringing had instilled within her a strong disapproval of men wearing hats inside a church building (although there seemed to be nothing wrong with a flashy Easter bonnet worn by the ladies). This example may seem trivial and silly, but it is an example of the way traditions can easily be considered "right" and any infraction of them may be considered "wrong."

epieikés – equitable and true to the spirit of the law

What are some "Christian" expectations you can think of that are based on human traditions or opinion, but don't have their basis in Scripture?

_____

_____

Many of the expectations we place on other Christians are not based on Scripture.

To finish this illustration, we need to look back at the quotation above that describes the person who is not only gentle but also open to reason. The description, according to James 3:17, of the person who is open to reason is also one who is easily-persuaded. Without reading the rest of the definition, this would seem to fly in the face of all Christian belief! Aren't we supposed to be firm in our belief of our God, Savior, and Scripture? Yes, indeed we are. The rest of the definition explains that we are not to be weak, gullible, or naïve, but to be willing to consider the opinions of others "**when unalterable theological or moral principles are not involved**." Simply stated, if Scripture doesn't say that men shouldn't wear hats into the church building, and there are no other scriptural implications that it is a sin, we need to be open to the possibility that it may not be a sin at all. In weighing our traditional opinions on the scale of Scripture, we may find that many of our "hang ups" aren't things God cares to put much emphasis on at all. It is important for us to realize that we need to extend the freedom Christ died for to our brothers and sisters.

When unalterable theological or moral principles are NOT involved, extend freedom.

The tricky part about this is identifying these areas in our own lives. How do we identify areas of personal opinion when we've been raised believing they are absolute truth? The key is staying open to reason. As others cross our path who don't exactly share our opinions, we need to ask ourselves if Scripture supports our disagreement with them or if this might be a time when we get to practice this "willing deference" to others. Choosing to allow them to exercise their freedom in Christ may just knock their socks off with gentleness and grace! Give it a try!

Something very important to consider is that the Holy Spirit works uniquely in each of our lives. There will be areas in each of our lives that we feel convicted about, even though they are not unalterable theological or moral principles (something that Scripture is emphatically for or against). Romans 14 tells us, that if we are convicted about something and continue on with it anyway, we are sinning. Within the same chapter, it is stated that a fellow Christian can participate in the same action and not be sinning. It is wrong for the convicted Christian to continue against his conviction, but it is also wrong for him to expect all other Christians to fall in line with his convictions. Again, this is ONLY speaking of things that are **not** clearly stated in Scripture. This is not permission to commit murder if you don't feel convicted about it! Scripture is emphatic concerning right and wrong, but there are areas where a willing deference to each other is emphatically necessary as well.

Consider this: One girl consistently comes to church wearing jeans, while another may always wear dresses. It is important for neither of them to be offended by the other, no matter where their own conviction lies. If the girl who consistently wears dresses feels that she would be disrespecting God, and therefore sinning by wearing jeans to church, then **for her** it would be sin and she needs to hold to her conviction. But, because Scripture doesn't address this topic directly, it would show the gentleness of wisdom if she were open to reason, accepting that the other girl in jeans may not share her conviction. The girl in jeans, as well, would need to be respectful of her fellow dress-wearing Christian and not condemn her for her convictions, nor try to press her own liberty onto her.

The Holy Spirit works uniquely in each of our lives.

The list of examples could go on and on. Those who feel that the only way to truly worship in song is through praise music need to be gentle and open to reason with those who feel adamantly about hymns, and vice versa. A person who feels that they would be sinning by going into a restaurant that serves alcohol must adhere to that conviction, and yet respect the liberty of the one who is able to dine at Applebee's without conviction. The bottom line is that there must be pure wisdom to begin with, and after that, there must be a willingness to be gentle and open to reason. The purity of wisdom will recognize actual sin as clearly-defined in Scripture and stay away from it; while the gentleness of wisdom will provide for the situations where conviction and liberty are involved.

Being open to reason requires accepting one another's convictions and liberties.

What are some areas in your own life where you may have expectations of others that are based on your own traditional opinions or convictions and not necessarily dogmatic scriptural truth? Are you willing to learn to be gentle and open to reason in an effort to show the gentleness of wisdom?

_____

_____

Read Proverbs 16:21

Have you ever heard the phrase, "You catch more flies with honey than with vinegar?" If our traditions and opinions are making others feel uncomfortable because they don't share them yet feel we expect them to, we aren't exhibiting the love of God and are guilty of acting like Pharisees. We are to hold to our convictions, but also be filled with gracious love toward others that reflects God's grace and mercy as well as His righteousness. We aren't going to attract people to a loving God if they can't see His love through our gentleness and willingness to be reasonable.

People are attracted to a loving God when they see His love through our gentleness.

Pure wisdom will help you discern right from wrong as you obey the conviction of the Holy Spirit and search the Scripture for truth. As you do, your pleasant words, or sweetness of speech, will promote God's love to those around you much more than harsh dogma. The grace of God should soften us; which will show up in our interactions with others.

What are the next two descriptions of wisdom in James 3:17? _____

Hand in hand with being softened, wisdom shows itself in our lives through mercy. James has already described mercy in 2:8-13 as impartial love for all without exclusion. Mercy shows love even when judgment may be deserved. Only the gentleness of wisdom can show this sort of kindness, for it is so much easier to ridicule when it is deserved than to show mercy in the moment.

Good fruits and mercy are closely tied together in this verse, implying that acts of mercy bring forth good fruit. This good fruit is harvested in the lives of those giving the blessing as well as those receiving the blessing.

*adiakritos –
unambiguous,
without uncertainty,
undivided,
whole-hearted*

Finally, what are the last two descriptions given for wisdom? _____

Adiakritos means "unambiguous, without uncertainty, undivided, whole-hearted." In true James fashion, he had to throw in that true wisdom is not double-minded! It is unwavering, steadfast, and sure. It is set upon Scripture and does not waffle in opinion.

Closely-related, godly wisdom knows no hypocrisy; it is sincere. *Hypokrisis* was a word used to describe an actor playing two parts in a production, switching his mask quickly to give different impressions of himself at different times. Wisdom from above is genuine, tried, and true. You will not find a truly wise person of God speaking one way to some and quite another elsewhere. Those who hold godly wisdom are sincere at home, at work, and at play; there is no shifting of their character.

*hypokrisis – used
to describe an actor
playing two roles*

We have all been tempted to be one person in certain groups or situations, and a completely different person in others. What situations are most difficult for you to maintain your Christian character? _____

_____

James sandwiches his description of the gentleness of wisdom between bookend descriptions of peace. No doubt, true wisdom can only be harvested in the soil of peace. Whereas those who boast of flawed wisdom promote "disorder and every evil thing," those who seek and know God's righteousness, pursue lives of peace and produce peace as an out-flowing of their wise and merciful conduct.

*Are there aspects of
godly wisdom you
need to work on? Are
you in need of a good
brain washing, too?*

That was admittedly a lot to learn in one day. Let's review quickly: Godly wisdom is pure, peaceable, gentle, reasonable, full of mercy and good fruits, unwavering, and without hypocrisy. After thoroughly examining the practical side of what true gentleness of wisdom is, which of these attributes are you able to recognize in your own life? Are there areas you can identify that you might need to work on? Sometimes what I think I need is a good brain washing! We think of being brainwashed in a negative sense. But, when I know that my own faulty thinking is what is cluttering my mind, keeping me from realizing the peace I need in order to understand true wisdom, I truly pray that God will wash my mind clean and speak His wisdom to me so that I might understand Him more. Does your mind need washing, too? Are you willing today to ask Him to still your mind, so that you can hear His voice past all the distracting noise?

WEEK FIVE: A PEACEFUL AND HUMBLE FAITH

Day One – Conflicting Interests

Chocolate-covered strawberries. My grandma's porch swing. Moonlit nights. Conflict. Yes, these are indeed a few of my favorite things! Well – almost. Conflict. As much as we may try to avoid it, it seems to show up everywhere, including our study today. When James wrote his original letter to the churches, it had no chapter breaks and no divisions between verses. It was one continuous letter that flowed from one thought to the next.

Read James 4:1-2b.

I can't imagine that James intended for there to be a break in thought between his discourse concerning using the tongue with peaceable wisdom and the current section on conflict. Conflict cannot be fed without the tongue, bitter envy or selfish ambition, and it will not be fueled by the gentleness of wisdom. Therefore, these two chapters blend together seamlessly.

Conflict cannot be fed without the tongue, bitter envy, or selfish ambition.

James poses a question for his readers and immediately answers it in the form of another question. What did he identify as the source of their quarrels? _____

In the same way that he doesn't allow us to blame our temptations on anyone but ourselves (1:14), James makes us take responsibility for our disputes and quarrels as well. Certainly, Satan and his demons promote spiritual warfare that can lead to all kinds of conflict, but we cannot escape the entire burden of responsibility. Conflict causes all sorts of disorder, and James 3:16 told us that disorder and every evil thing originates with jealousy and selfish ambition. However, we choose whether or not those characteristics rule our hearts enough to cause conflict.

hédoné – pleasure, lust, strong desire

In the second question, James identifies the source of quarrels and conflict as being our pleasures. The Greek word for pleasure in this verse is *hédoné*, meaning "pleasure, lust, strong desire." It is the same root from which we get "hedonistic" and speaks of that which is enjoyable to the natural senses. Something interesting to note is that these pleasures do not necessarily have to start out as inherently bad. There are many things in this world that God intended to bring us good pleasure, but when we allow our focus to get out of balance, even they can turn into a selfish desire.

God gave us many good things in which to take pleasure; however, we can become easily frustrated if we can't have them and others do.

What are some good and healthy pleasures that you enjoy?

_____

_____

God desires for us to find good, pure, and wholesome things to take pleasure in. However, if life doesn't readily afford them to us, we may allow our pursuit of them to frustrate us and our focus may become unhealthy. We've just learned that sin causes confusion in our minds. When anything we find pleasure in consumes us to the point that we cannot find contentment without it, disorder in our mind is promoted, which can consequently create disorder with others in the form of conflict.

Imagine this illustration (it shouldn't be too hard for most of us)! A mother and toddler are at the store in the toy department. When they pass a particular toy that catches the child's eye, the youngster must have it NOW – because **this** toy will bring them such pleasure. There really isn't anything wrong with the toy or with them enjoying the thought of having it. The problem comes when the mommy says no and the child decides they literally CANNOT live another day without this particular toy! Suddenly a healthy desire for a wholesome pleasure has turned into irrational behavior and the conflict between mother and child begins. A healthy desire quickly turned into selfishness, which altered rational thinking and led to irrational actions in a matter of moments. As much as I'd love to say that we are above this as adults, I believe we all know better.

A healthy desire can quickly turn into selfishness.

Read James 4:2a, b.

"You _____ and do not have; so you commit _____.

You are _____ and cannot obtain; so you _____."

The beginnings of both of these statements identify the underlying issues, and the endings show our human tendencies. As much as it hurts our pride to be compared to a toddler, the fact of the matter is, when we want what we can't have, we can act like spoiled little brats. It would be easy for us to jump to the conclusion that we are "in the clear" on the first indictment because we've probably never committed murder, but a closer look into Scripture may tell us differently.

Read Matthew 5:21-22 and 1 John 3:15.

With what do these verses equate hatred? _____

James is saying that those of us who lust and become envious for what we cannot obtain, go so far as to hate those who can have what we do not, which leads to quarrels and strife. Let's remember our historical context for a moment. These were persecuted Jewish Christians who were struggling tremendously. They may have truly felt that the things they greatly desired were justified, but their desires consumed them to the point of hating others; it was causing enough dissension within the church that James caught wind of it. I'm certain that tensions were running high within the churches at this time, and it is at such times that conflict is anxiously waiting at the door.

It is much easier to lash out at others when your tensions are running high. How have you seen this truth played out in your life? _____

_____

When tensions are running high and conflict ensues, we run the risk of doing things we never intended to do. We may also say things we ordinarily wouldn't say, possibly things we don't even mean. As mentioned last week, we all have things we wish we could "unsay" and undo in our pasts. It is so important not to make decisions in the heat of conflict. When we do, our words and attitudes can become murderous. **We need to proactively and specifically try NOT to hurt each other**.

In my household, there are certain excuses concerning conflict that aren't even given anymore, because everyone in the house can already parrot back the response they will hear from Mom. Anytime hurtful words or actions rear their ugly heads in our home, followed by excuses such as, "I didn't mean to hurt you," or "I wasn't trying to make you feel bad," my response quickly follows, "But did you try **not** to?"

If we are going to allow God to be seen through us, then even in the privacy of our homes and around our families who see us at our worst, we have to make a serious effort to see with His eyes of grace, touch with His hand of mercy, and love with His unconditional love. We must be willing to swallow our pride in order to stop conflict before it begins. If conflicts do occur, we must have the self-control to stop and ask ourselves in the midst of them if our words and actions are truly necessary, or if they are simply adding fuel to the fire.

For others to see God in us, we must see with His eyes of grace, touch with His hand of mercy, and love with His unconditional love.

Have you ever been in an argument with someone and thought, "They aren't seeing things as they really are here. They're so far off-base that their thinking is completely irrational."

Are you willing to consider the possibility that, at times, it might be you whose "perspection" is clouded with sin and pride, rather than the conflict being anyone else's fault ? (See page 16 for a reminder of what "perspection" is.) _____

Let's face it, conflict is downright hard, and any time multiple people get together, there's bound to be some. What we each need to focus on is our own responsibility in each matter.

Read Romans 12:18 and Hebrews 12:14.

In both of these verses, the emphasis is put on "you" for keeping peace. We cannot be responsible for how others are going to react in conflict, but we are entirely responsible for our own attitudes and reactions. No one else can **make** us respond with unreasonable emotion; we choose to. I previously mentioned that I often ask myself if what I'm about to say may be something I could regret, keeping in mind what I want a given situation to look like five years from now. Similarly, I find it helpful to weigh the gravity of a situation before acting on it. For instance, I ask myself whether or not the subject of the conflict is going to matter in the least 20 years from now. If not, it may just be best to let it go. I have plenty of conflicts in my past that I didn't let go of at the time and I look back on them with deep regret. It is those regrets that remind me not to make the same mistakes again. I sometimes wish that on the mornings of those regretful days, I would have had some warning that "today" would be a day I would forever remember. Now, in waking up each day, I've learned from my regrets and choose to say that on this day, "I will guard my speech and actions if conflict should arise, for although I cannot retract what I've already done, today I can prevent any future damage I may still do."

We are each responsible for keeping the peace, and for our actions during conflict.

Proverbs 19:11 says that wisdom gives us patience, and it is to our glory to overlook an offense. Think back over the last several conflicts you have encountered. How could choosing to overlook an offense have been a wiser choice?

_____

_____

Let's briefly look at a few examples of conflict given in Scripture. Not all conflict looks alike, but there are consistent lessons we can learn from each.

Our first example will be King Saul and David. King Saul was envious of David, and it consumed his very being. From their first encounter until their last, David did nothing to provoke Saul, and yet Saul's envy led to one of Scripture's most famous conflicts. God had laid His hand on David's life, and although David knew that one day he would become king, he did not pursue that position and he did not covet what Saul had. In fact, he humbly submitted to Saul as king and chose not to take his life on multiple occasions. Yet, David's popularity grew steadily and as a result, Saul's hate for him also grew. Saul possessed the crown, and yet he was insanely (literally) jealous of what David had that he did not; namely, success in battle and the love of the people. Just as James pointed out, envy fueled the conflict.

Some battles simply aren't worth fighting. It is to your glory to overlook an offense.

I'm using this particular conflict because we often hear that "it takes two to tango," meaning that in every conflict, there are two sides and both must be somewhat at fault. Although this is usually true, there can be cases where one person is living smack dab in the middle of God's will and conflict still finds its way to him. This was the case for David. There are times when Satan plants a bulls eye right on a person who is living for the Lord and does what he can to take him or her down by means of conflict and strife, even without them contributing to the battle. Jesus, Himself, was a perfect example of this. Conflict surrounded Him on every side, but it was due to the bitter jealousy of others, not as a result of any wrongdoing on His part.

It is possible to be in the center of God's will and in the center of conflict due to no fault of one's own.

We can learn from the examples of both Saul and David in this situation. Saul was so overcome with envy and jealousy that he refused to let go of the hate that consumed him. I'm sure he felt justified in his anger because he felt that his crown was threatened. Due to his clouded thinking, Saul likely would have told you that the conflict was David's fault. But, by refusing to let go of his jealousy, Saul lived the rest of his years in an extremely tormented state. His hatred for David became an obsession in his life, which caused him to lose all focus and rationale. As a result, he could no longer hear God or be effectively used by Him.

We may have no choice in whether a conflict starts or stops, but we can do everything possible not to contribute to it.

David's life, on the other hand, was obviously affected by Saul's hatred and constant murder attempts. But the consistent, God-honoring choices he made kept him blameless in the matter and available for great use by the Lord. Although he could have easily justified retaliation, as he knew that God intended for him to eventually be king, David allowed God to handle the matter and he **never** allowed a revengeful spirit to overcome him when dealing with Saul. From David's beautiful example, we can learn that although we may not have started the conflict, and we might not be able to stop it, we can do everything in our power not to contribute to it.

Are your reactions to conflict more like Saul's or David's? Do you feel your opinions, feelings, and positions must be vindicated now by your own efforts, or do you allow God to work things out in His way and in His time?

_____

_____

Our second and third examples of conflict will resemble what we may face more regularly, for many times, our actions don't resemble David's example above. Our next example will be that of Joseph and his brothers. In this situation, there was absolute guilt, fueled by jealousy and anger, on the part of the brothers, while there was quite possibly unintentional fault on the part of young Joseph. Many a sermon has been preached concerning Joseph's lack of discretion in "bragging" about his dreams to his brothers who did not want to hear that they would one day bow down to him. We can't know for sure what the intent of Joseph's heart was. Perhaps he was bragging; perhaps he was just amazed at the visions God was giving him. Either way, he did contribute to the conflict because, due to immaturity, he apparently hadn't learned the value of biting his tongue when tensions began to run high.

In many conflicts, both parties share in at least part of the responsibility.

We can again see from the brothers' example, that when we allow envy and jealousy to overtake our hearts, we become consumed to the point of extremely irrational behavior. I don't assume any of them were probably the type to murder a family member, and yet James tells us that our lusts and envies can drive us to murderous extremes, whether emotionally or physically.

Joseph gives us a look at the person who comes out on the other side of the conflict and has grown in wisdom through experience. He did show immaturity in his words, which promoted conflict. But, he grew in wisdom through his experiences and later learned not to bolt ahead with his emotions, even when he knew he was in the right. Through much experience with trials, conflicts, and hardships, Joseph changed for the good.

Like Joseph, we can change, for God can change our hearts.

Change is always possible; we cannot hide behind the excuse that we are simply confrontational people saying, "That's just the way I am." Like Joseph, we too **can** change, for God **can** change our hearts. Psalm 51:10 says, *"Create in me a clean heart, O God, and renew a right spirit within me"* (ESV). We all know what our natural human tendencies are in the midst of conflict. But, the cry of our heart needs to be that God would help us to break the spirit of anger that fuels conflict and give us a renewed spirit that He can use as an instrument of peace. It's not enough to ask God to help in the heat of the moment, although I would suggest it as additional help! We need to ask God for an "attitude transplant" like the one Joseph had. It grew him up, it built his faith, and it prepared him for every trial and conflict ahead.

What begins in hatred can end in love if one party is willing to put love and forgiveness ahead of their need to be right.

Joseph showed the wisdom of learning from his past conflict in the way he handled future conflicts later in life. After reaching "superstar" status in the kingdom, Joseph could have done tremendous harm to his brothers when they suddenly appeared in his presence, had he harbored bitterness toward them all those years. But, the way he handled the past during his present circumstances entirely altered the course of their future. What had begun in hate, ended in love and miraculous healing, because one man was willing to put love and forgiveness for others ahead of his need for vindication. A restored relationship was more important to him than getting his side of the story settled once and for all.

Are you looking for miraculous healing in a situation you're facing? If so, how much love and forgiveness are you willing to lavish on another by means of controlling your own response to conflict? Will you trust God and allow Him to take care of the rest?

_____

_____

Jacob and Esau were both motivated by envy over what the other had.

The final example of conflict we'll examine lies between Jacob and Esau. In this case, both brothers are worthy of great blame. Jacob was envious of Esau's birthright and blessing, and perhaps the favoritism of their father. Esau was envious of the birthright and blessing after Jacob "repossessed" both of them, and he may have resented the favoritism Jacob was shown by their mother. These two give us a classic example of purely selfish conflict. Both were motivated by their envy for the pleasure of life they were certain they couldn't live without. Both wanted what the other had; both were driven to hate, and one even threatened murder. They were both flat out wrong.

This set of dysfunctional twins shows us what to avoid. Their example shows us clearly that lives can be entirely altered and ruined by an obsession for what we "must" have, and James tells us that this is the source of our quarrels. It would be tempting to say, "I don't obsess over wanting any "thing." My conflicts usually involve times when someone wrongs me and I want it made right." The need to be proven right or innocent can have just as much to do with "fulfilling our pleasures" as anything tangible. Appeasing our own pride in order to have the satisfaction of feeling that justice for our own purpose has been served is a way of feeding our selfish pleasure.

The need to be "right" can be as much of a source of conflict as anything tangible.

In what is your true pleasure found? Is it found when your own heart and feelings are finally heard and vindicated, or when God's heart is seen through you?

_____

When you constantly strive to be heard, do you really ever find peace, or do you find it is a never-ending process, much like a hamster on a wheel?

_____

To be used by God, we must let go of our need to fight and hold on to His promise to take care of us His way.

In your effort to make your opinions and feelings heard in the midst of conflict, do you consider the damage you are contributing to the situation, or do you bolt ahead without considering the cost?

_____

Read Romans 12:19

Conflict is consuming. It is a tool of the enemy to steal our concentration. To focus on God the way He intends, He needs our full focus all day, every day. When we are consumed with conflict, we find ourselves mulling it over in our heads over and over again. We replay conversations, script new ones, prepare defenses for future battles, etc. If we desire to be effectively used by God, if we want to move forward in His will and allow Him to show us the best He has for us, we must LET GO of our need to fight and HOLD ON to His promise to take care of it all in His own time, in His own way. In essence, we need to take a holy "chill pill" knowing that vengeance is His.

James had just given us instructions for living in peace. I don't think there is any coincidence that he established his stance on that fact directly before covering the topic of conflict. In his constant argument against the double mind, he again points out two things that simply cannot coincide. Peace, and the wisdom it produces, cannot live in tandem with a spirit that produces conflict. We must pray for a renewed spirit that can see and think with the eyes and heart of God in order to put our own selfishness aside.

What are you willing to do to diffuse conflict in your life? Remember, you may not have started it, and you might not be able to stop it, but you can do everything in your power not to contribute to it.

Peace, and the wisdom it produces, cannot coexist with a spirit that produces conflict.

_____

_____

_____

_____

Day Two — A Greater Grace

You may have noticed yesterday, that although we read James 4:1-2, we didn't cover the final sentence in verse 2. Although this sentence does refer back to the previous thought, it more readily ties in with the sentences that follow. This is where we will pick up our reading today.

Read James 4:2.

We can create turmoil by wanting what we don't have, and by taking matters into our own hands.

In essence, James is saying, "You're fussing with each other because your hearts are unsettled. Your hearts are unsettled because you want what you don't have. You don't have, because you don't ASK!"

Have you ever walked in on an argument between your children that could have been avoided had they just consulted you first? Their turmoil was fueled not only by what they wanted, but by their desire to take the matter into their own hands. Had they asked you, the answer may have been a quick yes or no and there would have been no need for them to argue among themselves.

All too often we do that with God. We get so wrapped up in our worlds, so frustrated with the way we want things to go, or maybe with the way we want others to act, that we forget God's place in the equation. At this point, James takes the emphasis away from the conflict between people and refocuses his attention on each individual's failure to acknowledge God in every matter.

Our Heavenly Father wants to give us good and perfect gifts. He is just waiting for us to ask.

Read Matthew 7:7-11.

There are things, dear friends, that God is just waiting for us to ask Him for, things that He longs to lavish upon us as a loving Father. Just as an earthly father desires to give good things to his children, our heavenly Father wants to give us good and perfect gifts so much more. But, oftentimes, He waits for us to ask. James says, *"You do not have because you do not ask!"* We are to live in an ongoing, healthy relationship with God where we are in constant communication with Him. When that is not a priority in our life, and we fail to come to Him for our needs, as well as our heart's desires, we may be missing out on beautiful things that He is just waiting for us to ask for.

Selfish desires show up in wrong motives when we pray.

Yet, there are a couple of disclaimers. Read James 4:3.

You ask and do not receive, because you ask with _____,

so that you may _____.

James isn't telling them that they will receive everything they ask for, promising them riches, health, and fame if they only ask for them. Immediately after he tells them that they have not because they ask not, he says, "When you do ask, you don't receive because you're asking with the wrong motives!" Again, he takes them right back to the source of their quarrels – their selfish desires, which he now says can show up even in their prayers. The individuals are not in right relationship with God, which is made evident by the apparent self-focused, rather than God-focused, prayers. Because this stirs up sinful frustration within the individual, it causes them to act irrationally and stir up conflict within the church body.

Since this causes so much personal, as well as corporate, disruption, it is imperative for us to seek to maintain a healthy focus on the things that God would choose for our lives rather than what our sinful natures desire. If we strive to be spiritually-minded, our desires will line up with what God desires for our lives, and our motives in our requests will be pure.

Read 1 John 3:21-22.

What condition is given for approaching God with confidence?

_____

Our hearts must be right when we take our requests to God.

Our hearts must be right when we take our requests to God. We can confidently place our requests before Him, only when we are living our lives seeking to keep His commandments as His servants.

Read 1 John 3:24. The one who keeps His commandments _____ in Him.

The NASB uses the word "abides" in this verse. Other translations use the words "lives, fellowships, remains, dwells, and continues." All of these translations accurately portray the essence of the verse. The Greek word for abide is *menó*, meaning "to remain, stay, wait for, await." Those living a life worthy of coming with confidence to the throne of God are those who are living out His commandments **because** they live their lives "remaining in Him." God is not a "go to" God where we simply bring Him our Christmas wish lists when we have desires of our own. It is only when we are consistently remaining in Him, abiding in Him, fellowshipping with Him, and waiting on Him, that we are able to come to Him in confidence.

menó – to remain, stay, wait for, await

When I think of the word abide, I think of it as somewhat of a comfort word. We don't abide in things that we dread. To abide in something, is to nestle ourselves right down into the middle of it. If we are abiding in our heavenly Father's arms, we are so closely knit with Him that we see Him, hear Him, and recognize Him in everything around us. When we allow ourselves to become this close to Him, it is our heart's most sincere desire to please Him and follow His commandments. Anyone who truly knows the Father and knows the security of abiding in those heavenly arms, is head over heels in love with Him and wants to do everything in their power to serve Him in any way. This is the child of God who can come to the Father with confidence in their requests.

How do you approach the Father in prayer? As a demanding child making selfish requests of "Santa," or in quiet confidence because you have been abiding in His loving arms? How can you abide in Him more this week?

To abide in something is to nestle ourselves into the middle of it.

_____

_____

Abiding in the Father, and having constant fellowship with Him is only part of what is required for receiving what we ask for in prayer.

1 John 5:14 says – "*This is the confidence which we have before Him, that, if we ask anything according to His will, He hears us.*"

According to this verse, how must we ask God if we want Him to hear our request?

_____

We must ask according to God's will if we want to be heard.

We are to pray according to God's will. Our requests cannot be filled with selfish motives; they must align with the heart of God.

How do you know if what you are praying for is in God's will or not? What do you think it means to pray according to His will?

_____

_____

When you are submitted to His will, you can find peace in His answer, whatever it is.

When we are abiding in God and He is abiding in us, we will know immediately that there are some things that we should not even entertain the thought of requesting in prayer, because it is simply out of line with what He would ever desire for us. Truth be told, when we are not abiding in Him and are not trying to align our thinking with His own, we are entirely capable of doing this. But, there are obviously times when our prayers can be pure in their intentions, yet we are not sure what God's final will is in a given matter. It is at these times that we can approach Him in the confidence of a clear conscience, knowing that our requests and heart's desires are pure. At this point, we must submit ourselves to His will and find peace in whatever His answer is. Praying according to His will doesn't mean we will always know the exact thing to pray for, but with an honest heart, we will pray for His will to be done (Matt. 6:10).

According to James 4:3, it is evident that, at times, we do not receive what we request of God because our requests are simply to fulfill our sinful pleasures. What are some examples of requests you previously made that you can now see were more for your pleasure and not aligned with His will?

_____

James equates praying with selfish motives to spiritual adultery.

_____

Read James 4:4.

James begins his next thought with, "You adulteresses!" You may wonder, "Why the harsh language?" He is reprimanding the person who prays to God, claiming to be His servant, and yet she prays with selfish motives, which shows that she is actually a servant of self and the world and not of God. She "wants to have her cake and eat it too" and God says, "No deal."

What does verse 4 call friendship with the world? _____

We cannot live for ourselves and live for God at the same time.

What does it call the man who wishes to be a friend of the world? _____

It is so easy to read these verses and dismiss ourselves from them, thinking that we aren't friends with the world if we aren't committing overt sins. But, the verses directly before these statements simply focused on the selfish intentions of the mind and heart in prayer. If our mindset and "heartset" are self-seeking and not God-filled and grace-filled from abiding in God, then we are living in hostility toward God and making ourselves His enemy.

Once again, we see James tracing the origin of the problem back to our old enemy, "double-mindedness." We cannot live for our own selfish pleasures and live for the Lord at the same time. Oftentimes, the Old Testament referred to those who were unfaithful to God as adulterers. Time and time again they turned away from God and worshiped false idols, committing spiritual adultery. We are the bride of Christ, and we will see in the next verse, that He takes that very seriously.

Read James 4:5.

James is clearly frustrated with the recipients of this letter. He has just called them adulterers and he begins the current verse by asking a pointed, rhetorical question. He is quite literally saying, "Do you think God is just wasting His breath when He says that He is jealous for you?" God is rightfully jealous for the love of His bride. He paid an unthinkable price in order to call us His own; we owe Him a lifetime of gratitude, and He expects it.

God is rightfully jealous for the love of His bride.

Just this last week, tears streamed down my cheeks during our Sunday morning worship service while we sang the song "You Are My King." The words *"Amazing love, how can it be, that You, my King, would die for me…"* suddenly pierced my heart. Images of a king sitting on his throne with his subjects all around flooded my mind. The thought of that king stepping down from his throne in order to take the death penalty of a guilty subject who knelt before him moved me to tears. Knowing that I was that guilty subject and that my King did that very thing for me is truly almost more than this heart can bear. Oh, how great a debt I owe – amazing love, how can it be?

But, in our case, the love story doesn't end there. Our King died in order to rise again and take us as His bride. Women swoon at love stories where a man is willing to lay down his life for the woman he loves. Movies romanticize this type of thing, and viewers are moved to think that they would do anything for a man who loved them so much. Ladies, that is exactly what has been done on our behalf, and our King deserves our endless love and faithful service.

Read Zechariah 8:2. While this verse obviously speaks of God's chosen people, Israel, it reveals to us His jealous nature for His people. We, the church, are His bride and His jealousy extends to us.

"With great wrath I am jealous for her…" It's a beautiful love story, but it's serious business, my friends. He paid the price, He's offered us joy beyond imagination for all eternity, and He's offered us His peace in this life. But, we are not to take those gifts and live our lives selfishly. We are to live understanding the debt of life we owe and realize that His jealousy comes mixed with wrath when we turn away from Him and don't make Him the priority of our lives.

Our King deserves our endless love and faithful service.

Are you living as a faithful wife of Christ? Of what other "loves" might He be jealous?

_____

_____

Read James 4:6.

Let's review. Our self-seeking hearts are made evident even in our prayers, and our friendship with the world is hostility toward God. He has every right to be angry and jealous of our spiritual unfaithfulness, but thankfully, it doesn't end there.

Fill in the blank according to verse 6. *"But, He gives us a greater* _____.*"*

Although God is serious in His jealousy, although He is the righteous Judge whose standard is perfection – **He gives us a greater grace.** This is such a short sentence, it can get glossed over so easily. We have a debt that we cannot pay. Christ had to die for it. Although our lives are still owed to the One who is worthy, when we fail to live our lives perfectly, His grace is sufficient to meet the standard of His own jealousy. He is Jealous God, He is Righteous Judge, but He is also Grace, and Mercy, and Love.

He is Jealous God, He Righteous Judge, but He is also Grace, Mercy, and Love!

I'm reminded of a note I saw hanging in a bathroom recently. I was visiting my brother's family and neatly taped to the children's restroom cupboard was a note that said,

"Dear Kids,

Do not put wet towels back into the cupboard or I will beat you.

Love, Mom"

God follows His discipline of us with grace and love.

I must explain that my tiny sister-in-law would never hurt a flea. But, obviously she needed to get a firm point across to her kids who were not meeting the "bathroom standard" that she had set. Notice, though, how she finished the note - "Love, Mom." She knew she was being funny, but just in case, she reassured her kids of her love. What a cute example of the way God is toward us when He must be firm with us, yet in His love, chooses to follow it with grace. He looks at us through righteous eyes that expect our very best, and He will discipline us accordingly when we fail to live for Him. But, He follows it with grace and love that doesn't give up on us when the "wet towel" ends up in the bathroom cupboard. He gives us a greater grace.

What are some areas in your life where you frequently stumble and fall for which God has to repeatedly give you His greater grace?

_____

_____

Those who humble themselves before the Lord will receive infinite grace when they stumble.

To whom does the end of verse six say He gives this grace? _____

It is the one who humbles himself before the Lord, allowing God to have His will in his life rather than seeking his own satisfaction, that will receive infinite grace when he stumbles. God opposes the proud and doesn't hear their selfish prayers as they have declared themselves His enemies. But, to the humble – those who are willing to pray, "Not my will but yours," those who are willing to be the faithful bride who lives her life in gratitude for the price paid for her hand – to such as these, He gives grace beyond reason.

If God had a note hanging in the "bathroom" of your life, what would it need to address as He firmly, yet graciously needs to ask you for **all** of your faithfulness to Him as His bride?

_____

_____

Day Three – Joy Comes in the "Mourning"

Yesterday, we left off with *"GOD IS OPPOSED TO THE PROUD, BUT GIVES GRACE TO THE HUMBLE."* Our next verse in James brings us to a "therefore" moment. Do you remember what question we need to ask when we come to the word "therefore" in Scripture?

(Hint: Week 2 Day 3) _____

Read James 4:7a

There is grace for those who will humbly submit to God.

This verse begins with *"Submit therefore to God."* Therefore refers back to what was previously stated and is followed by a command related to how to respond. So, what has James said? In a nutshell, he has stated, "We humans are a mess. We're self-absorbed; we have our selfish motives that lead to conflict in our own lives and the lives of others, we're friends with the world and enemies of God. Even then, however, God will give grace to those who are **humble** – THEREFORE SUBMIT TO GOD!"

What does the word submission mean to you?

_____

First, submission is **not** abject humiliation and forced obedience. It is a willing deference to another, a rearranging of one's priorities for another, which results in obedience. In reference to God, it means to forego what we feel is important and do all in an effort to please Him.

Submission is a willing deference to another, voluntarily placing one's priorities under another's.

On a daily basis, who do you serve with even your most trivial actions? Do you think about God's place in all you do, or is He an afterthought for whom you do **some** specific things, but not **all** things?

_____

"Submit to God" is such a broad statement. It entails surrendering every tiny facet of our lives to God! Where do we start? Thankfully, James lays out some simple guidelines to follow in order to live humbly in God-honoring submission.

Read James 4:7. What is the command following submission? _____

What is the promise that comes with that command? _____

anthistémi – to stand against, oppose, withstand, set against

In order to humble ourselves and rightly submit our lives to God, we must resist Satan and the things that Satan loves. Remember, Satan isn't actively behind every temptation to sin, but his fingerprints are all over every sinful act, and we must learn to resist attitudes and actions that would portray any likeness of him within us. I absolutely love the Greek word used for resist in this verse. *Anthistémi* means "to stand against, oppose, withstand, set against." It isn't a timid, feeble attempt to survive temptation and hope that Satan, or the temptation, will eventually just go away. This type of resistance doesn't play defense. No, it is a bold, offensive stand against sin, a direct opposition to Satan, a mind set against anything ungodly, and a will that chooses to withstand the attack of the enemy with firm resolve. Make no mistake, this tells us that the truly humble Christian is **strong**! To make such self-disciplined decisions day in and day out takes strength of character and fierce determination.

What happens when we resist the devil? _____

Read James 4:7-8.

In these verses we find a series of cause and effect statements. If we boldly stand against sin, Satan will flee and temptation will subside. When we remove one thing, it makes room for another.

If we boldy stand against sin, Satan will flee and temptation will subside.

According to verse 8, when we remove sin, who has room to draw near? _____

If we put aside our sin, we are sacrificing the part of our thoughts, desires, and motives that make us double-minded. It is the single-minded person, who strongly resolves to live solely for the Lord, that finds security in His nearness. Our sin pushes us away from God, yet when we resist, He is able to draw near.

We know we need to submit. But, how do we do that? We resist sin and draw near to God. How do we draw near to God? We realign our character to match His. How do we do that? I'm glad you asked. ☺

What command is given after we are told to draw near to God? _____

Our sin pushes us away from God, yet when we resist, He draws near.

James gives us a quick list of commands that are intended for instruction in keeping our hearts aligned with God's. The first of these commands is to "*cleanse your hands.*" When we are saved by grace, we are washed clean by the blood of the Lamb. Sin doesn't change that eternal status, but we can certainly get our hands messy from time to time while living in this fallen world. Sometimes we just need a good hand washing.

Here James calls for a "**re-do.**" Our hands symbolize our outward actions, the things we **do**. We need to look at our lives, our actions, our external behavior, and decide whether or not they line up with God's standard. If they don't, we need to recognize sin for what it is, wash up, and get right.

Read Psalm 24:3-4.

If our hands (our outward actions) don't meet God's standard, we need to wash them.

According to verse 4, list the first two requirements for the one who can stand before the Lord (or in James' words – "*draw near to God*").

_____

According to James 4:8, after cleansing our hands, what are we commanded to do as we submit to God?

_____

Not only do we need to "re-do," we need to "**re-think.**" Both the psalmist and James agree that purifying our outward behavior is not enough; a purified heart is required of the one who desires to stand before, or draw near to, the Lord. The Pharisees prided themselves on their impeccable outward appearance, but they were rotten where it mattered most – in their hearts. We've already seen that our outward actions can't help but demonstrate our inward attitude; these verses merely support the fact that both have to be clean to be in right standing with God.

Read James 4:9.

Fill in the blanks: Be _____ and _____ and _____.

Well, isn't that just the cherry on top of a great big bowl of ice cream? Why in the world would James tell us to be miserable and mourn and weep? Does he want us to be perpetually dismal, gloomy, and forlorn? Didn't he even begin this book by asking us to consider our trials as joy?

What might James be implying when he gives such an instruction?

_____

A pure heart is also required of those who want to be drawn near to God.

James doesn't mean to imply that the Christian life should be bleak and depressing. Rather, he is calling for the Christian to **repent**. Be miserable living in sin, mourn for the place it has brought you to, for the effect it is having on your life, and weep for the distance it has placed between you and God. Repentance is a complete turning away from something, a new path chosen that entirely forsakes the old.

As I think about this picture portrayed of misery, mourning, and weeping, I think of past sins that consumed me – habits that I found addicting, sinful characteristics that I allowed to rule my life. I can quickly recall multiple seasons where I'd simply had enough of it, and frankly I'd had enough of "myself." I was literally sick of their effects on my life; I was tired of being ruled by things that were only dragging me down, and I hated who I had become at the hands of my own sin. These were times when I needed to open my eyes to who I was and literally mourn the loss of what I could have been due to what I'd become. I needed to repent and submit.

We are to be miserable living in sin, to mourn where sin has taken us, and to weep for the distance it has created between us and God.

Read 2 Corinthians 7:8-11.

Paul felt somewhat badly for hurting the feelings of the church in Corinth for the previous letter he'd had to send calling them out on their sin. But, not badly enough to regret sending it or to regret its effects. He hurt for them as they needed to mourn their previous state, but he knew it was necessary and was grateful that his bold words of chastisement brought his desired result.

What does verse 10 say their godly sorrow brought? _____

What does verse 11 say their godly sorrow produced? _____

_____

Godly sorrow leads to a hatred of the sin that once chained us down, and a healthy fear of ever returning to it.

When there is true, godly sorrow over one's own sin, it produces all sorts of positive reactions that become life-changing as a person moves forward. There is an eagerness to leave the old behind and move forward in freedom, a hatred of the sin that once chained them down, and a healthy fear of ever returning to that miserable state in life.

Verse 10: Godly sorrow produces repentance without _____.

Be miserable, mourn, and weep over your current state of sin, allow it to make you feel sick enough that you are ready to get well, but repent and move on in joy. Godly sorrow does not lead us to the pit of self-loathing. That is exactly where Satan wants you to find yourself, but God says, "Repent and move on." We need not keep any record of the past. God keeps no record, but Satan certainly wants us to. It's by this method that he tempts us to live in guilt and defeat. But, God wants us to only remember enough of our sin to have a healthy fear of ever returning to it. He doesn't want us to live under the weight of guilt, for that will only keep us from being useful for Him.

God says, "Repent and move on." We need keep no record of our past.

What healthy fears from the past have you developed that prevent future mistakes in specific areas of your life?

_____

What past regrets do you have that you need to let go of in order to move forward in the freedom of His forgiveness?

_____

James 4:9 – *"Let your laughter be turned into _____ and your joy into _____."*

Again, James is not calling for a dismal existence. He's told us to "re-do," "re-think," "repent," and now he is commanding us to "**rearrange**." We must rearrange our lifestyle, our commitments, our priorities, and our convictions, to match those of the Lord's. What formerly brought us laughter, we must now mourn over; what we previously felt would bring us joy, needs to bring us gloom if we realize these things were sinful. It is good for us to mourn the sinful things that we formerly thought would bring us happiness, because it is in this moment that we realize that our thinking was skewed and we open our hearts to new, godly thinking. We are to mourn for the state of our sinful hearts, for **then** we are prepared to humble ourselves.

We must rearrange our convictions to match those of the Lord's.

Read James 4:10.

It was when James humbled himself and realized that he'd been so wrong and that Jesus had been so right that God was able to effectively use him. Only when James realized that life wasn't about himself was God able to exalt him in his humility. It was necessary for him to realize that his selfishness had clouded his mind and that he wanted nothing more than to move forward with God.

Notice how our position, relative to God, progresses through these verses. The beginning of the chapter showed us the mess that sin and selfish ambition gets us into. The following verses show us how to make room for God to draw near as we resist sin and realign our hearts. Assuming we have followed those instructions, we can find ourselves, according to verse 10, in the presence of God, drawn near. Through this process we have humbled ourselves to the point where it is now HE who can exalt us. As we exalt ourselves, we push God away and don't allow Him to exalt us in the amazing ways He'd like. But, when we die to self, oh the amazing things He has in store for us.

When we die to self, He can exalt us.

Who do you think can exalt you better – little old you – or the Creator of the universe? In what ways do you need to humble yourself, so that God can exalt you?

_____

_____

Admittedly, this is a hard process and His "exalting" won't be the same as what your own would have been. But He will blow your mind with what you never expected or fathomed possible. We must, though, allow ourselves to come to a brokenness where we mourn who we are and what we've become in comparison to what He'd have us to be. It is at this point where we find true joy, not what we assumed was joyful that we must now consider gloom. What God has for us is joy beyond reason, joy that can be found in the midst of trials, joy that enables us to love unconditionally in the midst of hurt, joy that finds supernatural strength in our weakest earthly moments. But, this joy is a result of our humility, submission, and mourning. We often sing that "joy comes in the morning." May I submit to you that "joy comes in the **mourning**?"

Joy comes in the mourning over our brokenness.

Can you remember a time when God replaced your mourning with His joy?

_____

_____

Today is a good day to: "re-do" (wash your hands); "re-think" (purify your attitudes); "repent" and "rearrange" your priorities (submit).

Is there any sin you need to mourn now to allow Him to replace it with His joy? Remember, joy comes in the mourning.

_____

_____

Day Four – Godless Gossip

Even Christians have a tendency to eat our own with our words.

Yesterday, we ended by looking at the way God will exalt the humble man. Interestingly, in verse 11, James begins showing us ways that man exalts himself, actually going so far as to assume the role of God in the lives of others.

Read James 4:11-12.

Do not _____ against _____ _____, brethren.

By referring to his readers as "brethren," James reminds us that he is talking with Christians. How sad it is that he has to keep reminding fellow Christians about the dangers of their spoken words. But, the truth is, we have a tendency to "eat our own" with our words. It's ugly, and James needed to address it. We have already discussed the source of our words, and the fact that they are powerful tools, but today we are going to get specific concerning a few ways those words can cause trouble.

katalaleó – 1. to speak evil of / slander; 2. to rail at; 3. to talk down

The Greek word used for speaking against another in James 4:11 is *katalaleó*. This word includes the thought of gossip, but it reaches much further in its meaning. It means "to speak evil of, slander, to rail at, to talk down."

Using the definition above, list several ways in which we can "speak against another."

_____

_____

By speaking against others, we place ourselves in a position of superiority over them.

Verse 11 says that the one who speaks against his brother, speaks against and judges the law. This makes him not a "doer of the law," but a judge of it. The law tells us not to speak against each other and to love our neighbor as ourselves. When we speak against our fellow Christians as their judge, we are placing ourselves in a position of superiority over them. By doing this, we are assuming that our opinion in a matter is correct and theirs is incorrect. Speaking against them, in the manner portrayed in verse 11, shows that we have disregarded the part of the law that tells us not to do such a thing. Instead, we judge them concerning some other parts of the law that we are certain they have broken and need to be made aware of.

We disrespect God's authority by taking His matters into our hands.

According to verse 12, whose responsibility is judgment? _____

Fill in the blank: "...but _____ _____ _____ *who judge your neighbor?*"

In other words, "Who do you think you are? Who died and made you judge?" By exalting ourselves to the position of God in judging our brother, we are not only harming our brother, but we are entirely disrespecting God's law, as well as His authority in the matter. We disrespect God's law by disregarding a portion of it in order to promote our own opinions or preferences. We disrespect His authority by taking a matter out of His hands and placing it in our own. Either way, we are walking on dangerous ground. Let's first look at how being judgmental affects us personally, and then we will focus on how it affects others.

Read Matthew 7:1-5.

When we are working with children, especially siblings, it is painfully obvious that they are often quick to lay blame on kids around them. I have so often said to both of my girls, "You worry about you; I'll worry about your sister." Jesus is saying that very thing in these verses. How dare we use the time that should be spent on correcting **our** sins for pointing out what we deem to be the sins of others? When we break the law in order to point out our opinion of someone else's infraction of the law, we are nothing more than a hypocrite. Ouch!

By what standard does Matthew 7:2 tell us we will be judged?

_____

The more grace we lavish on others, the more grace God will extend to us.

I remember the time in my life when I so clearly began to understand the gravity of this message. I'd heard a lesson given on judgment versus grace and I started realizing that the more grace I lavished on others, the more grace God is willing to extend to me. But, the more judgment I dished out, the more severely I would be judged. As this soaked in, I found myself praying so much more for others, begging God to show them grace, knowing that I needed His grace just as badly, if not more. I cannot describe how this process softened my heart, making it more pliable and ready for God to use in the lives of others.

When others think of you, do they fear your criticism, or know that you will meet them with grace?

_____

When your family thinks of you, do they fear your criticism, or know that you will meet them with grace?

_____

I ask that second question because, sad as it is, we often over-criticize our families in ways that we would never consider doing to others outside of our home. It may be a universal truth, but James says it's universally wrong and should be stopped.

When we lead with criticism, we are inviting God to do the same to us. We are telling Him that this is the standard by which we would like Him to judge us. The thought of that literally scares me to bits! I never want to return to the harshness that once defined me, inviting equal harshness from the *"One who is able to save and destroy"* (James 4:12).

When we criticize others, we invite God to do the same to us.

Now that we've seen how speaking against others adversely affects ourselves, let's turn our focus to a few of the many ways it can devastate others. Remember, when we speak in this manner, we are exalting ourselves to the position of God. But, what does that really look like?

We said earlier that there were 3 parts of the definition of our Greek word *katalaleó*. The first one we will pay specific attention to is "to speak evil of, slander."

How is speaking evil of another, or slandering them, "playing God" in their life?

_____

JAMES - LIVING A LIFE OF FAITH

Did any of you mention the word, "gossip" in your response? Gossip is an ugly beast that wreaks havoc in the lives of the one being slandered, the one listening to the gossip, as well as the deliverer of the juicy bit of news. We've already seen that the deliverer is inviting judgment on herself. But, what of the other two?

What effects can gossip have on the victim who is the object of its focus?

_____

Read Genesis 39:6-19.

There is no such thing as harmless gossip. Gossip of any type can land others in a prison of hurt.

I wonder what Joseph would say to us if he were standing here today concerning the damage one person's words can do in the life of another. Potiphar's wife certainly stepped into the role of God, taking into her own hands what would become of Joseph after she slandered him to others. She was miserable, and if she couldn't have her way, she was going to make him miserable, too. She threw out her words carelessly because it mattered little to her what would become of him, and as far as she knew, it wasn't going to cause any discomfort in her own life. But, what of Joseph? Her careless words landed him in prison for longer than two years when he'd done nothing wrong. Punished and imprisoned for having done nothing more than stand for his integrity, his entire reality was changed due to what one person said and how others were forced to respond to it.

It would be easy to look at this extreme example and excuse ourselves from the application, thinking that we would never throw out careless lies about such a serious topic. But, gossip of any shape and size can land others in a prison of hurt. Even if the message relayed is not intended to be false, when we speak against another, we are casting that person in a negative light. Based on our messages, they are trapped by the negative impression we've made of them. You may think, "I didn't try to cast them in a negative light." My question back to you – "But, did you try **not** to?"

Remember, if it's not your story, it's not yours to share.

Consider this for yourself. With all you have on your plate, do you really need anyone else's gossip forming the opinions others have of you? Is digging yourself out from underneath false impressions created by the mouths of others really something additional you want to have to worry about? Ask yourself that very thing the next time you start to speak against anyone besides yourself. If it's not a burden you'd like to bear at the hands of another, don't take it into your own hands to burden someone else with it either. As we saw in a previous day, if it's not "your story," it's not yours to share – even as "a prayer request."

Can you see how gossip is a form of judgment and speaking against another? Is this a problem area in your life that you need to address? As you've read about speaking against another, has the Holy Spirit brought someone to mind – do you need to apologize?

_____

Read Romans 14:4.

Who are you to judge another man's servant? For you moms, what happens inside of you when someone speaks against one of your children? I know my kids aren't perfect, but they're MY kids and I know them inside and out. When someone else thinks they are "reading their hearts" and speaks out about them when they clearly have their facts wrong, I can feel the hair on the back of my neck raise like a momma cat protecting her kittens. I have oodles of illustrations I could give about their flaws and shortcomings (just as they could do the same about mine), but those illustrations would be balanced with unconditional love and grace, because I am their momma and I want others to understand the good in them even more than any bad habits or faults. God is like that with us. When others take the liberty to speak against us, thinking they know our hearts and motives, but not having our best interests in mind, God says, "That's MY child you're talking about!"

Imagine an owner of a business who has a dear, hard-working employee that he has employed for years. One day someone off the street randomly walks into that business and begins to critique his employee, believing he knows best. I can imagine the owner walking over to the critic and calmly saying, "Thank you for your input, but this worker and I go way back. This is **my** business and not yours, you have no right to give input on facts that you don't have." No matter how much insight we think we have into a situation, unless we are God, there is no way we have all the facts and we need to graciously bow out of the "conversation." It is not our place to assume the position of judge when so many extenuating circumstances surround every facet of life.

We simply can't know all the facts in all situations; therefore we should usually bow out.

I don't care how old I get, I will always love cartoons and a line from one came to mind as I wrote on this topic. In the movie, "How to Train Your Dragon," the Vikings had thought for hundreds of years that the dragons were mean, vicious beasts. But after capturing one of them and nursing it back to health, young Hiccup says, "Everything we know about you guys is wrong." The irony of this statement struck me. "Everything we **know**…" Rather, it should have been "everything we **thought** we knew…" We can be so assured that our opinion concerning others is right, but it can be so wrong. **We don't know what we don't know.** We have no idea how much more there is to learn about others and their situations; only God knows the heart of man. Let's allow Him to show us what we need to know about others instead of formulating our own opinions. In addition, we need to avoid leading others to form wrong opinions as well.

We don't know what we don't know. Only God knows the heart of man.

Do you form an opinion about every person or situation you hear about? Are you willing to begin saying, "I don't know all the facts, therefore I can/will stay out of it?" How might this attitude be beneficial to you and those around you?

Sharing gossip places the one we've told it to in a very awkward position.

_____

_____

Not only do we harm ourselves and the victims of gossip when we speak against others in this way, but we also cause hardship for the one we are speaking to. If I speak negatively with someone about another person, I have put something on their plate that God did not intend for them to have to deal with. Suddenly, I am forcing them to have to decide via second or third-hand information whether or not what I am saying is true and what they are going to do with it. In other words, when I tell "person A" something about "person B," "person

A" has to decide whether to believe me or to give the other person the benefit of the doubt. They must further decide whether or not to tell anyone else, keep it to themselves, or act on what they've heard. Truly, this is playing God and we need to keep well away from it. Who are we to think we should have such influence in the lives of others?

Describe a time when you were placed in an awkward situation when someone shared information about another person that you didn't need to hear. How did you handle it? Would you do something different next time?

_____

_____

katalaleó – to rail at

The next part of the definition of *katalaleó* emphasized today is "to rail at." In a sense, we play God when we rail at someone, too. By doing so, we are acting as judge, jury, and executioner as we pass them their guilty verdict and serve them their penalty in the form of a verbal bludgeoning. Ever been completely lambasted by someone's words? It's not much fun, is it? Ever been the one doing the railing? The next time the temptation to do so comes your way, remember that you are inviting the same measure of judgment on yourself from the One who would look at you and say, "That's MY child you're judging!"

What are the implications of this sort of "speaking against" another? First, we are giving the other person the impression that they are not worthy of being treated with basic human respect. The way you speak to, or at, another person conveys to them the value you place in them. Do your words value or devalue those inside and outside of your home? Second, the message of our words can burden them with extra baggage. Just as I asked earlier concerning gossip, do you really need others weighing you down with more baggage than you already carry by the hurtful impressions they scream into your lives? If we answer "no" to that question, is it fair for us to play God and do it to others? God has plans for His servants, and if we are weighing them down with hurt and baggage that they have trouble unloading, we've taken God's place and kept them from being able to do His will as freely as He'd like them to.

The way you speak to, or at, others conveys the value you place in them.

Words can easily form one's self-opinion. Recall a time when someone's words affected who you believed you could or couldn't be.

katalaleó – to talk down

_____

_____

How might the way you talk to others be affecting what they believe they could or couldn't be?

_____

_____

Closely-related is the last part of our definition for *katalaleó*. "To talk down" can hurt as much as either of the other two meanings. To criticize and condescend can make a person feel small, useless, unworthy, and may give them the impression that they will never amount to anything. God tells us time and time again in His Word how much He values us, how beautiful He finds us, and how much He loves us. I find it interesting that He, who has the right to judge, goes to every length to build us up, while we, who have no right to judge, go to great lengths to tear each other down. Let us all remember what Paul wrote to the Ephesians, *"Do not let any unwholesome talk come out of your mouths, but only what is helpful for building others up according to their needs, that it may benefit those who listen"* (Eph. 4:29, NIV).

Next time you're tempted to criticize another, take a moment and ask if it's really necessary. In the long run, is the criticism of any eternal significance? Even if it is, is it really your place to give it? Instead of sending a condescending message, could a message of grace potentially work a miracle?

Have you ever been in the middle of an absolutely rotten day when someone decided to nitpick you about the most trivial, insignificant, ridiculous thing? On a day like that, you may not even have the energy to respond with more than tear-filled eyes. That person didn't know where your heart was at in that moment, but their words hurt and it was the last thing you needed. Friends, this life is hard, and we are all carrying hurts that perhaps no one else even realizes. Before speaking against anyone in any manner, remember that you can't possibly have all the facts, only God does. Your words may be heaping hurt onto a heart that you don't realize is already breaking. God says, "Don't do it. I will judge when I need to judge. You worry about you. I'll worry about everyone else." Think before you speak. When we exalt ourselves to the place of God, we tread on dangerous ground. It will be hard to see the fingerprints of God on those we've covered with bruises. Make sure it's His impression being left on those He loves, not yours.

It is hard to see the fingerprints of God on those we've covered with bruises.

Day Five – Unexpected Construction

Yesterday, we looked at the way man exalts himself by "playing God" in the lives of others. Today, we will see how he can assume the role of God in his own life.

Read James 4:13.

To illustrate his point, James directs his attention to a planning businessman. This man has his eyes set on an end profit and has made a deliberate plan, with absolute confidence in its success. James isn't condemning the man's desire to make a profit; rather, he is calling him out on his arrogance and self-reliance.

Read James 4:14.

Why is it foolish to plan with absolute confidence in oneself?

_____

Five years ago, could you have possibly fathomed where you are right now?

We do not know what tomorrow holds! Think of wherever it was you were in life five years ago. At that time, could you have possibly fathomed where you find yourself right now? Although you may be working the same job, have the same friends, and keep the same habits, have circumstances and events altered your reality in the midst of those five years in ways that were entirely out of your control? I know that my life has been filled with changes that I never could have imagined, and I would guess the same could be said for most of us.

James says, "*…you do not know what your life will be like tomorrow.*" But, there is One who does. It is quite foolish for us to believe that we know more about our future than the One who holds the future in His hands.

It is foolish to believe that we know more about our future than the One who holds the future.

Imagine walking in on a group of children who are planning to play a game of street hockey after school. As an adult with a broader understanding of surrounding events, you know that this is not a good idea because road construction is scheduled to begin that very evening. You know that the condition of the road is going to be altered and not only will this not be conducive to their plans, it will be dangerous for them to try to play their game in the midst of the construction. The intention behind their original plan isn't wrong; you just know more about the situation than they do.

God knows about every upcoming, unforeseen "construction project" that is going to alter our path. Our insistence on sticking to unwavering plans on the paths before us must look foolish to His all-knowing eyes.

What are some of the "plans" we make, and what is our motivation in making them?

_____

_____

I grew up a very "plan-oriented" person. I've always been very organized and have liked having my ducks in a row. Giving this area of my life over to God hasn't been easy. I know the benefits of orderly living and have had to learn how to balance that with giving God the freedom to change my "structure." There is nothing wrong with being orderly; in fact, it helps simplify much of life. The issue is not with structure, but with an adamant, self-assured attitude that gives no consideration to God and leaves no room for Him to work in the midst of that structure.

In order to look at this practically, let's consider a popular Bible figure: Jacob.

Read Genesis 25:27-34.

Jacob manipulated situations by means of being a crafty planner, which left no room for God to work out the details in his life. In this case, his motive was his own **selfishness**. He had a desire to have what his brother, Esau, had and he was willing to do whatever it took to get it for himself.

Our stubbornness to stick to our plans must look foolish to God.

In this particular example, Jacob's motives were self-seeking, not giving thought or care to the hurt that his plan would inflict on his family. At times, we can be selfish in this manner. We may have our eyes so fixed on an end goal, that we don't give any thought to how the ripple effects of our plan may adversely affect, or even burden, others. We know that God is never in the midst of this sort of plan; He does not support the selfish desires of His spoiled children.

Consider your most significant plans; what possible costs are they placing on others?

_____

_____

Planning and structure are not the problem. Leaving no room for God to work in, or change, that structure is.

James 4:14 –

"You are just a _____ that appears for a _____ while and _____ away".

Think about that verse for a moment longer, letting its truth sink in deeply. Our lives are vapors; we are here today and gone tomorrow. How can we, mere mists, suppose we know more than our heavenly Father? Our God knows the bigger picture; He realizes every "construction crew" that is going to demolish the very ground we plan to walk on. He knows the "construction" that is going to take place in our own lives and in the lives of others, and He miraculously knows how every detail of that fits together from eternity past to eternity future. He's got the entire picture to organize, and when we have the audacity to think that our own selfish desires should have the right to alter that master plan, we will learn through much heartache that they don't after all. You are a mist; He is the Maker – leave the planning to Him.

God knows every circumstance that is going to demolish the very ground we plan to walk on.

Read James 4:15.

Realizing the brevity of our lives in the grand scheme should help us to have a God-directed perspective. When we come to this realization, we must alter our prayers to ask whatever we ask according to His will. James begins His "sample prayer" with such a broad focus that it covers all other things. *"If the Lord wills, we will LIVE..."* (emphasis mine) Our very lives are in His hands; whether we are here or gone tomorrow is completely at the mercy of His sovereign will. With this truth always at the forefront of our minds, we should understand that our own plans, even the smallest ones, are futile, and everything we do should be done with God's permission.

True or False: I always seek God's will for the direction of my life. _____

True or False: I generally make my plans first, and then ask God to bless them. _____

What can you do to bring God into your planning process? _____

_____

We often do everything we can to secure our own blessings.

We've seen one of Jacob's plans motivated by selfishness, let's continue with him and see what other motivating factors drove him in his ambitions.

Read Genesis 27:18-33.

Attaining his brother's birthright wasn't enough, Jacob wanted more. He was looking out for his future and he was motivated by a desire for **smooth sailing.** Indeed, this con job on his father was absolutely fueled by selfishness, but let's focus on the specifics. By attaining the blessing of the first-born son, Jacob thought he was sealing the deal on a cushy retirement! He would be blessed with material wealth, his own family would eventually serve him, and God's hand of protection would be on him. This plan was to attain the mother-load of all blessings. We all long for security, so can you blame him? This was the guarantee that the 401K was steadfast and secure, his climb up the ladder of success was certain, and his worries would be behind him (or so he thought).

We do this in our lives. We may not trick someone out of their own blessings, but we often do everything we can to secure our own. We make strategic investments, we settle ourselves in a choice house in a choice neighborhood, we find a church that meets all of our "requirements," we choose our children's schools where they will have the best, etc. We are on a constant search for what will make us "happy," and the plans we make for our lives revolve around that pursuit of smooth sailing. We may read that list and wonder what would be wrong with any of those goals. This is America after all, where we hold to the inalienable right to the "pursuit of happiness." There is nothing inherently wrong with this. The ques-

Invite God into the planning process and accept His answers.

tion is whether or not we invite God into the planning process and whether we will accept His answer or deny it if it doesn't match our plan.

I was driving down the highway recently and noticed a billboard for a "planned community." I found it interesting to compare that thought to our own lives. A planned community clearly defines what is and is not allowed within a housing development to promote the happiness and contentment for those who choose to live there. There is no tolerance for disruption of these standards. How often do we plan so stringently that we don't allow God to disrupt us by sending in a "construction crew" to come and fix our potholes? God knows that disruptions in our lives can be the very things that make us closer to the creation He wants us to be. We may desire smooth sailing, but we must still submit our plans to Him and ask Him if they are His will. His answer may be something entirely different than what we had hoped for. I have found that traveling the rough and rocky road can bring us to the most beautiful places. Certainly, we will experience a greater variety of scenery during this trip called life than if we'd stuck solely to our perfectly-planned paths. Oftentimes, joy is found in the journey; even when detours are involved.

I have always felt that one of the saddest parts of Jacob's story is that God always intended for Jacob to receive his father's blessing. His mother was given that promise when Jacob was still in the womb (Gen. 25:23). But, neither Jacob or Rebekah were patient enough to allow God to work out the details. When they thought that the timing was getting too close, they intervened and took matters into their own hands. Yes, Jacob received the blessing, but he suffered harsh consequences as well.

Are you willing to wait for God's timing or do you generally push forward with your own plans?

God can use the disruptions in our lives to make us into the creation He wants us to be.

_____

Have you regretted plans you made without God's input? If so, how?

_____

Read Genesis 27:41-45.

Verse 44 says that Rebekah told Jacob to run away and stay with Laban for a few days until Esau cooled down, and Jacob did so. This plan was for his future **safety** and **security.** Notice the specifics of the plan. He was to stay with Laban for a "few days." Whether what is meant here implies a few literal days or even a few years, God proved that their plans were futile compared to His sovereign authority. They made a hasty decision without consulting God, and their details didn't work out anything like they intended.

God determines the success or failure of all plans.

Read Proverb 19:21

God determines the success or failure of all plans. Whether we like it or not, it's out of our hands.

When Jacob and Esau had this falling out, they were 77 years old; Jacob did not return home until he was 97. He was swindled by an uncle who was even more shrewd at manipulation than he was, and he was forced to forego his own plans for reasons he'd never expected. He was safe and secure with Laban, but he never fathomed how long the "construction crew" would be working on this particular road. His plan worked out in the end, but the details that he thought he had control of were completely out of his power.

Even when our intentions are reasonable, we must submit our requests to God.

Even when our intentions are as reasonable as safety and security, we must submit our requests to God and ask Him for **His** will to be done, not ours. But, Jacob took no time for such things at this point in his life.

In what ways have you tried to create safety and security (for yourself or others) through your own efforts, instead of relying on God?

_____

_____

During the 20 years that Jacob was forced to work for his uncle, he did grow in his relationship with the Lord. But old habits die hard, and Jacob's knee-jerk reaction was still to plan quickly for himself without consulting with God. He continued to struggle with submitting to God's will when it differed from his own. Our next passage finds him at age 97, traveling home carrying his old habit in his back pocket.

Read Genesis 32:3-12.

What did Jacob do in verses 7 – 8?

_____

The time to pray is before we make our plans.

What did he do in verses 9 – 12? _____

When Jacob heard that Esau was coming with four hundred men, he instantly assumed the worst and made a plan motivated by a need for **survival**. *After* he executed his plan, he prayed; after he got all of his ducks in a row, he went to God. Certainly there couldn't be anything wrong with seeking to assure one's survival, could there?

Look again at James 4:15: *"If the Lord wills, we will _____..."*

Our lives are in His hands, and as hard a pill as this may be to swallow, even our survival plans need to align with His will for us.

Oftentimes, when we are shifted into survival mode, our thoughts aren't entirely rational and we can make plans and decisions out of sheer panic. Jacob's plan to separate his huge entourage of servants as well as his family was strategically savvy. His plan, though, while apparently sound, was executed in panic.

Read Genesis 31:3.

God had just told him to return home, promising that He would be with him. The blessing that he'd received 20 years earlier had stated that his brother would eventually serve him. But, Jacob didn't recall God's promises in the midst of panic; he resorted to his natural instinct and made a swift plan.

Although it is difficult, we need to recall God's promises in the midst of our panic.

The next morning, he would find that his plan and panic had been for naught. Esau greeted him with kisses. This is easy to see as we have the hindsight view of their story in Scripture, but when we face our own urgent situations, it can be very difficult to not go into "quick fix" mode and do everything we can to survive an overwhelming hardship. We have many of our own promises from the Lord, but in moments of panic, they may not be what initially rises to the surface in our thinking.

We've all had crisis moments; times of fear and possible panic. When you find yourself in a fearful situation, do you respond like Jacob did and attempt to get your ducks in a row for God ahead of time? How might a situation have turned out better if you'd consulted God before making your plans?

_____

_____

Planning is not bad. In fact, Scripture teaches the wisdom of planning before making commitments, etc. It is our motive and our inclusion of God, along with submission to His ultimate will, which make the difference. Paul gives us a good example of this in the following passages.

Read Acts 18:20-21, 1 Corinthians 4:19; 16:7.

Paul had a consistent pattern of praying for things that he was certain had godly motives, yet he humbly submitted to the fact that God might have other plans.

Read Romans 1:9-10.

Paul had tried repeatedly to visit Rome in order to bring them the gospel. I don't believe intentions and motives can be any more pure than that. Yet, God, for reasons unknown to Paul at the time, repeatedly stopped him from making it there.

Make it a consistent pattern to pray in all things; humbly submitting to God's plans.

One of the most beautiful facts found in the historical context of the book of Romans surrounds this very issue. Paul desperately wanted to make it to Rome to share the details of the gospel, but due to the fact that God did not allow it, he was forced to write it all down in a letter. This letter, which became the book of Romans, gives the most exhaustive explanation of God's righteousness revealed in the gospel found in any one book of the Bible. Because he wasn't able to establish a church in Rome, Paul wrote them a letter that gave them every detail he would have shared with them had he been able to come in person.

Paul's motives were pure and his intentions were great, but God had a "construction crew" working in ways that Paul could not see, for which believers should be eternally grateful.

We have the book of Romans today because Paul did not get what he wanted years ago.

This is always the case. God knows best, absolutely. There is no getting around the fact that we can have the best of intentions, but if they do not work with God's will, the best intentions don't make the best plans.

With the benefit of hindsight, can you see the bigger blessing that came about because you specifically did NOT get what you hoped or prayed for? How? Remember, that blessing may have occurred in the life of another.

_____

_____

Christ prayed, "Father, not My will, but Yours be done." We cannot ask for more.

Read James 4:16-17.

In verse 16, James called out the planner who boasts in his arrogance. We, too, are called out by this passage in the same way if we look upon our own plans and take credit for those which have been successful, or look upon our future plans with absolute self-confidence. Even as our Savior prayed concerning His imminent death on the cross, He prayed, "Father, not My will, but Yours be done." We have no right to ask for more.

Verse 17 holds the reader accountable for all he has learned. He has been told that he is to submit to God's will in **all** things. Ignorance is no longer bliss after reading this passage, or the rest of James for that matter. To discount what has been taught, would now be sin.

We are accountable for all we have learned thus far in our study of James as well. We must be what God wants us to be, do what God wants us to do, speak as God wants us to speak, and sense what God wants us to sense.[26] Not allowing what we have read in God's Word to change our hearts, minds, and actions, is sin.

We must allow God's Word to change our hearts, minds, and actions.

We have completed four of the five chapters in James. Take a quick look back over the previous weeks; what have you learned to this point that you know you need to let change your heart, mind, and actions? Today is a great day to do the next right thing.

_____

_____

_____

_____

---

26   Walvoord and Zuck, *BKC NT,* p. 832

WEEK SIX: A PRAYERFULLY PATIENT FAITH

Day One – The Lord of Sabaoth

Welcome to the beginning of our last week together. It's gone quickly, hasn't it? We have consistently noted that the book of James was a letter written to Jewish Christians. This next portion of the letter, though, was a prophetic declaration concerning a particular, unsaved group.

Revisit James 2:1-7. Who was persecuting the Jewish Christians? *the rich*

James 5:1-6 is written about the unsaved, rich man.

Earlier in James, we were able to see that references to the "rich man" in Scripture do not always have to be negative. In this case, though, the rich are indeed being called out for their wrong actions. To make sense of this passage, and what we're about to read in Chapter 5, it may help to remember that what is true today was true back then as well; namely, not everyone who sat in church was saved. As my imagination reels, I can picture a hypothetical situation where the unsaved, rich oppressor has been shown his choice seat in the church, far from the poor man who was asked to sit on the floor. I wonder how he might squirm in his seat as this portion of the letter is read in front of the congregation concerning his own fate.

Read James 5:1-6.

klaió – to weep; ololuzó – to howl – both describe the reaction of the wicked to coming judgment

We know this portion of James was not written to accuse rich Jewish believers for multiple reasons. For one, the absence of James' consistent reference to them as "brethren" is quite conspicuous. Even more so, the strict accusation with no accompanying message of grace or deliverance also marks a stark contrast regarding who this charge is against. This is not to say that the Jewish Christians did not benefit from its inclusion in their letter, as this segment will remind them not to envy the evil rich man, but to have faith that God will judge them in His time.

James 5:1 *"Come now, you rich, ___weep___ and ___wail___ for your miseries are coming."*

James does not condemn wealth, just the love and misuse of it.

Elsewhere in Scripture, the words weep (*klaió*) and howl (*ololuzó*) are both used to describe the reaction of the wicked to the coming of the Lord in the end times. "In fact, *ololuzó* is found only in the prophets in the Old Testament and always in the context of judgment."[27] James knew this and chose to use this word as its judgmental significance would quickly grasp their attention and set the tone for the gravity of the message to follow.

Understanding the use of these words helps us accurately interpret the meaning of the rest of the passage. Based on this knowledge, what "miseries" were coming their way?

judgement of the Lord

This passage is announcing the final, eternal judgment of the unrepentant, rich oppressor.

---

27   Moo, TNTC, *James*, p. 164

As a reminder, neither James, nor any other biblical author, condemned wealth, but boldly rebuked an unhealthy love of, and misuse of, wealth.

Verse 1 tells them that their miseries are "coming," but verses 2-3 use the present tense to describe the demise of their riches.

What might have been James' motive in using this sort of wording?

to show how near God's judgement was

Even though James is warning them of the end times, the present tense depiction of material decay showed that the value of those material items are truly worthless even in this present life. Since they hold no spiritual value, they have no eternal significance. These "treasures" were no good to them now, and would certainly be no good to them in the end, when wealth has no way of saving them from the fire.

Material items hold no spiritual value; therefore, they have no eternal significance.

James uses interesting imagery when he refers to both silver and gold as "rusted." In this way, he effectively points out the temporality of wealth by stating that even precious metals, though they cannot really rust, will come to ruin.

James 5:3 – *"...their rust will be* __testament against you__ *and will consume your flesh like fire."*

The material items they held onto for security would be the very things that would bear witness against them, pronouncing their final condemnation. The treasures, themselves, are not inherently evil, but the fact that they are all some people have to show for when they meet the Lord, will seal their fate. Not only would the material items come to ruin; the love of them will bring man to ruin.

Not only will material items come to ruin, but the love of them can ruin us as well.

In what temporal things have you tried to find security? How secure have you really been in them?

Shelter. Household items, not running out of things.

Reread the final sentence in verse 3. The 1st century churches looked for the return of Christ to occur during their lifetime. As a result, those who truly knew Christ should have been living with eternity in mind, holding loosely to the things of this world. However, the unbelievers in their midst, were storing up treasure in what they thought were their literal "last days." Foolishly, they were hoarding when the end was near, but what they were really storing up was their own coming judgment.

Read Matthew 6:19-24.

Matthew 6 tells us that whatever we treasure will eventually capture our hearts as well.

It would be easy to look at the first 3 verses in James 5 and wonder what is so wrong with saving money. Isn't saving being a good steward of what God has given us? Matthew 6 clearly tells us it is the devotion to money that makes it a danger. When it becomes consuming and is what we truly serve, it takes the place of God in our lives and we tread on dangerous ground.

We will see in the following verses of James 5, that these rich oppressors were not just being savvy with their savings. They were hoarding, at a great cost to others, and ironically, to themselves as well.

Read James 5:4 and Deuteronomy 24:14-15.

According to Deut. 24, how often were the workers to be paid? *every day*

Why? *they are counting on you, their cries might be heard by the Lord*

In that culture, it was a life and death matter to withhold daily pay from a poor worker. A daily wage paid for daily bread for a laborer and his family. To withhold it was to potentially withhold life. Again, James uses the same imagery as he did in verse 3, stating that the unpaid wages literally cry out in accusation against them.

Read James 5:5. "*You have lived luxuriously* and self indulgence ..."

Those who had hoarded their wealth at the expense of other people's lives were doing it in order to live in luxury during their stay on this earth. Their focus was that of instant gratification in this life without any concern for eternity. Even though the Lord had told them to be watching for His return, they were only watching out for their pocketbooks, instead of investing their lives in the Kingdom of God.

James condemns hoarding wealth in order to live in luxury here and now.

Are you living your life as if you could be in your last days? If you knew you only had a few months to live, what would you hold on to? What would you release?

I would only hold on to what I really needed. Would trust the Lord to provide

What might you be hoarding? Are you holding onto something at the expense of others? What might it be costing others? Are you willing to loosen your grip just a little? Remember, two things cannot occupy the same space at once; what needs to go?

I'm holding on to my true self

Although this passage was written specifically about the hoarding of wealth on the part of the rich man, we as Christians can find spiritual application within it. The rich kept to themselves what they were obligated to share for the benefit of the poor. What they had to share was life-giving, and hoarding it produced deadly results. Hoarding our faith is far more costly than any tangible wealth we might keep from others. We are to share the salvation we've been graciously given with the spiritually-poor. When we withhold our faith and do not share the Word daily, we are contributing to their death, just as the rich man who didn't give daily wages to the starving servant. By withholding the gospel, we are contributing to their eternal death, a demise far greater than mere physical death. Those unpaid "wages" cry out in accusation against us. What is our excuse? What are we allowing to stop us? Are we allowing ourselves, in selfishness, to be content with the "luxury" of our own spiritual security, not caring that we are living in a lost and dying world? Do we simply assume someone else will "pay" the spiritually-poor what they desperately need in order to live? Are we willing to watch them starve while we take care of our own needs and discount theirs?

Two things cannot occupy the same space in your heart at one time.

At the end of James 5:5, we see that, just like the fattened calf, the rich oppressor was doing nothing more than fattening up his own heart for the imminent day of slaughter. His last days were coming, and he was preparing his heart to that end.

Our last days are coming. To what end are you preparing your heart?

_____

_____

Read James 5:6.

katadikazo – to pass sentence upon

Verse 6 gives further evidence that lets us know that this portion of the letter was directed toward the unbelieving listener, as it references the believer whom the rich man is oppressing. The Greek word for the condemning of the righteous man in this verse is *katadikazo*, a judicial word meaning "to pass sentence upon." Remember, these tyrannical, rich oppressors had drug poor believers to court and ruthlessly taken their property and possessions. We see in verse 6, that they had even gone to the extent of putting some of them to death. They stepped in to play the role of God and judge in the righteous man's life, and the previous verses have shown us that they will reap what they have sown; their judgment will be severe.

How did the righteous man respond to the persecution in 5:6? *They were not in opposition*

Our revenge stirs up trouble and pain; God's vengeance is just, pure, and brings benefit to us.

The image of the poor, believing laborer not resisting his persecutor is heart-breaking. But, the story does not end there.

We previously visited a verse in Romans that I would like to touch on again.

Read Romans 12:19.

Do not take vengeance for yourself; the Lord will take care of all things in His perfect time, in His perfect way. Your revenge will stir up trouble and cause you, as well as others, additional pain. God's vengeance will be just and pure and will work to the benefit of those who love Him.

No matter how silent God may seem at times, He always hears our cries.

Do you ever wonder if God is really listening when you ask Him to take care of a situation where you choose not to retaliate on your own? Reread James 5:4.

"The outcry of those who did the harvesting has *reached the ears*

of the *Lord Almighty* ."

Sisters, no matter how silent you may feel God is at times, the cry of His people **has reached His ears**. This portion of James was harshly prophesying against the unbelieving oppressor, but portions of it would have been encouraging to their victims. Many times, the persecuted Christians must have wondered if God was hearing their cries or if they'd been forgotten and left all alone. Had God abandoned them? Was He not returning after all? Did He even care to hear their cries? James assures them that, yes, He has.

The Lord of Sabaoth means the Lord of all armies, both seen and unseen.

We've all gone through "dark nights of the soul" – times when God seemed distant and uncaring. Describe such a time, and how God showed Himself faithful in the end.

_____

_____

The name of God used in this verse is the "Lord of Sabaoth." There are many names of God used in Scripture. Each points to a different attribute or characteristic of who He is, and the biblical authors appropriately used each name intentionally within the context of their surrounding verses. James chose this title, at this time, very carefully and deliberately. The Lord of Sabaoth means the Lord of hosts. It might not seem all that impressive until we realize that the "host" referred to includes His limitless, unseen, angelic armies fighting all around us. He is the God of armies. Not only does He have full control over earthly armies, but He has legion upon legion of physically-undetected, supernatural soldiers ready at His bidding.

In the book of Haggai, the Jews were being commanded to resume the rebuilding of their temple. They had built the foundation, but had ceased construction because of outside threats and legal action. When Haggai exhorted them to resume, they did so, but quickly became discouraged. As he urged them to persevere, he encouraged them by using the name "Lord of Sabaoth" 14 times within 38 sentences. As they said, "We can't go on," he reminded them that the Lord of armies beyond their wildest imagination had their backs. They needed to move forward; He promised to be their defense.

Read 1 Samuel 17:45 below.

> *Then David said to the Philistine, "You come to me with a sword, a spear, and a javelin, but I come to you in the name of the LORD of hosts, the God of the armies of Israel, whom you have taunted."*

You guessed it - the name David used here for God was "Lord of Sabaoth." This is a scene most of us readily recognize. Little David is preparing to fight giant Goliath and he comes in full confidence. Why would he have such confidence? David said in all boldness, "I come in the name of the God of armies, seen and unseen, and you have no chance of defeating what God wants to defend."

James intended to encourage his brethren in a beautiful way at the end of verse 4. We may not have readily recognized the Lord of Sabaoth or Lord of Hosts before, but I pray that after today, when you see your God referred to in this way, it will bring you great comfort and assurance.

That same Lord of hosts, who defended His people as they rebuilt their temple under opposition, the same Lord of Sabaoth, who brought victory to the Israelite armies again and again, hears our cries and will defend and avenge his righteous followers when they are wronged. In His time and in His way, He will make all things right. He is our ultimate protector against things seen and unseen at this present time and into eternity. *"If God is for us, who can be against us?"* (Rom. 8:31b, NIV). Do you need to be reminded of that today?

What "impossible" situation do you need the Lord of armies to march into today? Lift your voice to Him knowing that your cries will reach His ears. Feel free to write your pleas to Him.

deliver me from my job & my career Live for God.

The same Lord of Sabaoth still hears His children's cries. He still defends and avenges His own. He makes all things right in His time and in His way.

Day Two — Waiting...

In the previous verses, we saw that James had a harsh, prophetic message concerning those who were oppressing the poor believers. At the same time, we saw that this message was intended to comfort those being persecuted, as it reminded them that the "God of all armies" (Lord of Sabaoth) would hear their cries and avenge them.

Read James 5:7-8.

James' message – be patient until Christ's return.

Beginning in verse 7, James makes a very clear shift, as he once again addresses his listeners as "brethren." The use of the word "therefore" in this verse signals the fact that what he is going to say is based off the previous passage. In light of the judgment that is certain to fall on their oppressors, James makes a request of his Christian audience.

Psalm 37:1 Do not fret because of evil men or be envious of those who do wrong.

"*Therefore, be* ___patient___ , *brethren, until* ___the Lord's coming___ ."

Don't seek revenge. Don't envy their wealth. Don't loathe your own existence. Simply be patient until Christ returns. Did James really have to take us there? I mean, he's asked us to refine every area of our lives. But, patience until He returns or until we, ourselves, pass away? The thought alone can be so wearying.

Let's look at another similar passage. Read Psalm 37:1-11.

We all ache while we wait for Christ to return and make all things right.

Like James, the psalmist tells us not to fret because of the evil man. We're not to envy him or let his luxuries steal our focus. Instead, we're told to refrain from anger and wrath toward him. We are also told to delight in the Lord, commit our ways to Him, and be still while we patiently wait to meet Him face-to-face. We are told to trust Him and hold on as both punishment and blessing will come to those it is due.

Think about an ongoing trial you're facing. What about it requires the most patience? Are you making it harder by comparing what you don't have to what someone else appears to have? How can taking delight in the Lord, and keeping your eyes upon eternity, and off of others, help you endure?

heós – until

___Enduring my job and being the best I can be while I wait for a new direction___

Patience is flat-out hard, even when we have an absolute end in sight. Patience in waiting for the Lord to return and make all things right can seem unbearable at times. Repeatedly, different biblical authors cried out to God saying, "How long, O Lord?" as they suffered through this life. Just as they did, we ache for the day when pain of all types will be wiped away. As we ache, how are we to wait?

The word for "until" (*heós*) has a "pregnant" sense in verse 7. As we wait for the Lord, we have an anxious expectancy, **knowing** the "due date" is coming, although we cannot pinpoint His arrival. We know that it is entirely necessary for a baby to go through a full developing process while we await its delivery. In the same way, James describes a complete growing process that we must wait through before we are finally delivered into our new life in heaven. James uses a picture of a farmer to illustrate this waiting process.

The farmer anxiously waits through the full duration of the growing season for "the precious produce of the soil" to arrive. He waits through the early rains and the late rains. He waits as pestilence eats some of his crops, storms bend and break them over, and the sun scorches and burns areas that are too weak to withstand the heat. Yet, he waits, and in the end, life emerges complete, full, and worth the wait.

Likewise, we wait for our own lives to be brought to completion. We groan under the stress of our own pestilence, storms, and heat. Yet, while we wait, we are encouraged by the psalmist to be still, and by James to strengthen our hearts.

How can keeping your focus on the coming "harvest" help you weather the storms of life? Do you allow yourself to think about the promise of heaven, or do you think that's wasted time or just wishful thinking?

We need to be still and strengthen our hearts while we wait.

> be patient for the lord, the only thing that makes waiting worth it is living for God

How do we strengthen our hearts when the trials of life beat us down? The Greek word for strengthen in this passage is *stérizó*, meaning "to fix firmly, strengthen, establish, direct myself toward." This word gives the effect of being solidly planted and set fast. When inanimate objects become worn down, they become worn out, brittle, and frail. Their strength and endurance weakens. Living things, though, have the capacity to strengthen through hardship. A living tree, for example, is strengthened through pruning; a bone heals stronger after being broken. In the same way, if our hearts are firmly-rooted in Christ, and we are holding fast to the Word of God, we can be strengthened as the storms of life come. We can endure them with our eyes fixed on the coming of the Lord as the source of our hope. Notice the end of the definition of *stérizó* – "direct myself toward." Just as a plant, firmly-rooted in the ground, follows the path of the sun as it daily passes overhead, I am to be firmly-rooted in the soil of my faith, and deliberately direct myself toward the Son while I await His return. As we are still deeply-rooted in our faith and eagerly awaiting the fullness of the life awaiting us when our Savior comes, our hearts will strengthen in both the good times and the bad. Our strength is truly found in the source of life-giving Light that we must direct ourselves toward daily.

Read Revelation 22:20.

stérizó – to fix firmly, strengthen, establish, direct myself toward

In James 5:8, he tells us that the coming of the Lord is near. In Revelation, Christ, Himself, assures us that He is coming "soon." Yet, we often wait for "soon" with weary hearts, convinced that "soon" couldn't possibly come soon enough.

Soon. Christ said He was returning soon; yet, it's been more than 2000 years. Has this ever made you scratch your head in confusion? How would you explain His apparent "delay?"

> to him, it's not a delay.

The word for "soon" in Revelation 22 is *tachu*, meaning "quickly, speedily." It does not imply an immediate action, or even give allusion to something that will happen in a short time. Rather, it means that when an action does begin, it will be sudden and swift. Keeping this in mind, we need not become discouraged as if Christ has forgotten His promise. While we wait, we must stay firmly-established with a determined resolve to allow our faith to be strengthened, ready at every moment for His swift and sudden return.

Read James 5:9.

Oh, that pesky tongue keeps coming up! In trying times, it's so easy to grumble and complain. The word used for complain in this verse, *stenazó*, means "to groan, expressing grief, anger, or desire." Interestingly, it is a groaning due to pressure exerted forward, as in the pressure of childbirth. Depending on the context, it can refer to either an intensely pleasant or an anguishing pressure from what is coming on.[28] Again, as we expectantly await the coming of the Lord, we are both joyful at the promise, and burdened by our current "labor pains." During this sort of time, where there can be anxious unrest, we may tend to want to grumble.

tachu – quickly, speedily

When all is not as you wish it were, do you tend to grumble and complain? Or are you still and quiet as you wait patiently for God?

I complain to myself & God, but am learning to wait

stenazó – to groan, express grief, anger, or desire

When the going gets rough and the road gets long, we often complain. When we complain, we frequently do it in a way that blames others for our sorrows or hurts them as we "unload." Again, James reminds us of the danger in doing so. Our Judge will not only judge us in the same manner that we judge others, but He is "waiting at the door."

My children know what they can and can't get away with saying to their sibling in front of Mom. There have been times when I've waited on the other side of a door, listening to what they don't realize I can hear. God is no different. He hears it all, sees it all, and even knows the intentions of our heart behind it all. He is waiting at the door. What does He find on the other side? There have been times when I've heard enough and opened the door, announcing my presence, only to be greeted by my kids with bug eyes at having been caught. We don't know the day that Christ is coming, but we've been told that it will be swift when it happens. Do we want to be grumbling at one of His other children when He opens the door?

God hears all, sees all, and knows the heart behind every word and action.

Imagine for a moment that Jesus is standing on the other side of every door in your home or office. How would you change the way you talk to others?

I would be kinder, less judgmental. I would be humble.

Read James 5:10-11.

As another example of patient suffering, James refers to the prophets of the Old Testament.

---

28   Gary Hill, Helpsbible.com, http://concordances.org/greek/4727.htm

Many suffered merciless lives as they proclaimed the message of their God, only to be ignored, humiliated, and persecuted. Oftentimes, they must have felt they were doing nothing but beating their heads against a wall, making no progress with the children of God who refused to listen. They also lived with constant hate from the outside world that despised their very existence. They had much to complain about, but although they voiced their woes to the Lord and cried out to Him in anguish, they did not abandon or give up on God. As a result of their endurance then, they are considered blessed today.

As a prime example of a man who went through much and yet endured alongside the Lord, James reminds us of the story of Job. Job endured the loss of his family, his personal health, and his possessions. If anyone did, Job had reason to complain. He did question; he did struggle. But, he did not turn his back on God.

We can question; we can struggle; but we must not turn our back on God.

In order to find application for our own lives, it would benefit us to examine what Job truly had to endure. **In essence, Job wanted back what couldn't return and wanted to lose what he couldn't get rid of.** Death had ravaged his life and in this world, death is permanent. His grief and sorrow must have been all-consuming, as he suffered so much of it at one time. In rapid succession, he was told about the death of his 10 children, his livestock, and the loss of all his other possessions. Waves of grief must have overcome him again and again as reality continued to set in. The question "why" was at the forefront of his thoughts day and night. He was overcome with sorrow, and endurance seemed impossible, especially as he was forced to endure alone.

Whether we like to face it or not, death is an undeniable reality in this life. With death, comes grief. Describe a time you were forced to grieve the loss of someone, or something, you couldn't have back.

Permanent losses lead to great sorrow, making endurance seem impossible.

My grandmother.

Although Job endured his inner turmoil alone, he wasn't physically alone. While they tried, those with him didn't help him endure. In fact, they made his endurance more difficult. They were a great part of what he probably wished he could do without; but they just wouldn't go away. Although Satan took much from Job in his attack, he left him with what he knew would cause him greater pain. He was left with excruciating boils, a wife who discouraged him, and "friends" who forgot this wasn't "their story," and took the opportunity to share their hurtful opinions. The pain in his own body was something he couldn't escape. Chronic pain is enough to drive a person mad. Heaped on top of mourning the loss of all of his children, this additional, constant reminder of his new state of being must have been entirely defeating. If that wasn't enough, while doing everything he could not to turn his back on God, his wife told him to do just that. Then, his friends chose to share their "wisdom" to boot. At the peak of his suffering, Job's friends could hold their tongues no longer. To be perfectly honest, much of what they had to say was "wise" in general terms. Yet, they lacked the discernment to see that their "wisdom" did not apply to Job's situation. As they threw out advice based on their traditional understanding, they did not have the insight to realize that Job's trials were not intended for his discipline. They assumed, based on their

The right words, spoken at the wrong time, can be as devastating as the wrong words.

own beliefs, that there was a one-size-fits-all wisdom that Job must have been lacking, and their choice to lavish it upon him stung his very soul.

Think about a time when the advice from another person during your trials was hurtful, because they did not know what God was doing or have all the details.

New job opportunity

_____

Might you have hurt someone else in a similar way? How?

Yes, by giving selfish advice.

_____

hupomoné – endurance, steadfastness, patient waiting for

During this time, Job needed support, understanding, compassion, and love. However, we see none of that given to him, which added greatly to his trial, and yet he endured. Endurance in this passage is *hupomoné*, a compound word of *hupo* meaning "under" and *meno* meaning "endurance, steadfastness, patient waiting for." Whereas the patience referred to in verses 7 and 8 is a long-suffering patience with a loving attitude (*makrothumeó*), *hupomoné* refers to a patient, enduring attitude that denotes a strong, determined attitude with which we are to face hardship. In other words, Job "strengthened his heart" as we elaborated on in verse 8, even in the midst of the greatest struggles we can fathom. He was firmly-rooted and following the "Son" even when it seemed to make no sense at all.

Like Job, we are blessed because of the reward awaiting us in eternity.

Look back to verse 11. What do we count those who endured? *blessed*

I'm pretty certain Job wouldn't have told you that he felt blessed during this period of his life. But, remember what the beatitudes taught us on Day Five of Week One. Job was blessed because of the reward awaiting him in eternity after enduring with the Lord during this life that brought him such tremendous hurt. Even though he couldn't always readily see the reward, Job **always** had a reason to hope.

Verse 11. *"You have heard of the endurance of Job and have seen the _____ of the Lord's dealings…"*

telos – an end, purpose

The word for outcome in this verse should be somewhat familiar to us by now. We have seen a form of it multiple times and we are brought to it again. *Telos* is used here, meaning "an end, purpose." It speaks of the consummation of an end goal, a closure with all its results.[29] We've seen forms of this word used in the book of James as he has referred to a "perfect" result, a completion toward a given end, a peak of maturity (James 1:4). In the story of Job, we get to see *telos* in the outcome of the Lord's dealings with Job. As the story goes, Job's faithfulness held strong, and he was tangibly rewarded in the end. But, James shows us an even more beautiful outcome at the end of verse 11. The Lord's dealings with Job showed that He is full of compassion and He is merciful. Job let endurance have its perfect result, and despite his time of questioning and struggle, God remained compassionate and merciful.

---

29   Gary Hill, Helpsbible.com, http://concordances.org/greek/5056.htm

Job struggled, he hurt, he questioned, but his heart was steadfast in his unwavering faith, because he was deeply-rooted in truth. Living a life of faith takes both patience and endurance. We must have patience as we work through all of the many things James has told us we need to refine on the journey of our Christian walk. We must endure as the trials of life knock us down, even as we seek to be refined. We must not lose heart as we eagerly await the Lord's coming, even when our hearts are crying, "How long, O Lord, how long?"

As we consider all we have learned in these five rich chapters of James, we now find ourselves accountable for all we know. We must keep our guard up; we must keep our hearts right. Our Lord is standing at the door and His return is near. Until that day, we are living through the early and late rains, the pestilence and the storms. How will He find us when He returns? Will we have endured well, giving Him opportunity to show His compassion and mercy? If we have not so far, are we willing to begin today? Let us endure together, He's coming back soon…and oh the eternal glory that will be ours when He does.

> *Therefore we do not lose heart, but though our outer man is decaying, yet our inner man is being renewed day by day. For momentary, light affliction is producing for us an eternal weight of glory far beyond all comparison, while we look not at the things which are seen, but at the things which are not seen; for the things which are seen are temporal, but the things which are not seen are eternal. (2 Cor. 4:16-18)*

Day Three – Let Your Yes Be Yes

Yesterday, we focused on patience and endurance in the midst of suffering, while we saw the danger of using our words to complain and grumble against one another in such times.

Read James 5:12.

In the New Testament, we are ordered not to swear at all.

Today, we will see that when we are in the midst of hard times that we long to escape, times that tempt us to grumble, we may a have a tendency to run on at the mouth. One way we do this is by trying to validate our own side of things and our own viewpoints by ascribing God's name, ways, and support to them. If we can prove to others that God is on our side by assigning His name to our situation, we elevate ourselves and our point.

Read Matthew 5:33-37.

As you can tell, James was very closely restating the words of Jesus in verse 12 of his letter. Verse 33 of Matthew 5 refers back to the original Levitical law concerning oaths. Leviticus 19:12 stated, *"You shall not swear falsely by My name, so as to profane the name of your God; I am the LORD."* Unlike the words of Jesus and James, this law only forbid the breaking of an oath made in God's name, for it would profane the name associated with it. In the New Testament, though, we find the order not to swear at all.

Although some have believed that this instruction prohibits Christians from taking **any** oaths, official oaths to authorities don't seem to be the issue. Rather, the concern seems to revolve around personal, voluntary oaths.

In your opinion, what danger could there be in making personal oaths?

Making a commitment of self, without God, could be impossible. There are so many things out of our control

A man's word should be enough, without having to swear by any other means.

The primary issue here seems to be associated with the value of one's word and the potential for bringing irreverence to God. A man's word should be enough, without having to swear by any other means. His goal should be to live in such a way that when he is questioned, his answer is readily accepted because he has always been proven reliable and trustworthy.

When someone says, "God as my witness," they are attempting to give credence to their particular claim. Though not always, at times this effort is fueled by pride. Pride is hard to swallow, and it certainly rears its head when we are placed in positions of vulnerability. Let's look at a few ways that our pride may lead us to swear oaths while we're vulnerable.

"God as my witness, I **know** I'm right about this!" At times, we can be absolutely convinced that we are right on a subject, and to bolster our argument, we pin God's name to it. The truth is, no matter how sure we are of ourselves, or a situation, we have already discussed the fact that none of us possess the capability of knowing every detail surrounding any circumstance. There is always room for error when humanity is involved. In swearing by God's name, we subject His reputation to something that has the potential of proving fallible.

Even Ivory is only 99.44% pure soap. ☺ Can you remember a time when you felt **100% sure** about something, only to realize later that you were not **100% right**? How might remembering this possibility help you avoid swearing in the future?

In swearing by God's name, we put His reputation at risk.

_____

_____

On the flip side of that coin, there are times when our pride doesn't like to admit that we are wrong. We tread on dangerous ground when we swear by God as our Witness that something we fully know is wrong, is indeed right. It hurts our ego when we have to admit defeat, or a lack of knowledge where we feel we should have it. It is at times like these when we may be tempted to swear something falsely simply to save face. Saving face at the cost of using the name of the Almighty God in vain is no laughing matter. His reputation means everything to Him; it should mean everything to us as well.

We should not make commitments without considering if we can fulfill them first.

Whether we swear by His name or not, by simply taking on His name as a Christian, we constantly put God's reputation on the line. Have you let your pride get in the way of admitting when you're wrong? How may this have affected the way others view God as a result?

_____

_____

"I swear I'll do it!" Not only do we swear by our accuracy at times, we also may have a tendency to swear by our ability. We often make commitments to carry out actions without weighing the possibility that we may not be able to fulfill the promise. At times, with the best of intentions, we make promises that are beyond our ability to fulfill. Just as we are not able to know every detail of other's lives, we are also not able to know if our own circumstances will allow us to keep the commitments we swear to. In Luke 14, we find Jesus addressing the crowds about the cost of being His disciple. There, Jesus spoke of the wisdom of considering the personal cost before making personal commitments. "Who begins a building project," asks Christ, "without determining if he can afford to complete it?" Or, "What king goes into battle against another without first calculating if he has enough troops to win?" To start something, but not complete it, is not only foolish, it opens us up to the ridicule of others as well; i.e., it tarnishes our name and the name of God.

God's reputation should mean everything to us.

One of my daughters has always had an innate sense about this. Even when she was little, I would ask her to do a task and without fail, she would reply, "Mommy, I promise I'll try." Sometimes I would get frustrated with her because I wanted her to tell me that she would absolutely fulfill the obligation I had placed on her. But, in reality, it was much better for her not to make an absolute commitment to do something in a future moment that she did not hold in her own hands. Her intentions were to follow through, and she usually did. But, in her caution, she kept herself from giving her word when extenuating circumstances could have prevented her from completely delivering.

It is better to promise to try, than to promise to complete.

In the same way, we need to guard the reputation of our word as well as God's name, for we reflect Him as Christians, when we promise to fulfill even the smallest commitment.

Would you say that you are largely regarded by others as a "woman of your word?" Do you carelessly make promises without considering the impact if you don't keep them?

_____

_____

We need to guard the reputation of our word as well as God's name.

There are also those times when we may commit to something that we have no intention of following through on in the first place. Have you ever asked one of your kids to clean their room and have them respond with, "Okay," yet see no intention of follow-through? Surely they just forgot! Truthfully, there are times when a quick "yes" is given to appease the one asking. It may be embarrassing to admit that we don't believe we can handle a task, or we may be embarrassed to admit we simply don't want to. We may not want to "face the music" of saying "no," and so we give the answer we believe someone wants to hear in order to settle the moment without subjecting ourselves to scrutiny, judgment, or further discussion on the topic.

Admitting we cannot, or do not want to, fulfill a task can be humbling. We might feel that we are admitting inadequacy, or revealing some shortcoming, which hurts our pride. We don't relish the thought of looking like a failure to others, and in that fear, we may agree to do something while planning to conveniently "forget" or find a way to back out at a later time. The irony in this situation is that the latter (planning to not keep your word) is the only actual failure in this scenario. An honest admission of inability or lack of desire to fulfill a task is not sinful – lying, however, is. When we give our word and do not keep it, we shed doubt on the integrity of that word. After multiple incidents of such, our character can prove to be entirely unreliable.

There is nothing wrong with lacking an ability. However, saying you'll do something and not following through is wrong.

In Matthew 21, Jesus told a parable about a man who had two sons. *"He came to the first and said, 'Son, go work today in the vineyard.' And he answered, 'I will not'; but afterward he regretted it and went. The man came to the second and said the same thing; and he answered, 'I will, sir'; but he did not go. Which of the two did the will of his father?" They said, "The first."* Making a promise and not following through is to be outside the Father's will.

As Christians, we always reflect the God we claim to serve.

Have you ever said that you will do something fully knowing you won't? Why? What would be the outcome of simply saying you can't, or won't, do something instead?

Yes, in many social situations re: Christmas parties I don't really want to go to

James tells us that our "yes" needs to mean "yes" and our "no" needs to mean "no." As Christians, we constantly reflect the God we say we serve. When our "yes" is "no," it reflects poorly on Him and we misrepresent His character. When James tells us not to make oaths, he is telling us that we shouldn't need to. If our "yes" is always "yes," then people will come to rely on our word without any need for attaching an oath to it. "We should never need to use an oath to prove that 'this time I really mean it!' Instead we should always 'really mean it.'"[30]

30   Zane C. Hodges, *The Epistle of James*, p. 115

When we get into the habit of not staying true to our word, we damage our name. Oh how we often long for gold, silver, and other wealth. But, ladies, a good name – our good name – is to be valued above all these (Pro. 22:1). Others will come to the place where they know they cannot rely on us. We often need to ask ourselves where we stand in reference to this. Based off of how we live our lives and fulfill our commitments, what messages have we conveyed concerning the value of our word? Do our children know that when we commit to do something with or for them, that we will follow through? Do our spouses know that they can rely on us and the commitments we've made to them? Do our friends know that they can come to us with any need because they can rely on our character to be true and our follow-through to be dependable? Do our churches know that when we commit to fill a position, that they will not need to worry about our level of commitment? Do they know that our "yes" means "yes" and that because we have given our word, we will give our utmost devotion to keeping it?

If our "yes" is always "yes," people will rely on our word without the need for an accompanying oath.

What are the ripple effects of having an unreliable reputation?

People lose their trust in us

A good name is to be more desired than great wealth, favor is better than silver and gold (Proverbs 22:1).

The ripple effects of unreliability are vast. When we give others our word, they place their hope and trust in us. When we don't keep our word, that hope is dashed. Proverbs 13:12 puts it this way, "**Hope deferred** *makes the heart sick, but desire fulfilled is a tree of life.*" (emphasis mine) Are we trees of life to others, or are we making their hearts sick? Raising children who cannot trust us will greatly affect the way they raise their own children and relate to others (including their future spouses). A lack of dependability with a spouse, even in things that may seem trivial, wears down a relationship and has the ability to wreak havoc in a home. Friends who can't be found trustworthy, end up losing friendships. Churches suffer greatly when volunteers don't take God's work seriously, showing up when they feel like it, not giving their commitment serious consideration because they consider church work "optional."

The ripple effects of unreliability are vast.

These effects ripple beyond a list that we can begin to comprehend. But, the greatest detriment done in breaking our word is the harm done to God's name. God's "yes" is an absolute "yes." We need not worry about Him being fickle. His Word is true and without hypocrisy. The gift of salvation that He offers us is offered in absolute truth; His commitment to hold us securely once we have accepted Him until the day He brings us home, is unconditional. His "no" is also an emphatic "no." What God is against is irrefutable. The sins that He lines out in Scripture are not to be questioned or debated. He is unwavering, He is just, He is true. There are many people, though, who will never crack open a single book of the Bible to hear His truths directly from Him. Because of this, He relies on His people to represent His character. Just as we are able to fully rely on God's "yes" and "no," others should find that same characteristic in us, which should, in turn, draw them to the God whose character we exude.

God's "yes" is an absolute "yes." He is never fickle.

God relies on His people to represent His character.

Your life may be the only glimpse of God others ever see. Based on your "yes's" and "no's," are they getting an accurate view of Him? If not, what needs to change? To whom have you made yourself accountable for the promises you make?

Day Four — Restoration and Righteousness

In this final chapter of James, he has brought us full circle back to the place where we began in Chapter One. Two days ago, we revisited the topic of pain and suffering, and the need to endure with our eyes patiently fixed on the Lord, as Job did. Yesterday, we saw that during times of trial, when our patience may run thin, we need not rush into making oaths that cannot be kept. Today, we will see that "suffering in some form or other is sure to come, and the sovereign remedy for all suffering is prayer."[31]

Read James 5:13-18, giving special notice to each mention of the word prayer.

"Suffering in some form is sure to come; the sovereign remedy is prayer."

You may have noticed that the words "pray" or "prayer" are the common thread woven through every verse. As noted before, repetition in Scripture is never a coincidence. James clearly wants to end his letter with a bold emphasis on prayer.

Prayer is lifting our voice to the Lord, silently or aloud, in order to communicate with Him. Verse 13 covers the fact that we need to do that in all situations and circumstances. When we are hurting, lift it to the Lord. When we are joyful, do the same. We often go to God with our hurts, but forget to lift a prayer of praise during good times. But, it is during those times of prayerful praise that we acknowledge all of the good He has provided in our lives. When we have taken the time to do that, we can draw from those times of joyful communion with the Lord, during our future times of drought. Praise fills the well of the heart and provides residual refreshment to draw from in times of suffering.

Under what circumstances do you most frequently go to the Lord in prayer? Do you remember to go to Him with praise, or are most of your prayers a vocalizing of hurts and needs? How can you bring more balance to your prayer life?

I should praise him more, I should pray for others more

We are to lift our voice to Him in all circumstances – painful and joyful.

The next two verses of James have caused endless debates over the years and were even the basis for the adoption of "Extreme Unction," or "Anointing of the Sick," into the Roman Catholic list of sacraments. The use of these verses to support Extreme Unction was based on the belief that they refer to physical healing. The New International Commentary of the New Testament states, "In the 16th century, at the Council of Trent, the so-called Sacrament of Extreme Unction received authoritative definition in the Roman Church, that Council declaring that this manmade Sacrament is 'implied by Mark, and commended and promulgated by James the apostle and brother of the Lord.' There never was a more glaring travesty of Scripture."[32] Translating these verses in such a manner is the basis for all debate concerning their meaning. Due to the original Greek language used and the context of the surrounding verses, it is my belief that this passage does not relate to physical healing. I'll explain more as we proceed.

---

31   Alexander Ross, *The New International Commentary on the New Testament, Commentary on the Epistles of James and John*, p. 97

32   Ibid. p. 99-100

Have you ever read these verses, prayed earnestly, and wondered why physical healing did not occur? What went through your mind as you watched a loved one succumb to illness?

Yes, I have prayed For healing that has not come

So far in Chapter 5, James has covered oppression by the unsaved rich and how to respond to that sort of suffering. He also addressed the fact that some of his Christian readers might be participating in actions and conversations (as a response to this suffering) that may cause them to fall under judgment. James even warns them that the Judge is standing right at the door. To best understand verses 14-16, we need to place them in line with the context of the previous verses, as well as the ones yet to come. We will also look at the Greek to more closely evaluate the passage.

asthenei – to be weak

Fill in the blank according to James 5:14. *"Is anyone among you ___ SICK ___?"*

The Greek word for sick in this passage is *asthenei*, which literally means "to be weak." "There is no reason to consider 'sick' as referring exclusively to physical illness. Though it is used in the Gospels for physical maladies, it is generally used in Acts and the Epistles to refer to a weak faith or a weak conscience."[33] The Greek word, *kamnonta*, used for the "sick person" in verse 15, supports this understanding as it literally translates "to be weary." By understanding this as well as the chapter context, we realize that James was referring to those who had become morally and spiritually weak and weary due to their sufferings. Their "sickness" is of a spiritual nature, and it is they who should call on the help of the leadership of the church.

kamnonta – to be weary

Why call on others in the church? Read 1 Thessalonians 5:14.

We as Christians are commanded to "help the weak." The word for weak in this verse is the same word we find in James 5:14. Those who are struggling in their faith, because this life is bearing down on them, need the prayers and encouragement of fellow believers. When a believer comes to the point where he realizes that overcoming the sin that has entrapped him is more than he can handle alone, it is greatly beneficial for him to come to his fellow believers for prayer, support, encouragement, and accountability. Of course, even a private, repentant heart is heard by God, but isolation from others makes walking away from sin and back into spiritual restoration much more difficult. This is one of the many reasons we are commanded not to forsake the gathering of ourselves together (Heb. 10:25).

Those who are struggling in their faith need the prayers and encouragement of fellow believers.

Because sin is dark, it likes to be hidden. Have you wrestled with temptation to hide your sins? If so, what could your fellow sisters in Christ do to help you through it? What can you do to help others when they are weak?

pray. Stand with me

Call the presses – I don't iron!

I must confess, I don't iron. I know, that's quite a silly confession that has nothing whatsoever to do with sin. But, the fact of the matter is, in doing so, I was open and honest with others concerning something I might find somewhat embarrassing to admit. In being vulnerable in that manner, I've allowed others who also don't iron to realize that I can fully relate to them in that. I've allowed you to see that I'm not the perfect "June Cleaver" and have hopefully also let you know, through my confession, that I don't have high expectations of others concerning such things either.

---

33   Walvoord and Zuck, *BKC NT*, p. 834

As absolutely laughable as a confession about ironing is, (except possibly to my mother), it does give us a glimpse into the possible benefits of confession. When we share our vulnerabilities with others, we let others know that they are not alone in their own struggles and we allow them to see that we are human and relatable as well. It is in this way that those in the body of Christ can build one another up and be a soothing balm, a healing agent in one another's lives. No, this does not suggest that we need to share every private sin with the public, nor does it mean that we have to make regular confessions in front of an entire congregation. But, when there is an entrapment of sin consuming a believer to the extent of making him spiritually "ill," James instructs him to take it beyond his isolation and humbly ask for forgiveness and help.

When we share our vulnerabilities with others, we let them know they are not alone in their struggles.

Because our culture does not relate to the anointing of oil, the next part of James' instruction seems obscure to us. The word used here for anoint, *aleíphō,* simply means "to rub with oil." This is not the same as the ceremonial or ritual anointing (*chrio*) that we see mentioned other areas of Scripture. Rather, it is a mundane form of anointing, not used as a means of divine physical healing, but as a means of refreshment and encouragement.[34] A few other examples of this sort of anointing in Scripture are listed below:

Luke 7:38 – the woman "poured" (*aleíphō*) perfume on Jesus' feet

Luke 7:46 – a host "put oil" (*aleíphō*) on the head of his guest

Matt 6:17 – one who is fasting should not be sad and ungroomed, but should "put oil" (*aleíphō*) on his head and wash his face.

aleíphō – to rub with oil as a means of refreshment and encouragement

"Thus, James' point is that the 'weak' (*asthenei*) and 'weary' (*kamnonta*) would be refreshed, encouraged, and uplifted by the elders who rubbed oil on the despondents' heads and prayed for them."[35]

Verses 15 and 16 go on to say that the one who is weary from sin and defeated by spiritual discouragement, will be restored by the prayer offered in faith. If this verse were referring to physical healing, many a Christian with deep faith in God, would wonder why his faith was not enough to claim the absolute assurance given here that *"the prayer offered in faith **will** restore the one who is sick."* (emphasis mine) In fact, if physical healing was always assured to those who pray in faith, many would never die. But, James speaks of spiritual healing as he encourages the one trapped in sin to confess. Once a person is willing to humble himself enough to openly confess and seek the help of other Christians, he is willing to repent and seeks to do right. To this person, restoration and healing is assured.

James speaks of spiritual healing as he encourages those trapped in sin to confess.

According to James 5:16, fill in the blanks:

"The _____ prayer of a _____ man can accomplish much."

I believe this verse may cause many Christians quite a bit of doubt and pain as they wonder why their prayers don't seem to get answered. When we pray in faith and nothing seems to get accomplished, what went wrong? Were we not "righteous" enough? Where is the fine line that makes us righteous enough for our prayers to be effective?

On Day Three of Week Three in our study, we discussed three large words that I mentioned

---

34   Daniel R. Hayden, "Calling the Elders to Pray," *Bibliotheca Sacra* 138. July–September 1981:264.

35   Walvoord and Zuck, *BKC NT*, p. 834-835

were at the core of our Christianity: justification, redemption, and propitiation. We are going to revisit them today, and this will hopefully give evidence to the fact that understanding the concepts behind these words will help us with understanding many other areas of Scripture. If you recall, propitiation was what was required to appease the wrath of God. Christ's death propitiated God and paid our penalty (redemption). When Christ propitiated God, it was then possible for us to come to God and ask for the gift of salvation. When we do that, He (as sovereign Judge) pounds His gavel upon the courtroom bench and declares us justified. To be justified is to be declared **righteous**. In fact, righteous (*dikaios*) means "just in the eyes of God." You did **nothing** to become righteous, you can do **nothing** to become more righteous. You were **declared** righteous because the righteous Son of God stood in your place and paid the price for your sin. It is not your righteousness that God sees, but Christ's righteousness in you. Therefore, the righteous man is the saved man. The effective prayer of a **saved** man can accomplish much! I don't know about any of you, but that brings me a sigh of relief.

dikaios – just in the eyes of God

Yes, we as Christians are able to walk in a "righteous lifestyle." We also know, from the example of the backslidden Christian referred to earlier, that we are able to choose to walk in an "unrighteous lifestyle." It is true, that when we have broken our fellowship with God, that it inhibits our prayers. But, when you are walking in line with God's will and you feel that prayers are not being answered in the way you hoped, you need not fear this verse is telling you that you have not achieved a level of righteousness worthy of having effective prayers. As we've learned, even in the most trying times of our lives, it is not always God's will to remove our trials, but instead for us to endure and grow through them. This does not question our status as "righteous" in the sight of God.

Have you questioned whether or not the reason some of your prayers went unanswered was related to your lack of "righteousness?" How does seeing that the effective prayers that accomplish much come from the saved person encourage you?

The righteous man is the saved man. Therefore, the effective prayer of the saved man accomplishes much.

_____

_____

The other word I would like to examine in this verse is "effective." If we aren't receiving the answers we want to our prayers and we know it isn't because we haven't achieved some perfect level of righteousness, could it be that we aren't praying "effectively?" The Greek word used here is *energeó*, which means "I am at work, am operative, accomplish." It is a word that involves action. I'm certain that you recognize the word "energy" in its root. It isn't a magic recipe for a perfect prayer; rather, it is saying that prayer is a work in action, an act of faith (James 1:6) that produces action. We are taking action in order to ask a God of action to move in our situation. So, the **active** prayer of a **saved** man can accomplish much. When we are living our life in fellowship with God, we can go to Him with confidence that our prayers can move mountains if it is in accordance with His will to act in that manner.

energeó – I am at work, am operative, accomplish

How active are you in your prayer life? If you are not actively going to God in prayer, should you expect Him to be active in answering?

_____

_____

Read James 5:17-18.

To illustrate the power of prayer, James invites one last Old Testament character to our study – Elijah. In doing so, he stays with his own context that has revolved around those who need spiritual healing due to sin. The drought brought on the nation of Israel by Elijah's prayer was due to their sin of idolatry under the evil king Ahab. Elijah prayed that the rains would cease, and they did. He further prayed that they would resume at a later date, and the skies opened up and poured down rain (1 Kings 17-18).

According to James 5:17, what kind of a man was Elijah?

he was just like us

Elijah was only a man like the rest, yet he was a man of faithful prayer.

It was important for James to point out that Elijah's prayers were not more potent because he was a prophet. No, Elijah was a man with a sin nature, with emotions, with ups and downs in this life. He was only a man, yet he was a man of faithful prayer. We see in this verse that he prayed "earnestly." There again, we have a word that could cause us to fear when our own prayers seem unanswered. Did I perhaps not pray "earnestly" enough? The Greek words used for "prayed earnestly" are *proseuché proseuchomai*, which literally translate, he "prayed with prayer." "Here the point is not that Elijah put up a particularly fervent prayer, but that praying was precisely what he did."[36]

Prayer is to be our way of life. It is to be on our breath at all times as we walk through our day. God is not to be pulled out of the closet for random needs and shoved back in when we don't feel we care for any more of His input. He is with us always, and we are to include Him in our every moment.

proseuché proseuchomai - prayed with prayer

Read 1 Thess. 5:17. *pray continually*

Praying without ceasing doesn't mean we are to be on our knees in prayer 24 hours a day, 7 days of the week. It means that as we go about our daily business, God should be included in it all. We are to be in constant communication with Him; considering Him in our every word, consulting Him in every action. Allowing Him to speak to us in every area of our lives is the way in which we take all that we have learned in His Word and LIVE it in an active life of faith. We cannot live that kind of active faith without inviting Him into our every action. We do not welcome Him into every action unless we proactively commit to communicate with Him in every moment.

Prayer is to be on our breath at all times.

Will you commit to do that today? Will you make a commitment to begin inviting God into every moment of your life? Will you invite Him into your smallest decisions? Will you commit your time to Him as you drive in your car instead of allowing your mind to wander every which way? Will you ask for His guidance **while** you're in the middle of conversations so He can season your thoughts and words? The more we do this, the more readily His words are on our lips as we go throughout our day, and the more His words are on our lips, the more others are drawn to Him through the grace of our testimony. The ripple effects are beautiful and mighty, but it all begins with prayer. Will you be a woman of prayer?

---

36   Adamson, *NICNT, James*, p. 201

Day Five – The Power of Prayer

I t is hard to believe that we've arrived at the final day. What an extraordinary journey this has been for me. I hope and pray it has been a meaningful time for you as well. Let's dig in one more time and finish strong!

Just as we saw that the illustration of Elijah dealt with a nation who had fallen away in sin, the final two verses of the book of James flow directly from that idea and deal with individuals who had fallen away in sin. Had the previous verses been talking about physical healing, these final two verses would have seemed disjointed from the rest of the chapter. We will see today, however, that because they dealt with spiritual weakness, they fit beautifully within their context.

Read James 5:17-20.

We briefly covered Elijah yesterday, but today, I'd like the opportunity to further elaborate on the significance of some of the details of his story. Having now read verses 19 and 20, I'd like to look back at Elijah with eyes that have seen the full surrounding context.

According to our homework yesterday, why did Elijah pray for drought?

_____

The nation of Israel had fallen into sin and needed spiritual restoration. Something needed to be done and prayer, imploring God to act, was Elijah's greatest option. About 3 ½ years into the drought, Elijah decided to confront Ahab and his false prophets, challenging them to a duel between the one true God and Baal. In the midst of presenting his challenge, he turned to the people of Israel and boldly called them out for being double-minded.

Read 1 Kings 18:16-21.

When Elijah confronted the people, what was their response? _____

These were God's chosen people! They'd been the recipients of great miracles due to the work of their mighty God. Yet now, not only were they guilty of bowing before false gods, but when confronted with the truth – they stood silent. Ladies, we do not have to be walking in overt sin to be spiritually "unwell." When we stand silent in the midst of a world that is blatantly turning their backs on God, we are contributing to the demise of the Christian faith in this world and are setting ourselves up for spiritual apathy. These things ought not to be!

Describe a time you stood silently when you probably needed to speak the truth in love. What were the results of your silence?

_____

_____

Read 1 Kings 18:22-37.

Elijah knew his greatest option was prayer.

When we stand silent in the face of godlessness, we're contributing to the demise of the Christian faith.

After the prophets of Baal utterly failed in their part of the challenge, Elijah called out to God to demonstrate His power to the people.

According to verse 37, why did Elijah want God to answer his prayer?

_____

This question brings us to the heart of our lesson today. Elijah did not set up this elaborate plan in order to prove himself. In fact, his intentions were entirely selfless, for the life of a prophet was lonely, dangerous, and solely for the spiritual benefit of others. He was willing to live such a life because the people needed to be told of their God, and his ultimate goal at this moment was the turning of their hearts away from sin and back to God. Oh how we need like-minded servants today.

Elijah's goal was to turn the heart of the people back to God.

Read James 5:19-20 once more.

We have already focused on the one who turns away in sin. Today let's focus on the one who prays for him and redirects his path back to the Lord. The primary focus of our study has been on **living** out our faith. Doing so is necessary to demonstrate the sincerity of our faith, and we have looked at many practical ways to do that in our lives. But, why does it matter? Has the basis for all we've learned been to solely benefit our own lives? No, like Elijah, our active faith is to bring glory to God and, in doing so, draw others to Him, ministering to them in ways we wouldn't be able to otherwise.

Our active faith is to bring glory to God and draw others to Him.

According to James, "live and let live" is just not an option for Christians. Just like Elijah, our goal is to turn the hearts of others away from sin and back to God. The original Greek uses the word *planaó* for the one who strays from the truth. It literally means "to wander, lead astray, deceive." "It suggests one who has missed his path and is hopelessly lost. 'Planet' was taken from this Greek word to convey the idea that the luminaries were 'wandering stars,' not 'fixed' like the rest."[37] It is these wandering ones who need to be brought back into fellowship.

Are you willing to help restore a brother or sister who has wandered away from the faith? Have you benefited from a fellow believer lovingly helping you find your way back to the right path? If so, how?

planaó – to wander, lead astray, deceive

_____

_____

Verse 20 tells us the benefit of turning one back to the Lord. On the other side of that coin, what is the cost of living our lives for ourselves and not recognizing the tool we were created to be in the lives of others?

_____

_____

The word used for death in verse 20 is *thanatos*, and is the same word used in James 1:15

---

37   Walvoord and Zuck, *BKC NT*, p. 835

that we previously discussed. It can refer to both spiritual and physical death. Because verse 20 refers to a brother in Christ who has been turned back to the Lord, we know that the death he is saved from is not eternal death in hell. Rather, it is possibly either a "living death" that is indicative of a life lived outside of God's will, or a premature physical death due to the consequences of sin. Either way, the one who has taken the effort to help restore him has done him a world of good.

On that same note, this restoration will cover a multitude of sins. When one confesses his sin and turns back to the Lord, his sins are covered. This is a beautiful word, *kaluptó*, meaning "to cover, veil, hide, conceal, envelop." It is as if a veil covers the sin and frees the sinner to move forward without its taunting presence openly and consistently reminding him of his past sin. Have you had sin that has taunted you and held you tightly in its grasp? I'm sure you would be eternally grateful to anyone who would be willing to help you escape its torment. These verses tell us that through the power of prayer it is possible, and you are able to be that helpful agent in the life of another as well.

kaluptó – to cover, veil, hide, conceal, envelop

Let's take one more look in on Elijah. When we left off, he was praying that God would act so the people would turn back to Him.

Read 1 Kings 18:38-45.

According to James 5:18, what happened when Elijah prayed for rain?

_____

When Elijah's prayers were answered, the barren land once again began producing fruit. Just before this, in 1 Kings 18:39, when God answered his prayer to send fire from heaven, the people fell on their faces and declared, *"The LORD, He is God!"* One of Elijah's prayers produced fruit from land, the other produced fruit from the people. When sin is repented of, the repentant life **will** produce fruit. But, it comes back to being committed to prayer for one another. Hoarding our faith will not help others produce fruit; living for their advancement in the faith will.

Elijah's prayers produced fruit from the land and from the people.

When it all comes down to it, this concept returns us to our royal law – love your neighbor as yourself. We innately love ourselves enough to pray for God's best in our own lives, even when we are at our worst. Are we willing to take the time to do that for others? Are we willing to take time to share that prayer with them? Are we willing to give **all** of our "neighbors" that benefit and not only our closest friends? Who are you willing to love unconditionally beyond their sin in order to be a prayerful instrument of God in their restoration to spiritual health?

Who are you willing to love unconditionally beyond their sin?

Let's look at verses 19-20 from the NASB one more time.

> *"My brethren, if any among you strays from the truth and <u>one turns him back,</u> <u>**let**</u> <u>**him know**</u> <u>that he who turns a sinner from the error of his way</u> will save his soul from death and will cover a multitude of sins."* (emphasis mine)

As you can see, there is an emphasis in this passage on the brother who is restoring the wayward believer. Many non-literal translations of Scripture change the wording enough that it completely misses this important emphasis.

In these verses, James calls us to be sensitive to the spiritual needs of others. This is such hard work to do. Therefore, James tells us to encourage those who have been instruments in restoring a wayward brother. There is no doubt that this process can be trying, emotional, and wearying to the one who is investing his life in another. If we see those around us doing this sort of ministry, we are to encourage them along the way, for as they give of themselves, they need our encouragement to "refill their cup." The writer of Hebrews tells us to consider how we can *spur one another on toward love and good deeds* (10:24, NIV). Likewise, Paul reminds us to *encourage one another and build each other up* (1 Thess. 5:11, NIV). We are all called to be encouragers and, in essence, we should all be receiving encouragement and giving encouragement at all times.

In order to restore a brother in need, we must pay attention to those around us.

Who has been a consistent source of spiritual encouragement to you? Who do you know that cares for the spiritual needs of others? How can you be an encourager to them?

In order to recognize a brother in need of restoration, we must be paying attention to those around us, being sensitive to the needs of others. Again, this involves us entirely taking our eyes off ourselves and focusing on others in order to realize their need. It can be the smallest things that make the biggest difference in someone's life. A person who may feel like no one would miss them if they left the church might be entirely touched by an email that simply lets them know they were missed. Someone whose eyes are filled with tears may be moved to realize that you notice their hurt and care enough to extend a hug. One who shared a prayer request a few months ago may be blown away for you to follow up and check on them, because although they figure everyone had forgotten, maybe not **everyone** has.

Describe a time when someone displayed this type of care for you. What difference did it make to you at the time? Jot down the names of a few people you can minister to this week by expressing care and concern.

The words "I'll pray for you" should be followed by prayer.

Once we share that love and commit to pray for others, it is important for us to keep that commitment. The words "I'll pray for you" should not be thrown around without follow-through. We need to be diligent to pray for those we've told we would. We've seen in our study that the power of prayer is nothing to sneeze at; we must not just toss around such a powerful promise, it's quite a serious matter.

I have come to where I try to immediately pray for others as they come to mind. When the Lord allows someone to enter your thoughts, it's generally not a coincidence. Our minds are always busy thinking about this or that, so when others come to mind, instead of just "thinking" about them, stop and pray for them. There's truly nothing better you could do for them. No matter who they are – struggling or solid, friend or foe, lift them up in prayer and it will benefit you both.

Are you in the habit of praying for others when you say you will? What can you do to become more consistent in praying for others?

_____

_____

The truth is, we all need prayer; each person's burdens are significant.

Finally, as we consider the needs of others, we need to be willing to recognize their significance. We are quite a selfish lot, this human race. We assume each of our own sorrows are greater than the next person's. We even tend to compete concerning who's under the greatest amount of stress, who's endured the most pain, etc. We're all in this together. We've all endured hurt that is unique to our own situation and the truth is, we all need prayer. We all need serious prayer and in order for that to happen, we need to consider each other's burdens as significant and lift them up as such. If we are **all** doing that, then **many** should be lifting our burdens while we lift other's as well.

What is your reaction to the idea that other people's burdens are as great as yours? What benefits can you see in praying for the needs of others?

_____

_____

Lord, we pray that you will find us living a life of faith!

I can hardly believe our study has come to its conclusion. James has taught us that our faith needs to permeate every facet of our lives. He's challenged us with practical ways to do that, and has encouraged us by letting us know that the mighty Lord of Sabaoth is also the loving God of grace who walks with us every step of the way. Thankfully, He gives us each other for encouragement and strengthening through prayer. As we walk this life together, may we encourage each other to actively live this life of faith, **doing** the Word and not hearing only. May we show ourselves approved when our Judge, who is standing at the door, finds us enduring patiently and obediently for His return. Lord, we pray that you will find us Living a Life of Faith!

JAMES — LIVING A LIFE OF FAITH

Leader's Discussion Guide

The leader's guide is intended to offer suggestions for facilitating seven sessions of *James — Living a Life of Faith* by Angie Smith. We believe that women of any level of Bible knowledge can, and will, benefit from this study.

To be an effective group facilitator, you do not need to be a Bible scholar, or even a gifted teacher. The most important "ability" is "availability," and the desire to love women and see their faith in Christ, and knowledge of His Word, grow. Beyond that, all that is required is a little effort to promote the study within your church, and encourage the ladies to participate.

It is recommended that the study be conducted over a 7-week period of time, with each weekly session lasting 60 to 90 minutes. If you wish to offer the class time for prayer and fellowship, we certainly recommend 90 minutes; you will want a full hour for group discussion of the material. Alternately, you may choose to use the extended, 13-session study plan found in Appendix A.

Session 1 is designed to be a time to introduce the ladies to the study and to one another. During this time, copies of the study should be handed out and introductions of each participant made. Many groups may like to complete an ice-breaker, or some activity, to get to know one-another. Further ideas to promote group interaction will be provided under Session 1.

Beginning in Session 2 (when using the 7-week schedule), the participants will begin digging deeply into God's Word. Chapter 1 of James will be covered during Sessions 2 and 3. Each of the remaining chapters of James (2-5) will take one week (Sessions 4 - 7).

Remember, these are suggestions only. It is your group – adapt the schedule to meet your individual needs.

Lastly, emphasize to your group the importance of completing each daily assignment. Remind them that it is "only 6 weeks" of actual study. However, after 40 days of any new activity, they will have developed a new habit, a godly habit of spending a significant amount of time in God's Holy Word. What an awesome role you can play, sweet sister, in helping your friends develop such a wonderful, spiritual discipline. Pray for them each week, and know that we have prayed for each of the faithful daughters of the King who will lead them each week. Thank you for your willingness; may you, and your class, be incredibly blessed!

SESSION ONE — INTRODUCTION

Before the Session

- Have a copy of *James — Living a Life of Faith* available for each learner.

- Plan a welcoming, or ice-breaking, activity. For ideas, you may wish to visit one or more of the following sites: http://www.any-occasion-free-christian-game.com/christian-ice-breakers.html or

- http://christianicebreakergames.com/2009/05/christian-womens-retreat-icebreaker-games/

- In our group, we had the type of chocolate that has a "message" on the inside of the wrapper. Because much of James focuses on changing our perspective, the ladies were challenged to read their wrappers with a different perspective and share a biblical truth that supported or refuted the "wrapper wisdom" of the candy they unwrapped.

- Prepare an attendance sheet so members can have one another's names, phone numbers, and e-mail addresses. Consider the use of name tags for the 1st session or 2, if members aren't familiar with one another.

- Consider providing snacks for each session. As the leader, you may wish to provide each snack, or to increase class participation have members sign up on the 1st night to take turns bringing refreshments for the remainder of the study.

During the Session

- Welcome the women and hand out copies of the study.

- State that you believe groups learn better together if they know one another. Invite the group to introduce themselves and then complete the icebreaker or activity of your choice.

- Have the ladies skim the introduction and Week 1, noting the 5-day format. **Encourage the women to read the introduction, as it is key to understanding the context of the book of James.** In fact, Angie read the introduction aloud to her ladies during their own first session as it reads much like a narrative. Consider having one person read the body of the introduction and ask other women to read the verses given in italics throughout the reading for group participation.

- **Further encourage them to complete each day of reading and be prepared to discuss the material during the next session.**

- Ask them what drew them to studying the book of James, and at least one thing they hope to gain from it over the next 6 weeks?

- Consider ending each session with a time of group prayer.

- Have FUN! The attitude of the leader sets the tone for the entire group. Enthusiasm for studying God's Word is contagious, and it can begin with you!

SESSION TWO – JAMES 1:1-12

Before the Session

- Have class roster available for each member as they enter the room.

- Consider sending each woman an email during the week encouraging them to remain on schedule with their reading, and remind them of the next class time and location.

- Pray for each class member by name.

- Select several questions from the list below to ask during the session in order to generate discussion. In addition, consider highlighting insights from the homework that you would like to further discuss.

During the Session

- Welcome the women and allow time for prayer requests and general comments about the content of the week's homework assignments. Consider having the ladies write prayer requests on a paper to be emailed to the entire group the next day as sharing requests verbally can take a considerable amount of time.

- Ask as many of the following questions as you deem appropriate and that time allows. Try to balance questions about actual Scripture passages (marked with an "S") with personal application questions (marked with an "A").

- S: Who was James writing to? (1:1)

- A: Does the answer to the above question impact how you'll respond to what you read?

- S: According to James 1:1-4, how should we consider trials that come our way?

- A: When trials actually come, what is your knee-jerk reaction to them?

- A: What prevents you from seeing God's perspective in your trials?

- S: What are we to let happen as we endure trials? (1:4)

- A: In what ways have you seen your endurance grow from previous suffering?

- S: What must accompany our request for wisdom? (1:6)

- A: What might cause you to doubt God when you ask for wisdom?

- S: According to James 1:12, the man who perseveres under trial is called what? What will this person receive?

- A: How might keeping your mind focused on the crown of life to come help you persevere today?

- A: What one truth from this week will you seek to implement?

SESSION THREE — JAMES 1:13-27

Before the Session

- Consider sending each woman an email during the week encouraging them to remain on schedule with their reading.

- Pray for each class member by name.

- Consider another ice-breaking activity if you feel it would improve the dynamics within your group.

- Select several questions from the list below to ask during the session in order to generate discussion. In addition, consider highlighting insights from the homework that you would like to further discuss.

During the Session

- Welcome the women and allow time for prayer requests and general comments about the content of the weeks' homework assignments.

- Ask as many of the following questions as you deem appropriate and that time allows.

- S: According to James 1:13-14, what is the source of our temptation?

- A: Have you ever tried to blame temptation on God or on others? Why?

- S: Temptation does not come from God. According to James 1:17, what does come from God?

- A: For what good things are you most thankful?

- S: According to 1:22, what should our response to the Word be?

- A: Would you consider yourself a hearer of the Word or a doer of the Word? What would others say about you concerning this question?

- S: According to 1:25, what type of person will be blessed in what he does?

- A: Absorbing God's Word is meant to change our hearts first and then our actions. Do your actions indicate that your heart is right with God?

- S: How does James describe pure religion in the sight of God? (1:27)

- A: Based upon that definition, how pure is your own religion? What changes might you need to make?

- A: What one truth from this week will you seek to implement?

SESSION FOUR — JAMES 2

Before the Session

- Consider enlisting the help of one other participant in order to split the class roster in two, and contact each woman by phone to encourage and pray for them.

- Select several questions from the list below to ask during the session in order to generate discussion. In addition, consider highlighting insights from the homework that you would like to further discuss.

During the Session

- Welcome the women and allow time for prayer requests and general comments about the content of the weeks' homework assignments.

- Ask as many of the following questions as you deem appropriate and that time allows.

- S: According to James 2:1-7, what was not to be allowed within the church?

- A: In Day 1, Angie described 4 categories of people that Christ loves, but we may tend to avoid. They were: those of "questionable character," the "scary," the "awkward," and "the rude." Which are the most difficult for you to love? Why?

- S: To what is James referring when he mentions the "royal law?" (2:8-9)

- A: Loving others as ourselves is a very difficult calling. It requires us to love others at their worst and when our love is not returned. What have you found that helps you do that?

- S: What was the primary purpose of "the law?" (2:9-11)

- A: How can you remember what you have been saved from?

- S: James contends that faith without works is dead. (2:14-17) Do you agree?

- A: If others knew only what you did, and not what you said, what type of faith would they conclude you have?

- S: Who did James choose as examples of genuine faith? (2:20-26)

- A: Abraham was "the poster child" and Rahab, "the prostitute." Why do you think James chose them? Which do you relate to more? Why?

- A: What one truth from this week will you seek to implement?

SESSION FIVE – JAMES 3

Before the Session

- Is it time for some food and fellowship? Call the person who volunteered to bring snacks this week and thank her for her contribution.

- This week's lesson is about the power of the tongue. Consider bringing an article that discusses the impact of positive and negative words to share with the group. Alternatively, prior to the class, enlist a volunteer to share the impact someone's words (positive or negative) had on their life.

- Select several questions from the list below to ask during the session in order to generate discussion. In addition, consider highlighting insights from the homework that you would like to further discuss.

During the Session

- Welcome the women and allow time for prayer requests and general comments about the content of the weeks' homework assignments.

- Ask as many of the following questions as you deem appropriate and that time allows.

- S: With what warning does James begin Chapter 3? (3:1) Why?

- A: We are all teachers of someone somewhere. What are others learning from you by your words and actions?

- S: To what does James compare the tongue? (3:3-5) What's his point?

- A: On Day 2, Angie writes, "Harsh words can crush a spirit, silence is impossible to interpret, but a kind word is seldom misunderstood." Share an example of when words crushed you or lifted you up? When has silence been deafening?

- S: James is stumped at how two opposing things can come out of the same mouth; what are they? (3:9-12)

- A: In what ways have you "cursed" your fellow believer who has been made in the likeness of God? What can you do to put an end to it?

- S: In James 3:13, two types of wisdom are mentioned; what were they?

- S: How would you describe the "gentleness of wisdom?"

- A: Based upon the amount of time you spend listening to each (the world and to God), which would you honestly say is your primary source of wisdom?

- S: What were the characteristics of the wisdom that comes from above? (3:17-18)

- A: Part of gentle and reasonable wisdom is to recognize whether or not the expectations you place on others are Scriptural or your opinion. When theological or moral principals are not involved, how good are you at extending freedom?

- A: What one truth from this week will you seek to apply?

SESSION SIX – JAMES 4

Before the Session

- James 4 includes teaching on conflict. If you have members who would enjoy this type of activity, consider having 2 or more of them put together a skit of a common "conflict" they experience and act it at the beginning of class.

- Select several questions from the list below to ask during the session in order to generate discussion. In addition, consider highlighting insights from the homework that you would like to further discuss.

During the Session

- Welcome the women and allow time for prayer requests and general comments about the content of the weeks' homework assignments.

- Ask as many of the following questions as you deem appropriate and that time allows.

- S: What does James say is the source of our quarrels and conflicts? (4:1-2)

- A: In what ways have envy and lust for pleasures caused conflict in your life?

- S: What does James call friendship with the world? (4:4)

- A: In what ways have you become too cozy with this world?

- S: What commands are we given by James in vs. 7?

- A: What does submit mean to you? Is submitting to God easy or difficult for you? Why?

- S: What are we not to do to one another? Why? (4:11-12)

- A: Speaking against includes gossip, slander, railing against, and talking down about. Which of these are you prone to? How might remembering that God is responsible for judging others help you cease "speaking against" them?

- S: To what does James compare our lives? (4:14)

- A: You are a mist, and He is your Maker; but do you have trouble leaving the planning to Him? Why?

- A: What one truth from this week will you seek to implement?

SESSION SEVEN – JAMES 5

Before the Session

- Contact each member by phone or email, reminding them that they are in the home-stretch and to finish strong!

- If your group plans to continue with another study following James, have them bring ideas of what they would like to study next. Remember – after 6 weeks of studying God's Word, they have developed a new habit that you will want to help foster!

- Alternatively, consider taking another group of ladies through the James study – it is always exciting to help more women start this new, fun, and life-changing pattern!

- Select several questions from the list below to ask during the session in order to generate discussion. In addition, consider highlighting insights from the homework that you would like to further discuss.

During the Session

- Welcome the women and allow time for prayer requests and general comments about the content of the weeks' homework assignments.

- THANK THEM for sharing the last 6 weeks with you. Encourage them to continue in their own Bible study or to join a new study soon!

- Ask them to think back over the prior sessions and identify 1 or 2 of the most significant things they learned and how they plan to apply it in their personal lives.

- Discuss the idea of forming small groups to encourage and hold one another accountable for those changes. Remind them that it's easy to be a "hearer" of the Word; it's much tougher to become a "doer" of the Word! Support from another sister can be the help they need.

- Ask as many of the following questions as you deem appropriate and that time allows.

- S: The rich had oppressed the poor, and the cries of poor had reached God, who was called what? (5:4)

- A: How does thinking of God as the Lord of all armies, seen and unseen, impact your willingness to cry out to Him?

- S: What does James promise to those facing unfair, harsh oppression? (5:7-8)

- A: The Lord is coming "soon." How can keeping your focus on that promise help you through your current trials?

- S: Why should we, as Christians, not have to swear by any means? (5:12)

- A: Have you carelessly made promises without considering the impact if you don't/can't keep them? Describe a time when your "yes" was not a "yes" and the impact it had on those around you.

- S: T or F – James 5:13-18 promises physical healing? Support your answer.

- A: Have you prayed earnestly, and wondered why physical healing did not occur? What went through your mind as you watched a loved one lose their battle to illness?

- S: What are we to do when we encounter a brother or sister straying from the truth? (5:19-20)

- A: Caring for the spiritual well-being of others is hard, draining work. Think about those in your life who have been consistent sources of spiritual encouragement to you; how might you be an encourager to them?

- A: What one truth from this week will you seek to implement?

APPENDIX A

James – Living a Life of Faith

Alternate, 13-Session Study Plan

(Beginning with one introductory session, this alternate schedule then continues for 12 additional weeks of Bible study and discussion).

Introduction

<u>Session 1</u> – A Tried Faith *, Days 1 – 3

<u>Session 2</u> – A Tried Faith, Days 4 – 5

<u>Session 3</u> – A Tested and Triumphant Faith, Days 1 – 2

<u>Session 4</u> – A Tested and Triumphant Faith, Days 3 – 5

<u>Session 5</u> – An Active and Loving Faith, Days 1 – 3

<u>Session 6</u> – An Active and Loving Faith, Days 4 – 5

<u>Session 7</u> – A Controlled and Gentle Faith, Days 1 – 3

<u>Session 8</u> – A Controlled and Gentle Faith, Days 4 – 5

<u>Session 9</u> – A Peaceful and Humble Faith, Days 1 – 2

<u>Session 10</u> – A Peaceful and Humble Faith, Days 3 – 5

<u>Session 11</u> – A Prayerfully Patient Faith, Days 1 – 2

<u>Session 12</u> – A Prayerfully Patient Faith, Days 3 – 5

* Title of weekly sessions found in the Table of Content for easy reference.

as IAM ministries

The desire of as I AM ministries is to be a source of HOPE for the lost, PROVISION for the hungry, COMFORT for the broken-hearted, and INSIGHT for every Christian through the teaching of God's Word and the overflow of service that it inspires. At our root, as I AM is a Bible teaching ministry that produces Bible study curriculum and daily devotions. That is our root - but from every healthy root, there is growth and life. We believe that when we learn from God's Word, we should be inspired to be used as His hands and feet. Therefore, our ministry also creates opportunities for people to do just that. We want these to be hands-on activities where volunteers have a chance to look into the eyes of those they are serving and to show love through their own eyes and actions. Such opportunities include working in our community garden, which produces thousands of pounds of food for the hungry each year, and staffing weeks of summer camp that ministers to underprivileged children.

Jesus came to serve, and the masses were drawn to Him by His gentle and humble heart - the very heart He invites us to learn from (Matt. 11:29). We can teach for days, perhaps never being heard, but we can reach out in a moment of need, in order to make an eternal difference, and 'they will know us by our love.'

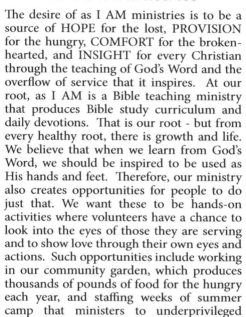

To support this work, or to schedule Angie and/or Dave to speak at your upcoming event, visit: www.asIAMministries.org

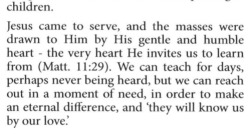

Notes:

Notes:

Notes:

Notes: